Housing and residential structure

Housing and residential structure

Alternative approaches

Keith Bassett and
John R. Short

Routledge & Kegan Paul
LONDON, BOSTON AND HENLEY

First published in 1980
by Routledge & Kegan Paul Ltd

39 Store Street,
London WC1E 7DD,

9 Park Street,
Boston, Mass. 02108, USA and

Broadway House,
Newtown Road,
Henley-on-Thames,
Oxon RG9 1EN

Set in 10/11 Linocomp Baskerville by
Rowland Phototypesetting Ltd
Bury St Edmunds, Suffolk
and printed in Great Britain by
Redwood Burn Ltd
Trowbridge and Esher

British Library Cataloguing in Publication Data

Bassett, Keith
Housing and residential structure.
1. Housing
I. Title   II. Short, John
301.5'4'091732   HD7287   79-42949

ISBN 0 7100 0439 7
ISBN 0 7100 0440 0 Pbk

Contents

Figures

Tables

Chapter 1

Introduction: approaches to housing and urban spatial structure

This book is concerned with examining the current state of knowledge concerning urban housing and residential structure in cities of advanced capitalist countries. In the subsequent chapters we will consider this state of knowledge in terms of the developments within four broad approaches as outlined in Table 1.1.

The ecological approach can be traced back to the writings of the Chicago school in the first third of the twentieth century. It is mainly concerned with the spatial patterns of residential structure while its theoretical underpinnings were initially derived from human ecology. The neo-classical approach, as the name suggests, draws its theoretical guidance from neo-classical economics and it is very largely concerned with the analysis of utility maximisation on the part of individual consumers in an atomistic housing market. The institutional approach has roots which straddle the Atlantic. In North America developments in political science have been adopted by some social scientists to focus on the institutional structure of land and housing markets around the broad themes of power and conflict. In Britain, developments in Weberian sociology associated with the work of R. E. Pahl have been used by some urban sociologists and geographers to analyse the institutional structure of housing with reference to the role of urban managers and the nature of housing constraints imposed on different types of households. The last few years have also witnessed the development of an explicitly Marxist approach to housing which draws upon historical materialism to focus on, amongst other topics, the position of housing as a commodity in a system of commodity production and the role of housing as an essential element in the reproduction of the labour force. Two important authors in this approach are Castells and Harvey.

The diversity of approaches to the study of housing is partly a manifestation of the complex nature of the topic. Housing is a heterogeneous, durable and essential consumer good; an indirect indicator of status and income differences between consumers; a map

TABLE I.I   *Four approaches to housing and residential structure*

Approach	Wider social theory	Areas of enquiry	Exemplar writers
1 **ecological**	human ecology	spatial patterns of residential structure	Burgess (1925)
2 **neo-classical**	neo-classical economics	utility maximisation, consumer choice	Alonso (1964)
3 **institutional**	Weberian sociology		
managerialism		gatekeepers, housing constraints	Pahl (1975)
locational conflict		power groupings, conflict	Form (1954)
4 **Marxist**	historical materialism	housing as a commodity, reproduction of labour force	Harvey (1973, part II) Castells (1977a)

of social relations within the city; an important facet of residential structure; a source of bargaining and conflict between various power groupings; and a source of profit to different institutions and agents involved in the production, consumption and exchange of housing. Such diverse characteristics make the study of housing a complex matter amenable to various interpretations. This draws the study of housing into the arena of interdisciplinary interaction and competing social theories. The particular area of reality which we call housing can be likened to a complex crystal with many faces. When held up to the light a particular pattern of reflected light is seen. Change the orientation of the crystal and a completely different pattern of reflected light is formed. In one sense the different approaches to housing can be seen as the different orientations of this multifaceted object producing different patterns when held up to the explanatory light.

These approaches differ because they draw their theoretical guidance and sustenance from various wider social theories. For example, the neo-classical approach draws upon the *weltanschauung* of neo-classical economics, the institutional approach is broadly based on the Weberian tradition while the Marxist approach gets its view of reality from historical materialism. The distinctions between the various approaches reflect not only differences in emphasis or type of questions posed, but they also reflect larger differences in the interpretation of facts and phenomena and in the explanation of social events. It is not simply differences between the orientation of the housing crystal but pronounced disagreement over the explanatory light to be used. The most significant disagreement occurs between Marxist and non-Marxist approaches. This gulf is not simply an area of disagreement over the interpretation of 'objective' facts, it is a fundamental difference in the pursuit of scientific knowledge.

A crude distinction can be drawn between the earlier developed ecological and neo-classical approaches which focus on equilibrium conditions, housing choices and social harmony and the more recent resurgence of interest in institutional and Marxist approaches which focus on disequilibrium conditions, housing constraints and social conflict. This switch in focus, which can be loosely dated to the late 1960s and early 1970s, is of course related to the nature of the wider social theories being brought to bear on the analysis of housing. However, this raises the question of why different social theories were being used at that point in time. At the risk of oversimplification, we would suggest that the reasons fundamentally lie in the changing nature of many advanced capitalist countries. The late 1960s witnessed the end of the post-war economic boom which unmasked the latent social conflict between different social groups and between capital and labour. This conflict, best expressed in the student and worker riots of France in 1968, called into question the implicit social consensus of contemporary social theories, and attention began to be paid to the conflict models derived from Marx and Weber. Within the housing sector the worsening housing problems in many inner city areas and the obvious constraints imposed by fiscal and government measures on entry into the various tenure categories raised doubts about the consumer sovereignty notions of neo-classical and ecological approaches. At this time, then, the social and housing scenes were receptive to radical shifts in the character of explanatory frameworks. Within academia these shifts were endorsed by the young Turks of the different disciplines eager to carve out a name for themselves. However, the desire for academic advancement only explains why these shifts take place; the direction of these shifts is largely guided by the changes in objective conditions which highlight the inadequacy of contemporary wisdom.

Paradigms and paradigm shifts

The term paradigm was first used by Kuhn (1962) to refer to a conceptual schema which defines both the objects and methods of investigation. For Kuhn, the history of certain subdisciplines in natural science is a history of the transition from one paradigm to another prompted by the inability of the previous paradigm to explain certain recurring facts and phenomena. In the course of normal scientific activity most natural scientists work within the guidelines of one paradigm, but as anomalies and unexplained facts are encountered then a revolutionary upheaval takes place, a paradigm shift, in which a new and better paradigm is fashioned to explain these anomalies and unanswered questions. This new paradigm then provides the guidelines for subsequent scientific enquiry until this paradigm, in turn, is faced with unexplained and unexplainable facts.

It has become increasingly fashionable to use the concepts of paradigm and paradigm shift in discussions of the history of ideas in the social sciences. Many authors, for example, have argued that the change in human geography from the ideographic to the more nomothetic approach of the 'new Geography' which occurred in the 1960s can be seen in terms of a paradigm shift. A similar use of the concept of paradigm shift has been applied to the history of economics by Johnston (1971). Can we use these concepts of paradigms and paradigm shift in the present discussion of different approaches to housing? Does the shift in the emphasis of housing research in the late 1960s to disequilibrium, constraints and social conflict constitute a paradigm shift? We would argue that such an application of Kuhn's ideas would be incorrect.

In the first place there are serious doubts about the validity of Kuhn's ideas in general which need not detain us here (but see Tribe, 1973). More importantly, even if we ignore these criticisms, such an application would be a corruption of Kuhn's ideas. Kuhn was at pains to point out that the concepts of paradigm and paradigm did not necessarily apply to the social sciences. In the social sciences there are a variety of competing social theories which at any one time will be used by different social scientists. Although one theory may be dominant, it does not pre-empt the use of others. In general, there is less purchase for the creation and maintenance of academic orthodoxy in the social sciences than in the natural sciences, and deviants from the consensus position, far from being ignored and abused, are often lauded. Paradigms, by definition, are hegemonic except in periods of paradigm shifts, but in the social sciences there are, in Kuhnian terms, multiple competing paradigm candidates in a stage of pre-paradigm development. Besides, the concept of a paradigm as used by Kuhn only applies to subdisciplines of natural science, but in the social sciences we are dealing with broad social theories, such as historical materialism, which span the present disciplinary boundaries. Historical materialism cannot be relegated to the status of a paradigm.

In the analysis of housing research we are looking at the application of different social theories to a particular area of reality. These theories have been established elsewhere and, although they may dominate in a particular discipline, they do not dominate research into housing and residential structure. For example, although the neo-classical school dominates contemporary economics, it does not dominate the housing research field. Within this area there is no hegemonic social theory, it is a poly-paradigmatic field of enquiry. Since the concepts of paradigm and paradigm shift are inappropriate for the social sciences in general and the housing research field in particular we will continue to use the term 'approaches' to refer to the application of different social theories to the analysis of housing.

Space and human geography

This book is written by geographers very largely for other geographers. However, this does not imply that there will be a desperate attempt to isolate a geographical angle on every matter. In other textbooks this is usually signalled by the extensive use of maps. We would argue that the concern with space, spatial relationships and spatial patterns in human geography has too often been advanced with scant regard to the societal background of spatial organisation. We would further argue that it is impossible to generate spatial theories independent of social theories. Spatial patterns and social processes are interwoven in a complex pattern; social relations are established through spatial relationships and spatial structure is formed by social processes. We cannot understand either spatial patterns or social processes without a consideration of the other. The concern with space in this book will therefore not be reflected in an attempt to forge a distinctly spatial theory, rather it will be a matter of emphasis; we will attempt to shine light more intensely on some parts of the social-spatial mosaic than others.

Aims and objectives

Our aim in this book will be to consider the different approaches to housing and residential structure in terms of the underlying assumptions, the character of exemplar studies and the type of questions left unanswered. Given the diversity of approaches and the often violent disagreement over fundamental assumptions we cannot offer a synthesis of the field, even if such a goal was desirable, but we will hopefully throw into relief the basic sources of disagreement and the main areas of controversy and consensus. Textbooks are too often written to establish a new paradigm or synthesis; this is not our intention. Disagreement between researchers is not a sign of ignorance or confusion to be cleared up by some eclectic paradigm-maker or synthesiser. For the purposes of informed debate it is essential to make the differences between approaches clearer; it is just as important to sort out fundamental lines of disagreement as it is to build conceptual bridges.

The structure of the book reflects our intentions. In Part I we focus on the essentially demand-orientated approaches of human ecology and neo-classical economics. Chapters 2 and 3 respectively discuss each of these approaches. In chapter 4 we discuss more recent advances from this demand-orientated perspective associated with behavioural considerations and urban modelling. Since these approaches have been discussed thoroughly in many other textbooks our exposition will focus on the underlying assumptions of these approaches rather than a blow by blow account of each single development.

In chapter 5 we briefly summarise the criticisms that have been levelled at these approaches and discuss the recent emergence of the institutional approach. So far, the institutional approach has consisted of an inchoate collection of individual case studies. In Part II we therefore attempt to generalise from these studies by hanging a discussion of the institutional approaches on the twin pegs of an analysis of private sector and public sector housing in Britain in chapters 6 and 7 respectively. Illustrative material from North America and France has been incorporated in certain sections of these chapters to aid the comparative analysis of institutional structures. Part III is devoted to an evaluation of the Marxist approaches to housing and residential structure.

After outlining basic Marxist theory and Marxist criticisms of other approaches we then go on to discuss both the current areas of interest and study, and the contribution of the two most influential writers in this approach, Castells and Harvey. It will become evident that our preferences lie in the application of a Marxist approach to housing and residential structure. However, this does not imply an uncritical acceptance on our part of work in this field. We are both aware of the enormous work that needs to be done in this area and the mass of unresolved questions and issues that remain.

PART I

Perspectives on housing and residential structure: early formulations, criticisms and recent developments

Chapter 2

The ecological tradition

The Chicago school

The ecological approach to cities and housing was first developed by a group of sociologists working in the first third of the twentieth century. They were based in Chicago, hence the widely used term to describe their place in intellectual history, the Chicago school. Throughout North America at this time the main locus of population growth was in the cities. Nowhere was this so evident as in Chicago, where the city was experiencing a massive population growth fuelled by migration from other parts of the country and from overseas, and where the main ingredients of America's melting pot were clearly visible in different residential areas. If Manchester with its smoking factories became the symbol of nineteenth-century Britain, then Chicago with its expanding industrial base and increasingly heterogeneous population became the embodiment of twentieth-century North America. The issues which dominated twentieth-century North American social life and social sciences – the assimilation of various ethnic and national groups and the conflicts between these groups – developed against the urban background of such cities as Chicago.

Unlike Engels in his analysis of Manchester, the Chicago school were less concerned with the examination of the city as a reflection and manifestation of the wider society and more with the analysis of the city as a separate entity. More particularly, they endeavoured to apply the concepts of ecology to a clearly demarcated urban arena.

To understand the conceptual framework of the Chicago school it is important to remember the pervading influence of various interpretations of the work of Charles Darwin and Herbert Spencer on the intellectual climate of North American social sciences twenty years either side of the turn of the twentieth century (see Hawthorn, 1976, ch. 9). In Darwin's theory, evolution was the result of the competition between species in the struggle for survival. Spencer argued that

9

human societies could be studied in a similar evolutionary approach and it is to Spencer that we owe the phrase, 'survival of the fittest'. A crude version of Spencer's theory, which was widely preached and heartily endorsed by the rich, stated that the rich were the strong and the poor were the weak in the struggle for survival and the obvious inequalities in wealth were natural, the product of the inexorable laws of evolution. Spencer's evolutionary doctrine with its emphasis on competition was accepted by a number of North American writers seeking to develop a 'scientific' sociology and it was influential in forming the character of the early social sciences in North America as a whole and the perspective of the Chicago school in particular.

The theoretical position of the Chicago human ecologists is outlined in a key article by Park (1936) where he argues that human society is organised into two levels; the biotic and the cultural. It is at the biotic level that the universal ecological processes of competition, dominance and invasion-succession occur. These impersonal forces, which relate to man as a species rather than to man as a repository of beliefs and values, work their way through the social system to create the patterns of residential differentiation. The cultural level of society is seen as a superstructure resting on this biotic level and although it is recognised that the cultural superstructure can restrict competition, the competition for space and the resultant spatial order are primarily a product of the ecological order.

> The incidence of this more or less arbitary control which custom and consensus impose upon the *natural* social order complicates the social process but does not fundamentally alter it – or if it does, the effects of *biotic* competition will still be manifest in the succeeding social order and the subsequent cause of events (Park, 1936, p.13: emphasis added).

The coalescence of these ecological concepts with an explicit model of the city is found in a famous paper by Burgess (1925). (The antecedents of this model can be found in the work by Hurd (1903) who argued that the patterns of urban growth were shaped by the operation of two processes, central growth and axial growth. Burgess was concerned with the first of these two processes.) In Burgess's model of urban growth (see Figure 2.1A) the zone of transition encircles the central business district (CBD) and the area of factories. The zone of transition, the area of old subdivided houses, is invaded by the growth of business and manufacturing concerns. In zone III are the workers who have escaped from the deteriorating conditions of the zone of transition but who need to remain close to their workplaces in the central city. In residential zone IV are the high-class apartment buildings and the exclusive areas of single-family dwellings and beyond this is the commuters' zone, zone V, which is the suburban area of single-family dwellings.

This model incorporated the precepts of human ecology and the specific character of contemporary Chicago (see Figure 2.1B). The Loop, the term given to the Chicago CBD, is the *dominant* element in the metropolitan community. The expansion of the CBD is the metronome of the city and when the CBD expands the other zones are pushed further and further outwards. A simple analogy is of a pebble dropped into a pool of water which creates concentric waves reaching out to the water's edge. In the residential areas the *competition* for space is reflected in the process of invasion and succession. When migrants enter the city they can only afford the cheap rented accommodation in the zone of transition. As the CBD expands the housing stock is reduced and the population is forced outwards, *invading* the other residential areas and eventually *succeeding* the previous population.

Burgess's model rests on the experience of Chicago in the first quarter of the twentieth century when the city witnessed successive waves of immigration. The vast majority of these migrants were poor and were only able to gain a foothold in the housing market by renting the cheaper housing in the inner city. Continued immigration on the one hand and the expansion of the CBD on the other resulted in some households in the zone of transition being forced outwards, thus creating a chain reaction with each preceding immigrant wave moving a little closer to the edge of the city. The steady march of sections of the population towards the suburbs was aided by rising real incomes which enabled households to buy or rent the more expensive housing.

Burgess's concentric model was used as the basis for subsequent empirical work in Chicago. On the one hand there were the studies concerned with the distribution of particular variables such as commercial vice (Reckless, 1926) and psychoses (Dunham, 1937), and on the other there were detailed examinations of particular neighbourhoods (e.g. Zorbaugh, 1929).

The approach of the Chicago school can be seen as the result of a marshalling of concepts derived from a specific intellectual milieu for the analysis of a particular city. At its worst the approach consisted of a crude form of social Darwinism, but at its best, especially in the studies of specific neighbourhoods, it led to a body of empirical studies sensitive to spatial variations, rich in detail and sympathetic to local conditions. However, even at its best the classical ecological approach did not adequately tackle an examination of the housing market processes which led to certain groups being located in particular areas of the city. This failure arose from the overall character of the ecological approach and in particular the abstraction

A

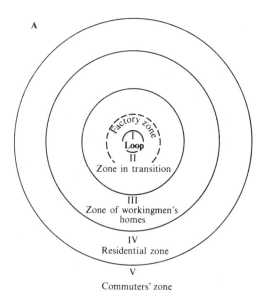

I
Loop

Factory zone

II
Zone in transition

III
Zone of workingmen's
homes

IV
Residential zone

V
Commuters' zone

B

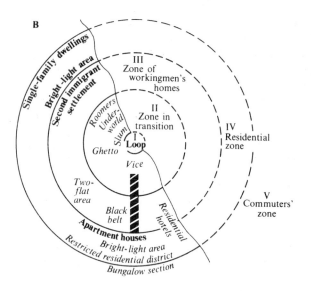

Single-family dwellings

Bright-light area

Second immigrant
settlement

III
Zone of
workingmen's
homes

Roomers

Under-
world

Slum

II
Zone in
transition

I
Loop

Ghetto

Vice

IV
Residential
zone

Two-
flat
area

Black
belt

Residential
hotels

V
Commuters'
zone

Apartment houses

Bright-light area

Restricted residential district

Bungalow section

FIGURE 2.1 *The Burgess model and contemporary Chicago (Source: Burgess, 1925)*

of the city as an independent unit. The demarcation of the city as a unit of study initially arose from the view that if an ecological complex, such as a foreshore or a deciduous forest, could be isolated for the purposes of analysis surely, the human ecologists argued, the city could be studied in similar fashion. The initial abstraction of the city as independent unit gradually fossilised into a reification of the city as an independent unit and this reification suppressed the creation of explanatory links in the ecological approach between the nature of the wider society, the structure of the housing market and the spatial arrangement of the city.

Despite these obvious shortcomings the ecological approach exercised considerable influence on subsequent research. In the following section we will examine the more important extensions and modifications.

Extensions and modifications

HOYT AND THE SECTOR MODEL

An extension of the concentric model was proposed by Homer Hoyt. (If Burgess concentrated on the first of the two processes identified by Hurd, then Hoyt concentrated on the second, namely axial growth.) In a monograph based on a very simple examination of twenty-five cities, Hoyt (1939) criticised the concentric model and suggested a sectoral pattern for residential areas. He argued that residential areas conformed to a pattern of sectors rather than of concentric circles. Some of his results, shown in Figure 2.2, indicate the sectoral pattern of high-status areas in six cities of the USA from 1900 to 1935. According to Hoyt these high-status sectors radiate outwards from the central city along established communication routes in the opposite direction from industrial areas and towards the homes of community leaders. Hoyt argued that the expansion of these sectors was initiated by the process of movement and consequent filtering. The growing obsolescence of existing housing prompted higher-income households to move into newly constructed dwellings. In the wake of this movement vacancies were created which were filled by lower-income households who in turn created vacancies which were filled by even lower-income households.

The filtering process was part-description and part-normative judgment on the part of Hoyt. Along with many North American economists, he believed that the provision of public housing would

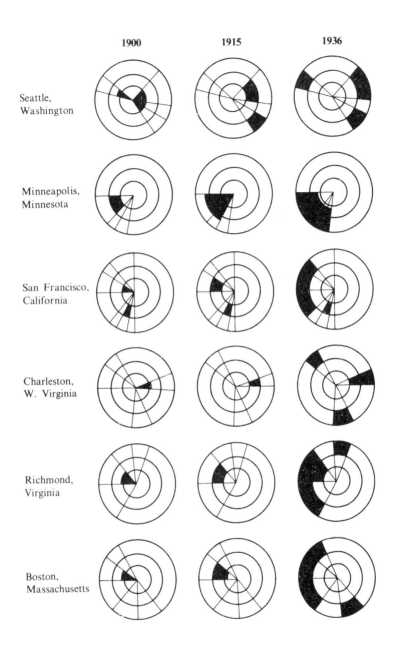

FIGURE 2.2 *High-rent areas in six USA cities (Source: Hoyt, 1939)*

undermine the values of United States society especially the belief in
the efficacity of the free market. His views are still shared by many,
especially those who justify the continuing emphasis on housing
construction for the needs of the higher- and middle-income groups
on the grounds that the filtering mechanism will ensure that everyone
will benefit.

The Hoyt and Burgess models can be considered as comple-
mentary. In particular Hoyt showed that within the sectors there was
a secondary zonal structure with rents and household status rising
towards the suburban ends of the sectors. More generally, both
models capture different facets of the spatial arrangement of North
American cities in the first half of the twentieth century.

CRITICISMS AND RESTATEMENTS

The ecological processes that were assumed to maintain the spatial
order described by the Chicago school did not go unchallenged.
Alihan (1938) attacked the fundamental distinction drawn by the
human ecologist between the biotic and cultural levels of society, and
she argued that it was impossible to distinguish between biotic
conflict and competition and culturally determined conflict and
competition. In a similar vein Firey (1945) criticised the explicit
assumption that cultural factors were mere superstructural elements
in the determination of land use. In an oft-quoted study he showed
that the continuing attraction of Beacon Hill in Boston for high-status
households was the product of sentimental attachments to the area.
Residential space was not merely the arena of biotic competition but
in some cases it could represent certain symbolic qualities and evoke
sentimental attachments.

These and other criticisms highlighted the crude distinction drawn
by the Chicago school between the biotic and cultural levels and more
generally drew attention to the neglect of cultural factors by the
human ecologists. The mounting criticisms prompted a restatement
of human ecology; in his book Hawley (1950) took up such a task. He
argued that the task of the human ecologist was the study of the
structure and functions of the community which was defined as a
territorially based system of human interaction. The development of
such a system was to be seen as the adaptive response of a population
to its environment. The understanding of how a population adapts to
a constantly changing environment was to be achieved through the
analysis of four variables; population, organisation, environment and
technology. Population was broadly defined as the members of a
community, organisation referred to the relationships between

community members and between the community and its environment. Environment was a blanket term covering all phenomena external to the community, and technology was defined as the tools, artifacts and methods used by the population (Hawley, 1971).

Despite these wide and somewhat loose terms of reference, urban ecology continued to be concerned almost entirely with the spatial patterns of residential differentiation. Subsequent developments are associated with Schnore, who received his early training from Hawley at the University of Michigan and whose work has been described as 'probably the most significant development in the field since Burgess and Hoyt' (Johnston, 1971, p. 141). Schnore's early concern was to test the relationship between socio-economic status and distance from the city centre implied by the Burgess model. In the zonal model proposed by Burgess there is a direct correspondence between distance and status of households and neighbourhoods with status rising with increasing distance from the city centre. In a number of papers Schnore (1963, 1964, 1966) investigated the differences between cities and suburbs in the proportion of households in various income and educational categories in two hundred urban areas in the USA. On the basis of empirical investigation into residential distribution of various income categories Schnore classified the cities into four groups:

Type A: The 'Milwaukee' type, consisting of seventy-four urban areas which showed the Burgess pattern of high-income groups in the suburbs and low-income groups in the central city areas.

Type B: The 'New Orleans' type, consisting of eighty-three urban areas which had both very high- and very low-income groups concentrated in the central city and middle-income groups concentrated in the suburbs.

Type C: The 'Fort Smith' type, consisting of nineteen urban areas which had high-income groups concentrated in the central area with low-income groups predominantly located in the suburbs.

Type D: The 'Des Moines' type, consisting of eight urban areas which had no identifiable pattern.

The results revealed that the Burgess pattern of status distribution was only of relevance to the older, larger cities of the USA. The newer, smaller and more rapidly growing cities had patterns of residential differentiation very different from the Burgess model.

Schnore's empirical work on USA cities and his reading of studies relating to Latin American cities prompted an evolutionary model of residential structure (Schnore, 1965). According to Schnore, in the pre-industrial city, a category under which most Latin American cities were classified, the high-status groups lived close to the city centre. With the onset of modernisation and the consequent rapid growth of cities, the central city became the main residential location of high- and low-status groups with the middle-status groups concentrated in the suburbs. In the final stage the centre became the area of residence for low-status groups with the higher-status groups located in the suburbs. The Burgess pattern of residential differentiation is the final stage of this evolution.

SOCIAL AREA ANALYSIS

The presentation of the method which came to be known as *social area analysis* first appeared in Shevky and Williams (1949). These two sociologists used census-tract data to examine the patterns of residential differentiation in Los Angeles. For each census tract of the city they identified three indices; social rank, urbanisation and segregation. These three indices were composite measures derived from census-tract variables. The social-rank variables related to occupation, rent and education, and the urbanisation variables related to fertility, female activity rates and the number of single-family dwellings. The segregation index was a composite measure of the segregation indices calculated for various ethnic groups. On the basis of these three general indices an eighteen-cell classification was used with each cell, or 'social area', containing those census tracts which had similar values across the three indices.

The initial reviews of this work were quick to point to the lack of theoretical justification for the selection of such indices and respective variables (e.g. Erickson, 1949). However, six years later Shevky and Bell (1955) presented social-area analysis as part of a deductive model of social change. The time-lag between empirical presentation and the theoretical justification, especially in the light of the intervening criticisms, has given rise to the nagging suspicion that social-area analysis as theory is little more than a retrospective rationalisation for previous empirical work. This charge was virtually admitted in Bell and Moskos (1964).

In their discussion of social area analysis as theory Shevky and Bell drew heavily upon the work of C. Clark (1940), Wilson and Wilson (1945) and a famous member of the Chicago school, Louis Wirth (1938). In summary, Shevky and Bell argued that the application of technological innovations led to changes in the nature of productive activity and in the nature of the economy as a whole. The consequent social changes that these economic changes produced were reflected in the *scale* of society. The theoretical construct of scale was defined as the number and intensity of personal and functional relationships. The transition from traditional rural societies to urban industrial societies, based upon changes in economic organisation, is characterised by increasing social scale, and this increase in scale is reflected in the range and intensity of relations, the differentiation of function and the growing complexity of organisations. These three orders of organisational complexity are associated with changes in the distribution of skills, in the structure of productive activity and in the composition of the population. The Shevky-Bell schema is summarised in Table 2.1, which shows that the three indices initially identified by Shevky and Williams are constructs of changes in a social system undergoing increasing scale.

TABLE 2.1   *The Shevky-Bell schema of increasing scale and social constructs*

Aspects of increasing scale	Changes in social structure	Constructs	Some derived measures
change in the range and intensity of relations	change in the arrangement of occupations based on function	Social rank (economic status)	occupation, schooling, rent
differentiation of function	change in life-styles	Urbanisation (family status)	fertility, female activity rates
complexity of organisation	changing residential location patterns	Segregation (ethnic status)	segregation of racial & national groups

(Source: Shevky and Bell, 1955)

This schema provides no real explanation of how the broad patterns of social differentiation are reflected into differences between households at the level of census tracts. It is an inferential leap from a broad theory of society to empirical regularities in the pattern of residential differentiation in which the explanatory links between the nature of the society and residential location of households are not examined. In general, the Shevky–Bell schema can be considered as a poorly argued rationalisation for the use of three indices. Nevertheless, the work of Shevky and Bell is not without merit. In the first place, social area analysis as method provided a convenient classification for the delineation of urban subareas and it provided a useful sampling frame for the execution of other types of research. In the second place, as subsequent work showed, the three indices which were identified proved to be important dimensions of residential differentiation, especially in North American cities.

URBAN GEOGRAPHY AND FACTORIAL ECOLOGY

The three extensions to the ecological approach we have just discussed occurred in the period roughly between 1940 and 1960. At this juncture one discipline in particular was to play an important part in the development of the ecological approach – human geography, or to be more precise, urban geography.

Before the 1960s studies in urban geography were, by and large, concerned with classifying different types of cities and with the analysis of the site and location of particular urban areas. Intra-urban studies were primarily concerned with the evolution of city form and Conzen's (1960) detailed examination of the morphology of Alnwick in Northumberland provides a classic example. The change in focus which became more apparent throughout the 1960s was precipitated by shifts in the methodology of human geography. The increasingly fashionable use of models and the growing application of quantitative techniques, the main outcomes of the diffusion of the 'new geography', shifted human geography, and urban geography in particular, from an ideographic to a more nomothetic approach. The new focus for urban geography was the development of models (Garner, 1967). 'Models' in this context was a shorthand notation for generalised statements about spatial patterns. The use and development of models was seen as the bridge to overcome the isolated parochialism of urban geography. Since urban geography had very few indigenous models, attention naturally turned to the models of urban ecology, as both disciplines shared similar interests in space and spatial patterns.

Eager to develop models and use quantitative techniques, the urban geographers could draw upon the spatial aspects of the Burgess and Hoyt models and the indices proposed by Shevky and Bell. The fusion of these elements became feasible with the development of computers which could handle the large amount of census data usually involved. The use of multivariate statistics, especially factor analysis and principal components analysis in the context of an examination of spatial patterns of residential differentiation, is generally referred to as *factorial ecology*. We will consider two exemplar studies which illustrate this approach.

Murdie's (1969) analysis of Toronto provides us with an example of a factorial ecology cast in explicitly deductive terms. Murdie fused the indices suggested by the social area analysts with the concentric and sectoral models of Burgess and Hoyt to suggest three hypotheses:

1 Economic status is associated with measures of income, occupation and education and is distributed in a sectoral pattern.
2 Family status is associated with fertility, type of household and

number of women in the labour force and is distributed in a
concentric pattern around the CBD.
3 Households of different ethnic status tend to group together in
residential space in distinct clusters.

The predicted spatial patterns of these three dimensions are shown
in Figure 2.3. To test these three hypotheses Murdie extracted 109
variables for over 200 census tracts in Toronto for 1951 and 1961 and

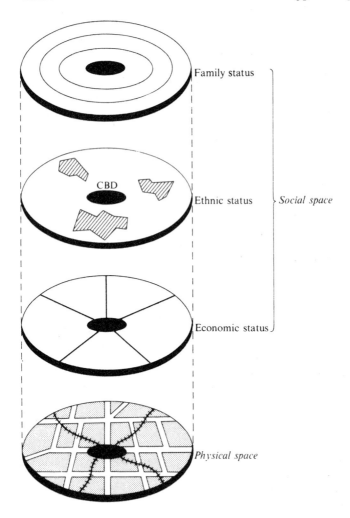

FIGURE 2.3 *Spatial dimensions of urban structure (Source: Murdie, 1969)*

performed a factor analysis on the 1951, 1961 and cross sectional 1951–61 data. The results showed that an economic-status factor, a family-status factor and an ethnic-status factor could be identified and the pattern of factor loadings revealed that the three factors were closely associated with the variables initially proposed by Shevky and Bell and suggested by Murdie's hypotheses. These three factors jointly accounted for 49.9 per cent of the variance in 1951 and 55.9 per cent of the variance in 1961. To discover the spatial pattern of the factor scores Murdie divided the city into six zones and six equally spaced sectors. Through the application of one-way and two-way analysis of variance he found that the economic- and family-status factor scores did have a sectoral and zonal pattern respectively while the ethnic-status factor scores had a distinct cluster-type spatial distribution. The initial hypotheses had been confirmed.

Robson's (1969) analysis of Sunderland was a more inductive factorial ecology of a British city. Robson selected fifty variables from the 1961 census for the small-scale enumeration districts and performed a principal-components analysis. The first two components, which explained 58.9 per cent of the total variation were identified by the pattern of component loadings to be social class and housing quality. Although the general picture did exhibit patterns of both a zonal and sectoral pattern Robson was at pains to point out the importance of local authority housing:

> The appearance of such large areas of local authority housing has made nonsense of the rings or sectors of the classical ecological theory. Indeed, the game of hunt-the-Chicago-model seems to be exhausted as far as the analysis of modern developments in British urban areas is concerned (Robson, 1969, p. 132).

On the basis of the component scores derived from the principal components analysis Robson demarcated distinct areas of the city. These areas formed the sampling frame for a study of attitudes to education, and the questionnaire results suggested that the area of residence had a strong association with a person's attitudes to education even when occupational status was held constant. In other words it appeared that the milieu of the urban social area had an independent effect on the individual's social outlook.

Robson's work was characteristic of other and subsequent factorial ecologies in two respects. First, the inductive approach became common. Census variables were selected and run through the statistical mill of principal components analysis or factor analysis, loadings were discussed with passing reference to Shevky and Bell while the maps of scores included some mention of the Burgess and Hoyt models. Second, the use of urban social areas, derived from the grouping of component scores, as a sampling frame for subsequent research became a standard research strategy (see Johnston, 1976).

In urban geography there was a marked bandwagon effect in relation to factorial ecology – a case of 'have technique, will travel', and throughout the 1960s and early 1970s a host of factorial ecology studies of British, North American and Australasian cities continued to appear in the literature. The method was also applied to cities in underdeveloped nations ranging from Calcutta (Berry and Rees, 1969) to Kuwait (A. G. Hill, 1973). Reviews of the literature concerned with the city population in advanced capitalist countries reported spatial patterns of residential differentiation that differed little from the findings discussed in Murdie's analysis (see Timms, 1971 and Johnston, 1971).

By 1973 one of the former practitioners could note the possibility of diminishing returns in the further use of factorial ecology (Robson, 1973). The explosion in the use of factorial ecology had, when the dust had settled, produced numerous empirical generalisations but little in the way of theory. However, the contribution of urban geographers to the ecological approach was not confined to the number-crunching exercises of principal components analysis. An important research strand has been the explicit testing of the spatial processes which were assumed to underpin the spatial patterns of the early models. Johnston (1969a), for example, examined the population movement patterns postulated by Burgess with reference to metropolitan London. For the period 1960–1 he found that immigrants from abroad were concentrated in inner city areas and their continued out-movement did appear to be initiating a process of invasion and succession. The processes implied by the Hoyt model have also come under scrutiny. Johnston (1966, 1969b) tested the hypothesis, explicit in Hoyt's model, that the location of high-status households should shift over time, with reference to Melbourne, Australia and Christchurch, New Zealand. He found that the centre of gravity of the elite residential areas in both cities was remarkably stable over time and argued that this reflected the social and economic power of the elite which enabled them to maintain the exclusivity of elite neighbourhood. Dzus and Romsa (1977), for example, have analysed the filtering process resulting from the construction of housing for the wealthy in Windsor, Canada. They found that few of the housing chains penetrated the poor areas of the city and even at the end of the chains the mean annual income of incoming households was relatively high.

Another important research strand was the elaboration of the generalised models of urban structure. For example, Schnore's work provided the basis for Johnston's restatement of the evolution of residential patterns. Johnston (1971, pp. 182–96; 1972) presents a cross-cultural model of urban residential patterns which has modernisation of society and resultant social changes as its independent variable. In the pre-industrial stage the elite are concentrated around the city centre. During the period of industrial take-off the higher-status households move away from the central city. Such movement is facilitated by transport improvements, and the lower status groups obtain housing by the filtering process or through employers or self-help construction. In the industrial stage the economy grows and the emerging middle classes attempt to translate their increased status and income into housing consumption. Two main types can be identified; the 'upper-class mimickers' who try to live as close as possible to the elite and the 'satisfied suburbanites' who are content to live in the less fashionable parts of the city. The post-industrial stage is reflected in the residential structure of cities by the rapid growth of middle-class suburbia which in spatial terms surround the elite residential areas. Into this sequence Johnston fits the experience of several countries: in the USA the middle classes reach their housing aspirations by personal savings; in New Zealand state funding is important; while in Latin America the satisfied suburbanites have emerged much sooner in the process of modernisation and can be found in the self-made residential quarter. An important theme running through Johnston's model, and one which distinguishes him from urban ecologists, is the concept of social classes, their emergence in the growth of capitalist societies and the resultant jockeying for position in urban residential space.

Conclusions

The ecological approach has largely consisted of an examination of the spatial patterns of residential differentiation. A concern with the description of such patterns is the thread that links the early studies of Chicago to the more recent factorial ecologies. The most important developments of the ecological approach from the Chicago school to the present day have taken two main forms. First, there has been a growing sophistication in the techniques employed to analyse such patterns with social-area analysis and then factorial ecology replacing the more simple tools of the early workers. Second, there has been a retreat from the ecological analogies used by Park, Burgess and other early human ecologists. The structure of residential space is now no longer seen as the expression of subcultural biotic forces.

An analysis of residential differentiation should concern itself with answering three questions. What groups in society are located where in the city? What are conditions like in these areas? How and why are these groups located where they are? From its inception the ecological approach was largely concerned with answering the first two questions, and, although the techniques have changed through time, the descriptive focus of the work has remained. The essential weakness of the ecological approach has been its failure adequately to answer the third question. This question can only be answered through an examination of the structure of the housing market, since it is the meshing of housing supply and allocation on the one hand and the pattern of housing demand on the other which structures residential space. The ecological approach, by considering the nature of housing supply and allocation in early-twentieth-century North America as a constant, given and often 'natural' variable, is unable to say anything meaningful about the structure of the housing market and consequently has little explanation to offer for the patterns of residential differentiation which it describes.

Chapter 3
Neo-classical economic models

In the previous chapter we have seen that those working within the ecological tradition consistently identified regularities in the spatial distribution of variables and characteristics associated with socio-economic status, family status and ethnic status. However, the developments in the ability to handle spatial data were not matched by the development of theory which could explain the processes creating and maintaining this urban spatial structure. Too often it was a case of empirical regularities in search of a theory. In contrast, the neo-classical economists had a well-developed theory of urban spatial structure and residential location. In this chapter we will examine the form and character of these neo-classical models. An examination of such models is especially pertinent given that the overall emphasis of these models, especially the focus on household preferences and housing demand, has become an integral part of the orthodox approach to cities and housing. To provide a background for such an examination the next section will outline briefly the general character of neo-classical economics.

Neo-classical economics: a general outline

Neo-classical economics began as a reaction to the classical economics of Ricardo and Marx (see Dobb, 1973). Developed by the English economist, Jevons, and the Austrians, Menger and Böhm-Bawerk, in the latter half of the nineteenth century, neo-classical economics shifted the emphasis in economic analysis away from the circumstances and conditions of production, the terrain of the classical economists, towards the preferences and needs of individual consumers.

Put at its simplest, neo-classical economics views society as a collection of individuals whose nature is assumed to be given. The realisation of individual preferences shapes the form of the economy and the nature of society. Put in an oversimplified fashion, neo-classical economics considers two sectors: households and firms. Households demand goods and services in the amounts and proportion which best satisfy their preferences; that is, they attempt to maximise their utility. Firms supply goods and demand land, labour and capital in the amounts and proportion which maximise their profits. The distribution of the value of net output between the three factors of production – land, labour and capital – is explained with reference to marginal productivity theory. According to this theory each of the three factors will be used until they cost more to use than the value they produce. The price for any factor is determined at the margin. In the marginal productivity theory of income distribution, for example, the rate of pay for any group of workers is assumed to equal the change in output that is associated with a variation of one unit in the size of that group. Under equilibrium conditions each of the factors will be paid according to their contribution to output. In the neo-classical framework incomes and scarce resources are allocated according to relative efficiency.

In its analysis of the economy, neo-classical economics makes four assumptions. First, the production of goods and services reflects the preferences of consumers. Second, all households and firms have perfect information. Third, from this basis of perfect information households maximise utility and firms maximise profits. Fourth, production is assumed to be flexible in that the factors of production can easily be interchanged.

As a consequence of this framework and the particular emphasis on equilibrium conditions, features such as unemployment, excess profits and the inflexibility of production are relegated to the position of deviations from the norm or as phenomena of only secondary importance. More generally, the view of the economy as a harmonious self-regulating mechanism which 'fairly' allocates scarce resources according to output obscures from analysis conflicts generated between workers, capitalists, landowners and landlords. In these respects neo-classical economics is partly a description of the private market system and partly a justification for it.

Although neo-classical economics is the orthodox economics in Western Europe and North America, and its assumptions and overall emphasis continue to provide the underpinnings of many studies of urban structure and housing,· in recent years it has come in for considerable criticisms. The inability of this form of economics to say anything substantive about some of the more pressing problems associated with the end of the post-war economic boom has stimulated the revival of interest in Ricardo and Marx and has prompted the growth of political economy (see Hollis and Nell, 1975; Rowthorn, 1974). The difference between traditional neo-classical economics and political economy is encapsulated by Nell (1972, p. 95), 'Orthodox economics tries to show that markets allocate scarce resources according to relative efficiency; political economics tries to show that markets distribute income according to relative power.' We will elaborate on the approach of Marxist political economy in later chapters but for the moment we can note that while neo-classical economics is the orthodox economics, it is not the only economics.

The trade-off model of residential location

The neo-classical models of residential location posit a relationship between the consumption of housing space and travel costs. The general hypothesis is that households trade-off travel costs (which increase away from the city centre), against housing costs (which are shown to decrease from the city centre) in an attempt to maximise utility subject to an overall budget constraint (Alonso, 1964; Kain, 1962; Muth, 1969; Wingo, 1961; Mills, 1972).

In the most limiting of cases a monocentric city situated in a featureless plain is assumed, with all jobs located in the city centre. Under conditions of perfect competition and complete freedom of choice households attempt to maximise a utility function consisting of housing and other goods subject to an overall budget constraint. Evans (1973) has suggested that leisure should be included in the utility function and that households are subject to a time constraint, as well as to a budget constraint. Within the context of comparative static-utility maximisation it is shown that the demand functions of individual households lead to the downward slope of the land-value and house-price gradients away from the central city.

The relationships between transport costs, housing costs and income are welded together in this framework to predict the location of individual households and of different income groups within the city. If a household's rate of pay increases and the space demands remain the same then the household should locate closer to the city centre. The same pattern should also be found if space demands remain the same but the household puts a higher valuation on leisure time since a location closer to work will decrease the amount of travelling time and hence increase the amount of leisure time. If, on the other hand, the rate of pay and valuation of time remain constant but the quantity of space demanded increases, then the household should move further out from the city centre to obtain the relatively cheaper housing space. This hypothesis, if correct, provides a rationale for the family life-cycle theory of residential mobility which predicts continued out-movement from the central area of the city as the size of household increases (see Abu-Lughod and Foley, 1960). In general, the rate of substitution between travel and housing costs are governed by the households' valuation of time and preference for housing of a particular density.

The residential distribution of households with different incomes is also explained with reference to density preferences, valuation of time and elasticity of demand for space and housing. Assuming a simple classification into high- and low-income groups, then the high-income households have the option either to live close to the centre thus reducing travel costs but having to face high housing costs or to take advantage of cheaper housing on the periphery and bear the higher journey-to-work costs. To explain the distribution of high-income households on the periphery the neo-classical models assume that the income elasticity for housing and space is positive and that higher-income households prefer low-density living. Low-income households thus live close to the city centre, consuming housing of higher unit price. It is worth noting at this point that the continued suburbanisation of jobs may mean that the higher-income households may not even have to face the penalty of higher journey-to-work costs to buy housing of a cheaper unit price as assumed in this trade-off model.

Two specific features of the trade-off model are worthy of attention. First, the explicit emphasis is on the structure of housing demand. The individual household provides the main unit of observation while the structure of household preferences provides the main explanatory variable. The analysis of housing supply and allocation in the neo-classical literature is conspicuous by its absence. One exception is the work of Muth (1969) whose book has been described as, 'arguably still the finest book on urban economics ever written' (Richardson, 1977, p. 18). Muth incorporates the production of housing and an analysis of producers' behaviour into his more sophisticated version of the trade-off model. For example, because land values decline from the city centre, Muth argues that this causes builders to use more land in relation to other factors of production with increasing distance from the city centre, and this in turn is one cause of the decline in population densities with increasing distance from the city centre.

Second, rent is treated as an asocial phenomenon, as a rational allocative device which allocates land to the highest bidder. Land is allocated to the household with the highest-bid rent function, which is the set of land rents the household is willing to pay in order to maintain a constant level of utility. Rent in the neo-classical models is entirely a function of accessibility. The competition for accessible sites cause rents in accessible locations to be high, and differences in the rent of different localities reflect differences in the accessibility of these locations. Within this framework of atomistic households freely realising their preferences and an urban land market dominated by differential rent, the neo-classical models seek to show how the housing market reaches a stable equilibrium.

Criticisms of the trade-off model are plentiful. The restrictive assumptions of a monocentric city, perfect competition and freedom of choice are frequently criticised. Kirwan and Ball (1973) question the assumptions of long-run supply-and-demand equilibrium and argue that the general equilibrium approach cannot handle the durability of housing or the high transaction costs of owner-occupier movement. Richardson (1971, ch. 1) maintains that journey-to-work costs are not a primary determinant of residential location; at best they are of secondary importance and for most income groups the residential location choice is constrained by the ability to get a mortgage. The importance of accessibility has also been questioned by the results of a number of empirical studies. Ball and Kirwan (1977), for example, show with reference to the Bristol housing market that the distribution of housing characteristics was at variance with the patterns suggested by the trade-off model; while Granfield's (1975) analysis of housing in Buffalo and Milwaukee has shown that income and race are more important determinants of residential location than accessibility to workplace. These and other studies suggest that accessibility to workplace may not be so important as the initial models have suggested.

The new urban economics

The mounting criticisms of the trade-off model have not restricted further developments in the neo-classical approach to residential location. Indeed Richardson (1977) suggests that since 1970 there has been a resurgence of interest and he has termed the most recent developments based upon deriving general equilibrium in a one-dimensional city as the new urban economics (NUE).

Despite Richardson's adjective, the latest version is still wedded to the older variety in its overall approach to residential location in that the utility maximisation of atomistic households is still the prime focus of concern. The more recent elaborations to the trade-off model have taken two directions. First, because the prediction of the standard model that the poor would live close to the city centre while the rich would live on the periphery is very restrictive, there has been some manipulation of the parameters associated with bid-rent functions. In the standard models it was argued that the poor would have a higher bid rent close to the city centre than the rich, as is shown in Figure 3.1A. In this case the poor were assumed to live close to their work in order to reduce transport costs while the rich were located on

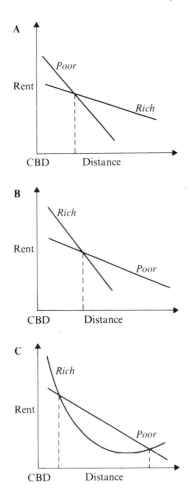

FIGURE 3.1 *Bid rent functions of rich and poor groups*

the periphery because of their high-income elasticity of demand for space. The main extension to this model has been to allow the income elasticity of demand for space and the valuation of travel time to vary in order to replicate the reality of different types of residential distributions (Pines, 1975). Figure 3.1B shows the case where the rich are assumed to have a higher valuation of time than the poor and thus have a steeper bid-rent function close to the city centre. This residential distribution is commonly found in cities of Latin America. Figure 3.1C describes the situation wherein the rich have a concave bid-rent function which twice bisects the bid-rent function of the poor and thus the rich are located close to the centre and also beyond the intermediate location of the poor. In this distribution the rich located in the central city areas are assumed to place a higher valuation on time while the rich on the periphery place greater emphasis on space. Such preferences are commonly associated with high-income households at different stages in the life-cycle; a higher valuation of time associated with households at the early stages of the life-cycle with greater emphasis placed on space by households at the middle stages of the life-cycle.

Second, greater realism has been added to the household decision-making process. In the classic trade-off model it was assumed that households traded-off accessibility and space in order to maximise utility. Yamada (1972) suggests that a household's decision is not simply a trade-off between accessibility and space but also includes a trade-off between space and leisure and between accessibility and environmental quality. Yamada argues that leisure and environmental quality are a function of distance in that a location further away from the CBD involves less time for leisure pursuits but greater environmental quality than a location closer to the CBD. Papageorgiou (1976) provides a further elaboration to the model of the decision-making environment of households to include a variable representing residential attractiveness and a composite index measuring environmental quality, housing quality and the social prestige of residential areas. The assumption that households make their residential location choices independent of other households has also been dropped in favour of the argument that an individual site is less important than the nature of the surrounding neighbourhood. Kirwan and Ball (1973) suggest that there is a neighbourhood preference premium which is the sum that a household is willing to pay in order to live in an area with a preferred socio-economic composition.

Conclusions

Any evaluation of the neo-classical location models must first of all consider their relative success in certain areas. In terms of replicating empirical regularities in the complex world of the land and housing markets of cities in advanced capitalist countries the neo-classical models have proved relatively successful. Mills's (1972) model of urban structure, for example, successfully predicts the decline of land values and population density from the city centre, both of which are found in most large cities of North-west Europe and North America. This is no mean achievement and Mills is justly proud in stating that these are dramatic results from a simple model. However, we must differentiate between the performance of models in terms of simulating or replicating reality and in terms of explaining reality. If the simulation studies in human geography have taught us anything, it is that one can easily simulate patterns without necessarily knowing the processes which maintain such patterns. The success of the neo-classical models in the former aspect is not under question but in the latter aspect there are a number of criticisms that can be made. The most general criticism pointed to in this chapter is that the models fail to consider the structuring of household housing decisions. Households do not make choices in a vacuum, rather the preferences that they express and the constraints that they experience are moulded by the nature of the wider social structure and by the more immediate effects of the specific character of certain systems of housing production and allocation. By ignoring these elements the neo-classical models provide little purchase for the explanation of the phenomena they so admirably replicate. More specifically, the models, by positing utility-maximisation behaviour on the part of individual households as the main explanatory variable, 'describe conditions when absolute and monopoly rents are insignificant, when absolute and relational concepts of time and space are irrelevant, and when the institutions of private property are notably quiescent in the land and property markets' (Harvey, 1973, p. 188). The level and nature of these abstractions raise serious doubts about the ability of the models to *explain* the reality of the land and property markets in cities in advanced capitalist countries.

Chapter 4

Behavioural perspectives and urban spatial interaction models

In the previous two chapters we have outlined the character and basic assumptions of two general approaches to the study of residential structure and housing. These approaches are of particular significance because they have provided the basis for, and guided the development of, subsequent work in this field. In this chapter we will consider the form and nature of two such avenues of recent research – the development of behavioural perspectives and the growth of spatial interaction models.

The behavioural approach

EARLY STUDIES

The development of the behavioural approach, by which we mean the explicit focus on perception and decision-making in the analysis of locational behaviour, can be traced back to the influential work of Kirk (1951, 1963) and Lowenthal (1961). Kirk argued that for too long geographers had made a sharp differentiation between man and environment. In contrast, he suggested that the important distinction should be drawn between the phenomenal environment, the external world of physical reality, and the behavioural environment, which was defined as the *perceived* environment in which phenomenal facts are organised and evaluated. It is the behavioural environment in which rational human behaviour takes place. In simple diagrammatic form, Kirk was arguing that geographers had been treating the man–environment relationship as pictured in Figure 4.1A and he was proposing the study of the relationship as suggested by Figure 4.1B.

The relationship between the external world and the perceived world was also discussed by Lowenthal. He argued that the external world, Kirk's phenomenal world, was refracted through the filters of

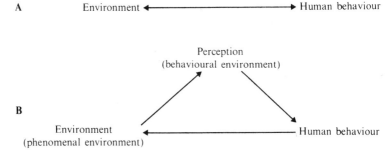

FIGURE 4.1   *Two alternative schemas for the man/environment relationship*

culture and the lens of personal experience and imagination to produce the perceived world in which locational behaviour takes place. Besides the accepted world shared by one culture, reinforced by training and teaching, there were also the slightly different personal viewpoints which were shaped by unique individual experience, imagination and memory.

These early papers by Kirk and Lowenthal drew attention to the importance of perception in understanding human behaviour and, for many, were timely reminders that the present *terra incognita* of geography were in the minds of men.

Several years later Wolpert (1964) pulled the discussion from the airy heights of broad generalisations to the more empirical level of a specific case study. For a region of Sweden he showed that the distribution of farm labour productivity varied significantly from the optimum productivity surface. Part of this variation was explained with reference to 'satisficing', as opposed to optimising, behaviour and to the effects of uncertainty reduction on the part of some farmers. The regional variations were explained in terms of regional differences in the level of information relating to techniques of production. Wolpert's paper is significant in two respects. First, it provides a good example of the role of perception, especially the importance of prior information, in influencing human behaviour and, second, it highlights the sub-optimal nature of behaviour which is at variance with the optimising assumptions of classic location models. This latter point was developed by Pred (1967), who attempted to introduce notions of sub-optimal satisficing behaviour into classic location models.

BEHAVIOURAL STUDIES OF HOUSING DEMAND

In urban geography the growth of behavioural research arose from the rising dissatisfaction associated with the inability of the factorial ecology method to explain how spatial patterns were created, maintained and/or changed. While the spatial patterns of residential structure had been identified by the plethora of factorial ecologies, the processes which shaped these patterns had all but been ignored. For many, the key to the problem of linking process and spatial form in an explanatory sense lay in the analysis of household behaviour, and many urban geographers began to consider individual household decision-making.

One topic was singled out for particular attention – residential mobility, the movement of households within urban areas. Robson was expressing a popular sentiment when he states, 'One avenue which does appear to offer considerable potential in throwing light on the structure of residential areas, however, is the study of mobility at the level of the individual household' (Robson, 1973, p. viii).

This avenue had already seen some traffic. In 1965 Wolpert had argued that aggregate models, including the gravity models, were of limited use in explaining patterns of mobility. To understand population movement it was essential, he argued, to comprehend the behavioural aspects of the decision to migrate. In viewing migration as an individual or group adaption to perceived changes in the external environment Wolpert proposed two concepts – *place utility* and *action space* (Wolpert, 1965). Place utility (note the explicit language of neo-classical economics) was defined as the individual's utility with respect to space. A household (Wolpert used the term individual) achieves a certain utility at its present location and perceives utilities at alternative locations. If the household perceives higher utilities at other locations then, if possible, the household will move in order to maximise utility. A household's action space was defined as those areas of the city which the household had regular contact with and to which it could assign place utilities. Later, Adams (1969) argued that this action space had a definite sectoral shape and that, since the action space was the decision-making environment for relocating households, the sectoral action space was reflected in the directional bias of intra-urban mobility patterns.

Wolpert's concepts of place utility and action space, and his later work (see Wolpert, 1966), were formalised into a model of the behavioural aspects of residential mobility by Brown and Moore (1970). In their model (see Figure 4.2) they visualised the relocation process as a two-stage affair. In stage 1 the decision to seek a new

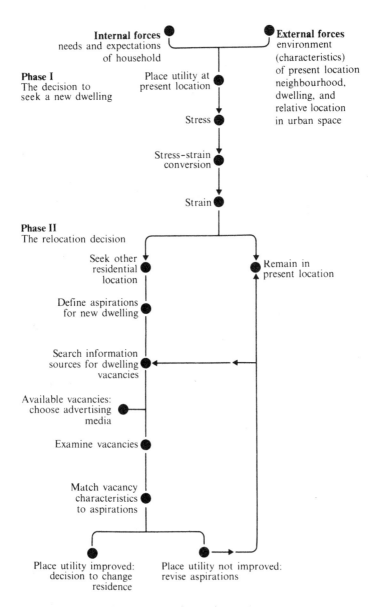

Internal forces
needs and expectations
of household

External forces
environment
(characteristics)
of present location
neighbourhood,
dwelling, and
relative location
in urban space

Phase I
The decision to
seek a new dwelling

Place utility at
present location

Stress

Stress-strain
conversion

Strain

Phase II
The relocation decision

Seek other
residential
location

Remain in
present location

Define aspirations
for new dwelling

Search information
sources for dwelling
vacancies

Available vacancies:
choose advertising
media

Examine vacancies

Match vacancy
characteristics
to aspirations

Place utility improved:
decision to change
residence

Place utility not improved:
revise aspirations

FIGURE 4.2 *A behavioural model of residential relocation (Source: Brown and Moore, 1971)*

36

dwelling is prompted by internal forces of household expectation and the perceived external forces of the immediate environment. If the level of stress created by these forces was greater than the household's threshold level and if higher place utilities were perceived in alternative locations then a decision to move was made. Stage 2 of the process consists of the actual move and includes the definition of an *aspiration region*, defined as the type and location of housing which is acceptable to the household, the search for and examination of vacancies and the choice of a specific dwelling.

This model stimulated a large number of studies into residential mobility. A consistent feature of these subsequent studies was that households were treated as autonomous decision-making units. The exclusion of considerations of housing supply and allocation was determined by the terms of reference laid down by Wolpert and Brown and Moore and by the adopted research methodology. The majority of studies either considered movers as an undifferentiated group or only studied specific samples of the population. To consider a group of movers as homogeneous or to only consider a homogeneous group of movers places the supply and allocation of housing as a constant, given variable.

One example of the behavioural approach can be seen in Michelson's (1977) study of relocating households in Toronto. Michelson's work is typical of the other studies of residential mobility in that the standard procedure of questionnaire techniques was used on a sample of high-income movers. However, the scale of the operation, a five-year longitudinal survey of 761 households, and its concern with post-move adaption and behaviour, makes it perhaps the most comprehensive study of residential mobility to date. Michelson studied the residential moves and subsequent behaviour of high-income movers into single-family houses and high-rise apartments stratified by location into downtown and suburban. The resultant fourfold destinations provided the comparative framework for his findings. To begin with Michelson attempted to discover how people found their new housing. His results showed that the mechanics of dwelling search varied between the different samples. For example, about 75 per cent of house buyers examined seven or more housing units compared to only 33 per cent of those who eventually moved into apartments. After a consideration of the push and pull factors associated with residential movement, the general picture of environmental choice for the four sample groups is summarised. Those moving into downtown apartments were generally younger than the total sample and placed greatest emphasis on location to the central city. Households moving into downtown houses were more affluent, placed great emphasis on home ownership and were concerned to reduce travel-to-work time and expenditure. Households moving into suburban apartments were those who wanted to obtain a suburban environment for raising children but were unable to afford suburban houses. Those who lived in suburban houses placed greatest emphasis on the prestige of residential areas, on home ownership, and on the desirability of a suburban location for the raising of children. Michelson's general conclusion concerning post-move adaption was that most households successfully adapted to their new environments and the majority were reasonably happy with their new dwelling. The greatest levels of dissatisfaction were expressed by apartment dwellers, but rising stress was contained in most cases by the expectation of future movement to a single-family house. Household satisfaction was found to be a function both of present dwelling and future expectations.

The substantive conclusions of this type of research into residential mobility in the private housing market of British and North American cities can be briefly summarised (a much fuller analysis can be found in Short's (1978) review article). First, the studies showed that residential mobility was mainly prompted by the new space requirements associated with changes in the family life-cycle. Second, the examination and search of dwelling vacancies was found to consist of a rather brief perusal of a few vacancies within previously known areas. Third, the dimensions on which households made their residential choice were found to include location, cost, dwelling characteristics, quality of the physical environment and the social status of the neighbourhood. The relative ranking of these dimensions varied between income groups, with higher-income households placing greater emphasis on social status of neighbourhood and quality of the physical environment, and also between age groups, with households at the middle stages of the life-cycle placing most emphasis on those characteristics of residential areas conducive to child-rearing.

On the one hand, some of these conclusions cast doubt on the validity of the neo-classical location models. It was shown that households varied in the criteria they adopted and that these criteria included more than a simple trade-off between accessibility and space. It was also shown that households had neither perfect information concerning vacancies nor perfect ability to use their information. In summary, the results showed that 'residential relocation man' was a far more complex animal than 'neo-classical man'. On the other hand, however, by continuing to assume that the household was the most important unit of study and that housing demand was the crucial element in the housing supply-and-demand relationship, this type of research offered little more than a slightly more realistic extension to the basic framework marked out by neo-classical economics.

By way of conclusion to this section we can note that the continuing interest in perception and behaviour by some human geographers has included a more explicitly phenomenological expression (Guelke, 1974; Ley, 1977). Ley, for example, argues that to understand group behaviour and individual decision-making it is essential to study the world of everyday experience. 'To understand the social process one must encounter the situation of the decision-maker, which includes incomplete and inconsistent information, values and partisan attitudes, short-term motives and long-range beliefs' (Ley, 1977, p. 502). Ley further maintains that only phenomenology, and particularly the phenomenological theory of social action proposed by Schutz (1967), can provide the basis for such a study. As yet there are few studies of housing demand which adopt a phenomenological perspective. It is difficult to imagine the form of such a study since in housing demand as in so many spheres of human action and behaviour the external constraints imposed and the choices conferred by the wider social structure play such an important role in structuring the individual's experience. The restricted analysis of social structure in phenomenology in general, and Schutz's theory of social action in particular, suggests that as far as the study of residential structure and housing is concerned phenomenology has very little to offer.

Social physics and spatial interaction models

SOCIAL PHYSICS

The methodology of the natural sciences, which aims to construct universal laws and principles to explain events in the physical world, has often been held up as the yardstick on which to judge the social sciences. Many have argued that the social sciences should adopt the methodology and basic aims of the natural sciences. This argument has been strengthened by the great success of the natural sciences in improving the material basis of human life and in the consequent enhanced status and prestige of natural scientists. The acceptance of this argument is the hallmark of logical positivism in general and social physics in particular. The aim of the social physicist is to construct universal laws for the explanation of social systems and human behaviour. The pursuit of such an aim can lead to two interrelated consequences. First, the elaboration of universal principles can lead to social systems and human behaviour being placed in the position of constant, given factors. As the white-coated natural scientist attempts to conduct experiments in highly controlled environments, so the social physicist can often eliminate all the historically specific aspects of social systems and human behaviour. Second, there is the consequent instrumentalist view of science. If human behaviour cannot be explained by universal laws, then there is a tendency in social physics to regard it as if it could; never mind the quality of the explanation, feel the width of the goodness of fit.

Perhaps the best example of the social physics approach is found in Zipf's (1949) work. Zipf's basic aim was to show that human behaviour could be considered under the general principle of minimisation of effort; this book is entitled *Human Behaviour and the Principle of Least Effort*. At one point in this book Zipf extends Newton's gravitational formula, $PiPj/Dij$, to the interaction between two cities where Pi and Pj refer to the mass (population) of cities i and j and where Dij is the distance between the two cities i and j. This gravity model is a direct extension of Newtonian physics to the field of human spatial interaction and provides the clearest example of the 'physics' in 'social physics'.

SPATIAL INTERACTION AND URBAN MODELS

The gravity model was subsequently refined by a succession of geographers and economists. In human geography the development of the gravity model in relation to population and commodity flows was only one aspect of the attempt to develop a more nomothetic approach based on the methodology of the natural sciences (see Harvey, 1969).

Modified forms of the gravity model were also incorporated into the large-scale urban models. The focus of these urban models is the activities of individual households, particularly their location and journey-to-work patterns, while their aim is to produce results which best fit the data relating to these activities. On the one hand, the development of such models throughout the 1960s reflected the opportunities afforded by the increased use of computers which could handle the large amounts of 'urban' data. On the other hand, the public need to control and manage urban systems also provided a considerable stimulus to further model-building endeavours. The traffic congestion and associated problems caused by the increasing separation between home and workplace and the rise in car-ownership in North American and British cities created a need for the prediction and extrapolation of present and future trends in order to provide an empirical basis for possible policy measures. The instrumentalism of the social physicists was in tune with the demands of the public policy makers. As one practitioner noted,

> The importance of the planning system in fostering such research cannot be stressed too much, for the continuing demand by planners for better tools to explore urban problems has helped to increase the relevance of urban modelling research; and it has meant that urban models have been built as aids to conditional prediction, rather than solely as aids to a greater understanding of urban phenomenon (Batty, 1976, p.v.).

One of the earliest models was formulated by Lowry (1964). In the Lowry model (see Figure 4.3) the distribution of basic employment is taken as given. This basic employment sector generates a dependent population which is located in zones by a gravity-model formulation.

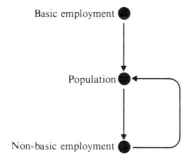

FIGURE 4.3 *A simplified representation of the Lowry model*

This population demands goods and services thereby generating a non-basic employment sector and these employees are located in zones, again by a gravity-model formulation. The linkage between the population and the non-basic employment sector shown in Figure 4.3 highlights the fact that the non-basic sector generates a dependent population who in turn require goods and services. By a series of equations (see A. G. Wilson, 1974, pp. 221–31; Batty, 1976, pp. 57–62) the Lowry model estimates the total population and total non-basic employment and allocates them to zones of an urban region. The whole cycle is repeated in an iterative fashion until convergence is obtained and the increments to population and non-basic employment become insignificant. In the household sector sub-model, Lowry assumed that workers were located around workplaces according to some function of journey-to-work costs. If T_{ij} is the number of workers who live in zone i and work in zone j then

$$T_{ij} = gE_j f(c_{ij})$$

where g is a constant, f is a decreasing function, E_j is the number of jobs in zone j and c_{ij} is the cost of travel from zone i to zone j. In the Lowry model workers are located in zones of an urban region according to a simple gravity-model formulation. The simple hypothesis which underpins the Lowry model and the residential location sub-models of subsequent statistical models is that workers tend to minimise the cost of the journey-to-work by locating close to their workplace.

Lowry considered workers as a homogeneous group and the housing market as an undifferentiated entity. This unrealistic assumption was dropped in later statistical models. A. G. Wilson (1974, ch. 10) attempted to remedy the unsatisfactory simplifications by introducing differences in income and house type in a simple disaggregated model of the form,

$$T_{ij}^{kw} = A_i^k \, B_j^w \, H_i^k \, E_j^w \, f_w \ (c_{ij})$$

where T_{ij}^{kw} is the number of w income people living in k type houses in zone i and working in zone j; H_i^k is the number of k type houses in zone i; E_j^w is the number of w income jobs in zone j; $f_w(c_{ij})$ is a function of the cost of travelling from zone i to zone j which varies with w income; A_i^k is a measure of the attractiveness of k type houses in zone j; and B_j^w is a measure of the attractiveness of zone i for w income groups. Batty (1976, ch. 10) presents two versions of a similarly disaggregated model cast in probabilistic terms.

By a series of equations such as those outlined the urban-model-builders have endeavoured to replicate residential and journey-to-work patterns in contemporary cities. Their treatment of housing has been simplistic in the extreme and has consisted of the basic assumption that households choose housing which minimises the cost of journey to work. The inability of this type of approach to say anything meaningful about the dynamics of the housing market is obvious, but for the moment we will discuss criticisms of these models which accept the validity of such an approach. Two main criticisms of these models have been made. First, it has been argued that, quite simply, the models do not work. In an empirical study of nine spatial inter-action models, Openshaw (1976) has demonstrated that the models provide a poor fit with the data; the models did not provide accurate descriptions of observed reality. In another paper the same author (Openshaw, 1977) drew attention to the effect of different zone systems on model performance. By calibrating four spatial inter-action models from data relating to journey to work patterns in Durham, Openshaw highlighted the important point that the values of the parameters in the model and overall model performance were crucially dependent on the scale of the zone classification.

Second, the lack of theoretical justification for the models has been consistently noted. Urban model builders are acutely aware that their models have only tenuous theoretical underpinnings. While the models may provide useful predictions for levels of interaction, based as they are on a Newtonian analogy, they provide no basis for an explanation of such interaction and provide little help with model interpretation. Although Wilson (1970) has shown that the gravity model can be derived statistically by utilising the concept of entropy (see Gould, 1972, for a simple explanation of Wilson's use of entropy and entropy maximisation), he is in effect merely providing an alternative analogy. Statistical mechanics like Newtonian physics only provide analogies for human behaviour, not explanations. Senior expresses a standard view when he states, 'a common complaint against current aggregate models of any type [is] that their relationship to the behaviour of the actual decision-making units is not examined' (Senior, 1974, p. 389).

These complaints have prompted a number of workers to establish such links. It is not surprising given the basic approach of urban modelling that the neo-classical economics has been seen as the basis for providing such links. Wilson (1974, p. 202), for example, claims that the entropy-maximising versions of interaction models can be seen as a statistical averaging over the utility-maximising behaviour of individual households. In other words the spatial interaction models are the aggregate outcome of many households all seeking to maximise utility. Wilson further claims that the entropy-maximising versions are an improvement on neo-classical models since they provide a precise meaning to the 'demand at a point' elusive in the neo-classical framework. A full review of the attempts by model builders to incorporate and extend neo-classical economic theory can be found in Senior (1974). In general, these attempts to show that the results of the spatial interaction models are in effect macro-level averages of the micro-level behaviour postulated by neo-classical economics. If behavioural geography has attempted to show that 'residential relocation man' is a more complex animal than 'neo-classical man' then more recent developments in urban modelling have attempted to show that 'spatial interaction man' is really no different from 'neo-classical man'.

Chapter 5

Power, conflict and urban managerialism

In the previous chapters we have described the basic framework of, and subsequent elaborations to, the traditional approaches to housing which focus on the activities of individual households and which are primarily concerned with the structure of housing demand. In this chapter we will examine recent alternative approaches to housing which focus on different topics and themes. The purpose of this chapter is to summarise the criticisms of the ecological and neo-classical analyses of housing made by these alternative approaches and to outline the general character of these alternative frameworks and the specific topics which they consider.

Criticisms

A number of criticisms have been levelled at the traditional approaches to housing and residential structure. First, it has been argued that the focus on household choices and preferences ignores the importance of housing constraints. Gray notes that, 'many groups are constricted and constrained from choice because of their position in the housing market, and by the individuals and institutions . . . controlling the operations of particular housing systems' (Gray, 1975, p. 230). A second and interrelated criticism has been that the focus on individual households ignores the effects of a number of diverse agents involved in the housing market. Households are not autonomous decision-making units; housing decisions are made in an environment created by interaction between a number of individuals and institutions which we can term 'agents'. These agents have differing aims and objectives; for example, estate agents have an obvious interest in increasing the turnover of housing, landlords are concerned with maintaining acceptable rates of return and developers are in business to build and sell houses at a profit.

Approaches to housing which analyse the housing market in terms of utility-maximising on the part of households and/or which focus only on household choices thus ignore the social realities of the housing market. Third, a more general criticism has been that the ecological and neo-classical frameworks have an implicit, and often explicit, assumption of social harmony which is at variance with the conflicts arising in society in general and in the housing market in particular.

These criticisms have led to the development of alternative approaches to housing. Two currents in recent research can be identified: a concern with the interrelationships between power, conflict and space, and a growing interest in the role of urban managers. The former flows from the work of North American political scientists and has been taken up largely by North American geographers. The latter flows from the work of British sociologists and has been taken up by British geographers. However, there is considerable overlap in terms of themes and concepts.

Power, conflict and space

The neo-classical and ecological approaches have been increasingly subjected to criticism by writers who have preferred to focus on social conflicts over land use rather than the social harmonies that seem implicit in earlier models. According to what we may broadly term, 'the locational conflict approach' changes in land use are not the outcome of the myriad decisions of individuals in a free and un-organised land market but rather the result of conflicts between interest groups with varying goals and differing degrees of power and influence.

An early statement of the position is found in an article written by Form as long ago as 1954. Form argued that, 'the image of a free and unorganised market in which individuals compete impersonally for land must be abandoned. The reason for this is that the land market is highly organised and dominated by a number of interacting organisations' (Form, 1954, p. 255). Form loosely described these organisations as 'land interested groupings' which included: real estate and building concerns; the larger industries, businesses and utilities of the city; home-owners and government agencies. He suggested that the different organisations could be studied in terms of the resources they could command, their function in the land market, their internal organisation and patterns of accountability, and their different images of the land market. Land-use changes were largely the outcome of conflict and bargaining between these groupings, and Form provided examples of zoning decisions to illustrate the way in which power struggles could end in economically powerful interests manipulating land-use changes for their own purposes.

The 1970s have seen a growing interest in the theme of locational politics and although much of this work is not a great advance on the earlier work of Form it has served to link discussion of spatial conflict with the mainstream theories in political science. Much of the debate has revolved around the question whether conflicts over space can be subsumed under a more general theory of conflict or whether they serve to define the distinctive nature of urban politics.

O. P. Williams (1971, 1975) has perhaps made the broadest attempt to link spatial processes and political processes in a distinctive approach to urban politics. Urban policies, he argues, have important implications for the distribution of real income, opportunities, costs and satisfaction, bringing advantages to some individuals and groups and disadvantages to others.

It follows that the organisation of space is inherently political; in fact urban politics is essentially about the allocation of favoured locations between different individuals and groups. The notion of spatial-externality effects, either positive or negative, plays an important part in Williams's analysis and finds similar emphasis in some of Harvey's earlier work. Local political activity, Harvey argues at one point, can be regarded 'as the basic mechanism for allocating the spatial externality fields in such a way as to reap indirect income advantages' (Harvey, 1973, p. 60). Similarly, Cox and Reynolds have claimed, 'much, if not most, political conflict in an industrial-urban society is, at least in part, the result of geographical externalities' (Cox and Reynolds, 1974, p. 22).

The emphasis on locational politics has been challenged in some quarters. Elkins has argued that 'what is unclear is the extent to which the allocation and distribution of location needs to be studied in a different manner from the study of other valued outcomes. That is, can it be claimed that a "distinct" social and political process has been isolated?' (Elkins, 1975. p. 169). Elkins concludes that the allocation of urban space does not differ significantly from the allocation of other types of value.

A suitable compromise position has been stated by Young. Location does have a special importance for the study of urban politics, 'space is not *just* a value allocated by the government/market nexus, but also has the characteristics of a power resource. As such, spatial allocations feed back into the urban political process in a more direct and immediate manner than do other goods distributed by the urban system' (Young, 1975, pp. 187–8). In this more limited sense an analysis of the relationships between location and power is an important dimension of urban political research.

The attempt to link the themes of location, conflict and power opens up an important avenue of research for geographers and provides opportunities for drawing upon the extensive theoretical and empirical work on conflict developed by sociologists and political scientists. We will return to various aspects of this work when we discuss urban politics and policy making in Chapter 7. For the moment it is sufficient to note the importance of the locational conflict theme for housing market studies. At a general level it implies a focus on the conflicts between groups and organisations with varying interests in the housing market – developers, landlords, estate agents, financial institutions, neighbourhood organisations and local government. At a more specific level it implies an attempt to link forms of housing to specifically spatial factors such as the pattern of externality effects which are of considerable importance in residential structures. For example, the organisation of residential neighbourhoods provides three major forms of externality effects – public-behaviour externalities, status externalities and property value externalities. As Cox (1978) has argued, when these externality effects have important social welfare consequences for residents, the housing market will tend to be highly structured in terms of social class, and local political processes are likely to revolve around attempts to control housing market processes to local advantage. The unequal distribution of power and wealth ensures that some groups are better able than others to influence housing-market processes and to reap the benefits of positive externalities.

Urban managers and the housing market

REX AND MOORE

An important contribution to the formation of what later came to be known as the managerial approach was the influential book written by Rex and Moore (1967). A paper by Rex (1968) summarises the main points of the book. In this book Rex and Moore provided a sociological analysis of Sparkbrook, an inner city area of Birmingham. In part, Rex and Moore accepted and extended the work of the Chicago school by considering the city as a sociological entity independent of the wider society, by studying an area of the city explicitly defined as a zone in transition and by postulating competition for housing as the crucial dynamic of the housing market. However, in discussing the nature of this competition for housing they drew upon the work of Max Weber.

One of Weber's main concerns was with the distribution of life chances, defined as the supply of consumption goods, external living conditions and personal life experience. Weber argued that the distribution of life chances and concomitant patterns of social stratification were a manifestation of the unequal distribution of power in society and this power and consequent stratification existed in three dimensions; the political, the social and the economic. In the economic sphere the term 'class' was used by Weber to distinguish individuals who have similar life chances and opportunities for gaining income. These opportunities are predicated upon the existence of a market in which individuals compete for the purpose of exchange while the life chances are determined by the market assets of the individual which include skills as well as property. Rex and Moore seized upon two elements in their interpretation of Weber: the importance of consumption patterns in defining class position and the differentiation of class positions within the broad categories of 'lack of property' and 'property'.

Threads of Weberian sociology were interwoven with those drawn from the Chicago school to produce the tapestry of housing classes. Rex and Moore rejected the cruder biological analogies of the Chicago school, but in viewing the city as an area of conflict they proposed the concept of housing classes. These classes arose from the conflict over the scarce resource of housing and were determined by the degree of access to housing. In order of prestige they identified the following housing classes which had distinct spatial distributions in British cities:

1 The outright owners of large houses in desirable areas.
2 Mortgage payers who 'own' houses in desirable areas.
3 Council tenants in council-built houses.
4 Council tenants in slum houses awaiting demolition.
5 Owners of houses bought with short-term loans who must take in lodgers to meet loan repayments.
6 Tenants of rooms in lodging houses.

These classes arise from the differing degrees of access to private and public housing and are determined by the income, occupation and ethnic status of individuals on the one hand and the allocation rules of the public and private sector on the other. In the private housing market those with capital can buy housing outright. The rest of the population who seek to enter the owner-occupied sector must satisfy the entry requirements of the building societies whose mortgage allocation policy is biased towards those with secure employment and with medium to high incomes. Entry into the public housing sector is determined by the allocation criterion used by the local authority. In Birmingham, Rex and Moore found that the local authority had a five-year waiting period and that on the recommendation of the housing visitor households who were eligible for public housing were placed either in council-built property or in the poorer quality housing awaiting demolition. The prejudices of the housing visitors and the five-year waiting period meant that New Commonwealth immigrants had restricted access to public housing in general and the better quality public housing in particular. Those households who are unable to obtain either owner-occupation or public housing can either save or borrow sufficient capital to buy the cheaper housing in the inner city or are forced to rent rooms in lodging houses. These, in brief outline, are the mechanisms behind the housing market which determine the housing classes proposed by Rex and Moore. Position in a particular housing class, for Rex and Moore, 'is of prime importance in determining a man's associations, his interests, his life style and his position in the urban social structure' (Rex and Moore, 1967, p. 39).

The interest aroused by the concept and classification of housing classes can be gauged by the large number of criticisms that have been directed against Rex and Moore. Pahl (1975, chapter 12) provides a summary of the arguments. Four criticisms have been made. First, the delineation of classes is based on a static snapshot of the housing market. Households often move from rented accommodation to either public housing or owner-occupation through the course of the family life-cycle. If a household does make such a move it is unlikely that social behaviour and position in the community radically alters because of changes in housing tenure *per se*. Second, in suggesting that conflict occurs between classes, Rex and Moore assume that all households desire the same type of housing. Conflict is generated by struggles over universally desired objects but Rex and Moore have yet to prove that there is a unitary value system in the sphere of housing consumption. Third, given this last point, it is not clear what is the basis of conflict between these classes. Why should private renters be in conflict with owner-occupiers? What exactly is the basis of conflict between housing classes 1 and 2? Finally, Haddon (1970) argues that the whole concept of housing classes is based on an incorrect reading of Weber. Weber defined class in terms of life chances associated with the disposal of goods and skills to achieve income. Haddon suggests that Rex and Moore have confused *disposal* and *use* of housing. The patterns of housing consumption, the use of housing, cannot be used to define class, even in the Weberian sense, since the use of housing is an index of achieved life chances not a cause. In other words, patterns of housing consumption are a reflection of social stratification and not, as Rex and Moore assume, a cause. Haddon goes on to suggest that it is not the degree of access that should be central to our analysis of housing but 'the means of access and the way a differentiated population negotiates the institutions and rules of eligibility of the "housing market" ' (Haddon, 1970, p. 133).

It would be tedious to list the many more criticisms, both general and specific, of Rex and Moore's work. In this particular context the important point to note is not that Rex and Moore were wrong but that their work and the subsequent criticisms shifted research towards the analysis of institutions and constraints in the housing market. By utilising Weber in the analysis of housing they launched the study of housing back into the mainstream of the sociological tradition and away from the murky waters of a discredited Spencerian approach. More particularly, with their emphasis on differential access to housing, Rex and Moore highlighted the importance of the allocation policies of public and private housing institutions and laid the basis of the managerialist approach.

PAHL AND SUBSEQUENT WORK

In a series of articles published between 1969 and 1974, the sociologist Ray Pahl codified the managerialist perspective (Pahl, 1975, chs 9–14). As a response to the uncritical acceptance of the assumptions of the Chicago school he developed a number of themes. It was impossible, he argued, to understand the city without a consideration of the nature of the wider society. The city was not a separate entity and urban patterns had to be related to the wider social processes. Second, he pointed to the need to consider the constraints which affected the life chances of different types of households; previous research had been too concerned with choices and not enough with constraints. The fundamental questions, he suggested, should be, 'Who gets the scarce resources and facilities? Who decides how to distribute or allocate these resources? Who decides who decides?' (Pahl, 1975, p. 185). Those who influenced the distribution and allocation of resources were termed the urban managers and included such diverse individuals as, 'public housing managers, estate agents, local government officers, property developers, representatives of building societies and insurance companies, youth employment officers, social workers, magistrates and councillors'. In a later paper Pahl expressed the original formulation as, the managers 'exert an independent influence on the allocation of scarce resources and facilities which may reinforce, reflect or reduce the inequalities engendered by the differentially rewarded occupation structure' (Pahl, 1977a, p. 50).

This managerial perspective was an important stimulus to research into housing in Britain. One reason for its wider adoption in Britain compared to North America lay in the greater role of planners, housing managers and the central and local state in general compared to the more *laissez faire* housing market of North America. The welfare capitalism of Britain, with its institutions of social and economic policy modifying the free play of market forces, has produced an easily identifiable bureaucratic layer in the British housing scene.

TABLE 5.1 *Studies of housing managers*

'Managers'	*Relevant studies*
Public housing officials	Gray (1976a): J. Lambert (1970): Damer (1974)
Public housing officials/planners	Paris (1974)
Planners	Dennis (1970, 1972): Davies (1972)
Local government officers/councillors	Muchnick (1970)
Estate agents	Hatch (1973)
Building society managers	Ford (1975)
Building societies/estate agents	P. Williams (1976)
Building societies/surveyors	C. Lambert (1976)
Housing associations	A. Thompson (1977)
Landlords	Elliot and McCrone (1975)
Institutions covered with housing in London	Harloe, Issacharoff and Minns (1974)

Table 5.1 provides only a small selection of the large number of studies devoted to analysing the role and effects of various urban managers. Gray (1976a), for example, was concerned with the effects of housing management officials in the local authority housing department in Hull on the selection and allocation of council house tenants, while Paris (1974) highlights the distributional consequences of the policies of the housing and planning departments in the clearance and redevelopment schemes that took place in post-war Birmingham. The inclusion of authors in this table does not imply that they all adopted the managerial thesis outlined above or that they were specifically stimulated by Pahl's papers, although both Gray and Paris clearly were, but merely that their focus of concern was on the actions, ideologies and consequent effects of various individuals and institutions involved in the supply and allocation of

housing. Although there is considerable diversity within this group of studies there are three broad recurring themes: Who are the individuals and which are the institutions which supply and allocate housing? What rules and procedures do they use to allocate housing? What are the effects of their rules and consequent actions on different types of households? This last question was generally subsumed under the explicitly distributional question of who gains and who loses.

The evaluations of the managerial approach (see Norman, 1975) have centred on the question what degree of autonomy do these urban managers have. Do they, as Pahl's restatement of the original formulation suggests, exert an independent influence? This formulation is difficult to sustain when we consider that scarcity and the allocation of scarce resources which is the nub of the managerial perspective are socially and economically determined. Urban managers allocate scarce resources, they do not themselves create scarcity; the urban managers are not autonomous agents. In this respect Williams (1978a) differentiates between early studies which in their explanations gave too much autonomy to managers – he terms this 'early managerialism', although others have called it 'naive managerialism' – and the more recent studies which have, 'a far more explicit concern with power relations, the nature of cities and the social and economic structure' (Williams, 1978a, p. 237). We will return to these issues in Part III of the book when we will discuss a Marxist evaluation of managerialism.

Urban managerialism as applied to housing is not a coherent theory of how or why housing is allocated in particular ways. Rather, it is a framework for study which suggests (a) that there are a variety of managers, including representatives of building societies, estate agents, landlords, public housing officials, etc., who have an effect on the allocation of housing; and (b) that a study of such managers and the institutions that they represent provides an understanding of the workings of the housing market and (in particular) how certain types of households are allocated certain types of housing.

Many of the limitations of the locational conflict and urban managerialist approaches will become apparent from a Marxist perspective developed later in this book. For the moment, these two approaches are valuable in taking us beyond the neo-classical and ecological frame-works to incorporate new themes – such as the role and effects of institutions and individuals involved in the supply and allocation of housing and the relationship between conflict, power and access in the housing market – which throw a different light on the nature of housing and structuring of residential space.

PART II

Institutional structures and constraints in housing markets

In the previous part we have discussed the development of different approaches to housing and residential structure. It would appear that the most promising field of enquiry is opened up by the approach which we considered under the broad theme of power, conflict and urban managerialism. In terms of explaining the structure of housing markets and of providing a more realistic framework for analysing the multidimensional nature of housing and residential structure this approach would seem to offer better purchase than the demand-orientated approaches of human ecology, neo-classical economics and the more recent developments in behavioural considerations and urban modelling.

What particular areas of enquiry are implied, and general themes raised, by the focus on power, conflict and urban managers? At a specific level, the locational conflict perspective, which we associated with developments in North American political science, points towards an analysis of the role of agents and institutions involved in the land and housing markets; more than this, it also implies that the nature of the conflict and competition between these different agents and institutions structures the broad character of land and housing markets. The emerging interest on urban managerialism, which has been most marked in Weberian sociology, similarly identifies institutions and agents as focal points of analysis but, in slight contrast, emphasises the role of such agents and institutions in terms of their effects on the housing constraints imposed on different types of households.

More generally, these two research strands point towards three main themes of enquiry:

1 the identification of agents and institutions involved in housing, their different goals, ideologies and relative power;
2 the nature of the interaction between these diverse agents and institutions and the kinds of constraints they impose on each other;
3 the effect of this interaction on the kind of housing constraints imposed on, and the nature of the housing choices afforded to, different types of households in different parts of the city.

In the subsequent chapters of this section these three broad themes will be used as the conceptual framework for exploring the nature of housing systems with particular emphasis on the British situation although international comparisons will be cited where appropriate. In using such a framework it is clearly desirable to adopt an holistic approach which stresses the mutual interaction of a system of agents and institutions. However, since it would be very unwieldy to attempt to consider the whole of the housing market in one broad exposition some kind of partitioning is necessary. We therefore propose to consider separately the private and public housing sectors. In the next chapter we will concentrate on the agents and institutions involved in the private housing sector, with particular emphasis on the interrelationships between such agents and institutions. In the subsequent chapter we will discuss the public housing sector with particular reference to the kind of agents and institutions involved in public policy formulation and implementation.

As we shall see, this institutional perspective provides a convenient way of organising information, a useful device for analysing the internal structure of the housing market and a handy peg on which to hand a discussion of facets left unexplored by the ecological and neo-classical approaches. Whether this institutional approach can lay claim to any greater theoretical substance is a question that will be discussed in the last section of the book, which considers Marxist approaches.

Chapter 6

The role of agents in the private housing market

There are a number of institutions, organisations and individuals, which for the sake of brevity we will term 'agents', involved directly and indirectly in the private housing market. The interaction between these agents creates the environment in which household housing decisions are made, housing choices are realised and housing constraints imposed. In this chapter we will seek to identify these agents, describe their involvement in the production, consumption and exchange of housing, and highlight their effect on the housing opportunities afforded to different types of households.

Figure 6.1 illustrates a rough categorisation of agents according to their position in the process of production of new housing, the process of financing the consumption of new and existing housing, and the process of exchanging houses between owners. On the production side it is logical to begin with the landowner. Land is an essential prerequisite for the construction of housing and, given a system of private property in which agents can own and control the use of land, landowners have a degree of influence over the supply and location of new housing. However, the development of residential land has increasingly taken place within the framework of zoning regulations and planning restrictions. This confers on planners the power to release or withhold land for house construction, which has obvious consequences for the location of new housing and less obvious implications for the price of housing. Perhaps the most important agent on the production side is the developer who assembles land, obtains planning permission, raises money to build the houses and in many cases acts as the builder. The decisions made by the builder/developer have important implications for the style, location and cost of housing.

At all stages of residential development the roles of financial institutions and government are crucial. In lending and advancing funds to other agents financial institutions become essential intermediaries at most stages in the construction process. They operate in a fiscal framework partly created by the government which can either stimulate or retard the mechanism of production.

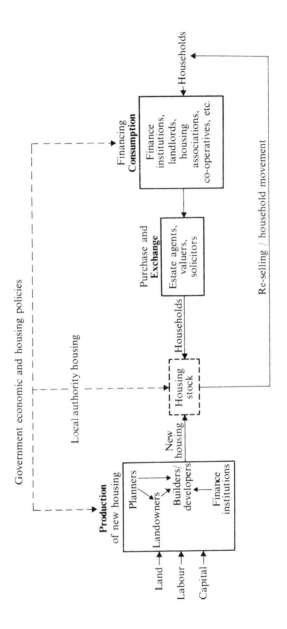

FIGURE 6.1 *The interaction between agents in the private housing market*

Housing, once produced, is placed upon the market like any other commodity. However, unlike other commodities, it cannot be directly purchased by households because of its very high cost relative to household income. Accordingly there are a number of agents such as mortgage institutions and landlords who act as intermediaries to enable households to consume housing services without immediately paying the full cost of the product. Finally, because households move in response to factors such as changes in family size and job location, it is necessary to provide mechanisms for selling and purchasing properties. A number of agents – estate agents, valuers and solicitors – act as intermediaries in these exchange processes.

This categorisation of agents and their interrelationships, although sketched with the British system in mind, is broadly applicable to a number of housing markets in Western Europe and North America. We will begin by examining more fully the agents and their interrelationships in Britain to show how different parts of a housing market interact before drawing some selected comparisons with the housing market in North America.

The framework for private market decisions

The various agents in the housing market operate in a framework created by the government institutions engaged in economic and land use planning. Three elements of this framework can be considered – land use policy, land tax policy and more generally, the broad nature of economic and social policy.

LAND USE CONTROL AND LAND USE POLICY

The land use system that has operated throughout most of the post war period dates from the 1947 Town and Country Planning Act. This Act embodied a general philosophy on the desirability of certain forms of urban change and growth. The fundamental objectives were to contain urban growth and renew the urban cores, to protect the countryside from unplanned urban sprawl and to create self-contained and balanced communities. To this end counties and county boroughs were designated as planning authorities and were required to draw up development plans and, in addition, legislation was passed to facilitate the establishments of green belts and New Towns. Behind the Act and its supplementary legislation lay the assumptions that comprehensive control by public bodies would leave only a small role for the private market and that the rate of urban growth would be low.

In practice this system was not fully implemented. Growth rates were higher than expected and as a result of policy changes in the 1950s local authority powers were largely reduced to negative controls over new development, and private speculative building became the norm. According to Hall *et al.* (1973, vol. 2, ch. 12) there have been three main effects of the post-war planning policy. First, containment policies were largely successful in slowing down the rate of conversion of agricultural land; second, even where unexpectedly high rates of suburbanisation did break through the land use controls, the greater control of employment decentralisation lead to an increasing separation between home and workplace; third, the constraints on urban growth have pushed up land and property prices at a faster rate than would otherwise have been the case, an effect which has had direct repercussions on housing densities, styles and quality. In terms of who gains and who loses, or more correctly who gains and who pays, the distributional effects of post-war planning in Britain have been regressive. Owners of land granted planning permission have seen a dramatic rise in the market price of their land, upper-income owner-occupiers in the green belts have had their quality of life protected and property values assured, while middle- to low-income households purchasing new property have been forced to buy expensive, high-density housing beyond the green belts. The preservation of the countryside has been bought at the price of long and costly journeys to work for many households. The cost of maintaining London's green belt, for example, has been borne by those households who had to travel further away from their place of employment.

LAND VALUES AND LAND TAX

The Achilles heel of the British planning system has been the inability to tax the gains associated with the increase in land values for land granted planning permission. The post-war period has been marked by several attempts to tax the gains from land development for the benefit of the community. The 1947 Act effectively nationalised development rights, established a fund to compensate owners for the loss of their rights and envisaged that ultimately all development gains would be subject to a 100 per cent tax. This system was dismantled by the Conservative governments in the 1950s.

A second attempt was made by the Labour government in the late

1960s. A Land Commission was set up to acquire a land bank for subsequent release to developers. This was backed up by a betterment levy of at least 40 per cent of all the development gains resulting from private land transactions. This system was ended by the incoming Conservative government of 1970. In both periods the operation of the levy seems to have had the effect of pushing up land prices and causing landowners to hold back land in the hope of a change of government. Both these factors increased the price of housing.

The latest attempt to secure public control over land and land transactions is embodied in the 1975 Community Land Act. In its original form this legislation envisaged the extensive purchase of land by local authorities below market value and a gradually increasing development tax on most private land transactions. However, after numerous concessions to developers and landowners the present Act will only begin to operate extensively after a long sequence of preparatory stages. It is too early, as yet, to see the precise impacts this Act will have on land values and housing prices.

ECONOMIC AND SOCIAL POLICY

Government policy also shapes or modifies the private market at the general level of economic and social policy. Governments, in pursuing macro-economic goals such as combating inflation, stimulating exports or deflating demand, carry through policies that effect the housing sector. Rates of housing investment and housebuilding activity may be deliberately used as a means of regulating the economy, for example through stimulating employment growth. To this end the government may directly influence local authority building whilst indirectly acting upon the private sector through credit control and interest rate policies. Over the last few years it seems more the case that the chief impacts on the housing sector have been the side effects of broader policies aimed at reducing inflation. For example, a policy of maintaining high interest rates may be necessary in order to finance government expenditure or control the money supply, but high interest rates affect the ability of builders to finance their activities and consumers to purchase the completed houses.

The broader social objectives of the government are also important in creating a climate for private market decisions. Successive governments have varied in their attitude towards owner-occupation on social and political grounds, with Conservative governments, in particular, seeing it as an essential support for the principles of private ownership and a source of social stability. The expansion and contraction of the private market has responded to a combination of ideological factors and the economic constraints imposed in the pursuit of macro-economic policies.

In conclusion, it is evident that government policy, at many levels, modifies market forces and interacts with them to shape the decision-making environment of housing producers and consumers. More details of specific policies will be brought out in the subsequent discussion where they are relevant to the actions of particular agents.

Production

LAND AND HOUSING: THE ROLE OF THE LANDOWNER

In a society where land is privately owned and is regarded as a source of revenue and profit landowners have certain powers to control the supply of housing. This power, now circumscribed by a variety of planning controls, was often vigorously exercised before the advent of planning regulations. Before examining the present role of land-owners it is useful to consider the role of landowners in the rapidly growing cities of the nineteenth and early twentieth centuries since this allows an examination of the role of landowners unsullied by planning regulations and incidentally highlights the imprint of the actions of past landowners on the urban fabric of some contemporary cities. The activities of past landowners lives on in the spatial structure of some contemporary British cities.

The influence of landownership on urban development can be seen with reference to the patterns of landownership and to the positive actions exercised by some landowners. Detailed studies of Leeds (Ward, 1962) and Bradford (Mortimore, 1969) have graphically shown how the patterns of landownership became the invisible skeleton for the growing body of the town. In Leeds the antecedent patterns of ownership influenced the design, layout and timing of construction of terraced artisan houses and in both cities the location of post-1914 public housing estates was dictated by the presence of large landholdings. The respective councils attempted to rehouse slum dwellers at densities of eight to twelve houses per acre, which required large sites, and the acquisition of these sites was facilitated by the existence of large compact landholdings. The location of these holdings dictated the siting of the public housing estates.

The existence of a large compact holding was also an important prerequisite for the development of high-status housing. The control necessary for this type of development was more easily assured when a single landowner owned a substantial plot of land. This is evident in the development of such high-status areas as Kelvinside in Glasgow and the Park in Nottingham where the land was owned by a small number of landowners who supervised the construction of housing in order to maintain the exclusive character of the area (see Simpson and Lloyd, 1977).

If landowners decided it was profitable to release land, they had the option of either selling it or leasing it to builders and developers. In the latter case profits accrued to the landowner through the increase in ground rents. Dyos (1961) gives the example of one estate in nineteenth-century London whose freehold groundrents increased from £2,000 per year to £21,000 per year after residential development had occurred. If landowners did lease their land the nature of the leases often influenced the character of the subsequent development. The quality and status of an area could be maintained by introducing restrictive clauses in the lease, which could range from stipulations on housing standards, the setting of minimum selling prices for housing to restrictions on the development of non-residential land uses. Perhaps the most vigorous landowner in this respect was the Duke of Bedford, whose attempts to maintain the status of Bloomsbury in London included the vetting of all goods sold by shops in the area and extended to the building of gates at the entrance to the estate to keep out the *hoi polloi* travelling to and from the newly built railway stations of Kings Cross and St Pancras.

The broad and pervasive influence of landowners on the growing cities of the nineteenth and early twentieth centuries is, perhaps, best summarised by Kellett,

> In many ways urban landowners were the most important single aspects of change . . . (they) profited at all stages of railway building and probably exercised the greatest single influence upon the selection of central sites, upon the location and character of suburbs; and even exercised a lesser though considerable influence upon the costs of the services offered (Kellett, 1969, p. 421).

Although the power of landowners to influence the overall character of residential development is now less marked than in previous periods, the ownership of a scarce and essential prerequisite for housing still gives contemporary landowners an important role to play in the changing patterns of ownership. The period since 1945 has seen a rapid growth in the landholdings of land and property companies who regard land primarily as an investment asset. Even more recently, since the early 1970s, these land and property

companies have been taken over by, or have become closely interlinked with, the major institutional investors such as insurance
companies and pension funds (Barras and Catalano, 1975). Land has
become regarded as a good investment because of its diminishing
supply and because it preserves its value in a period of rapid inflation
when industrial equities fail to provide adequate returns for the large
investment funds. Much of this investment has gone into land and
property in the commercial cores of cities (Ambrose and Colenutt,
1975), although institutional investors have also been building up
holdings of agricultural land (Munton, 1977). However, there is a
lack of published information on the precise patterns of landownership on the urban fringe, which is the crucial area for new residential
development. It is possible that ownership in these areas remains
relatively fragmented among many small landowners with one or two
traditional estates and a more recent growth of holdings by institutional investors and construction companies. The top 20 per cent of
large construction companies now prefer to hold land for residential
development in the form of land banks, some of this land with
planning permission and some expected to receive planning permission in the future. Although the main aim of these land banks has
been to secure future building activity, their existence allows
speculative gains to be made. Some of the largest construction
companies made substantial gains from their land banks as land
prices appreciated rapidly in the late 1960s and early 1970s.

The price that a landowner can obtain for his/her land depends on
a number of interacting factors. From the developer's viewpoint the
cost of land is a residual. Given the current state of interest rates and
mortgage finance, the developer will make an estimate of the selling
price of a house on the one hand and the costs of construction,
including an acceptable profit rate on the other. The difference will be
the amount the developer will be prepared to pay the landowner for
development land. If house prices are rising, the landowners can raise
their reserve price to ensure that they can capture part of this increase. However, the landowners' power in the market, which derives
from their ability to withhold land from the market, may be exercised
to ensure that they take a larger proportion of the total selling price of
houses, perhaps forcing the developer to economise by increasing the
number of houses per acre on the development. There are limits to
this power, for if the developers' profits are squeezed too low their
demand for land will drop.

The landowners' power is tempered by land use planning policies
and government legislation on land profits. Development control
means that there are effectively two markets in land: the market in
land with planning permission for residential development and the

market in land without planning permission, where prices are lower. The scarce supply of land with planning permission ensures that owners of such land can increase their reserve price. Furthermore, land tax policies may increase the price of land because since there is no tax on landholding, landowners will have few incentives to sell and they may hold back their land, which will reduce the supply of land and hence lead to an increase in land prices.

The ways in which changes in government legislation, housing demand and house prices interact to shape the market for landowners can be illustrated with several examples from the post-war period. In the period 1955–62 land prices rose steadily in line with house prices and construction costs, but between 1962 and 1970, and particularly after 1967, land prices increased more rapidly with landowners taking a larger and larger proportion of the total house price even though demand for housing was falling. This increase in the relative share of the price going to landowners is illustrated in Figure 6.2 for the western fringes of the London metropolitan area. This gain was

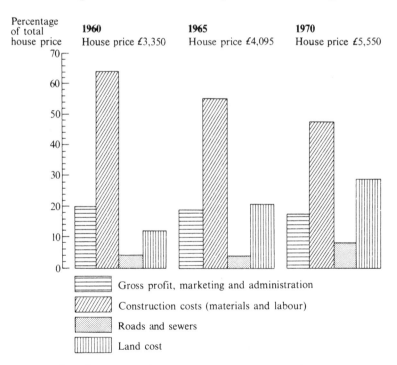

FIGURE 6.2 *Components of house prices in western London (Source: Hall* et al., *1973)*

caused by landowners withholding land from residential development, which increased the price of the available land. This scarcity
was partly a response to the introduction of the betterment levy by the
Labour government and the activities of the Land Commission
between 1967 and 1970 which caused landowners to withhold land in
the hope of a Conservative election victory and a change in legislation.

Figure 6.3 shows the pattern of land price changes since 1970. The
rapid increase in land prices between 1971 and 1973 was largely a
response to rapid increases in house prices. A high demand for
housing was made effective by the easy availability of mortgage
finance, but increases in the supply of land lagged someway behind
this increase in demand. In this context landowners were able to
divert part of the house price increase to themselves. The decline in
land prices after 1974 reflects the cuts in mortgage lending and the
decline in the rate of house price increases.

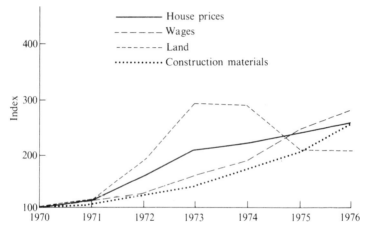

FIGURE 6.3 *Changes in land and other prices and costs since 1970*

The effects of such changes are not directly registered in the
housing market but are transmitted to the consumer through the
intermediary of the developer. The ways in which builders and
developers have responded to rising land prices and land shortages
will be outlined in the next section.

The above discussion applies largely to the role of the landowner in
the process of residential development. Within established built-up
areas residential land is mainly owned either by the local authority or
by freehold owner-occupiers. However, there are certain parts of

some cities where a leasehold system still survives, which provides potential gains for landowners. For example, 80 per cent of the houses in the Saltley area of inner Birmingham were leasehold in 1975 (Green, 1976). The area was built up at the end of the late nineteenth century on land owned by two major landowners who leased the land on 99-year leases to builders. The builders, in turn, leased the land to small landlords or local skilled workers. By the 1960s inflation had eroded the value of the groundrents of the original landowners and they sold off much of their holdings to two property companies who saw the opportunity for redevoping the area once the leases were terminated. This investment strategy was undermined by the 1974 Leasehold Reform Act and a shift in government policy away from redevelopment towards area improvement. In this context landowners stand to gain most by selling the freeholds of the property at the highest possible price to the occupiers.

In conclusion we can note that the overall importance of landowners in the production of housing lies in their ownership of a scarce and essential element in the production of housing. The power that this confers is used by all but the most traditional landowners to achieve maximum profits and increased revenue.

HOUSE CONSTRUCTION: THE ROLE OF THE BUILDER AND DEVELOPER

The agents involved in the actual construction of housing are builders and developers. A distinction could be made between the builder who constructs housing and the developer who assembles land, finances construction, obtains planning permission and arranges the sale of the product. In practice the divisions between the role of builders and developers have become less distinct as the larger construction companies now perform the functions normally associated with the developer.

In the nineteenth century the bulk of new housing was produced by a large number of small-scale developers and builders. Between 1870 and 1880, for example, 416 different firms were building 5,670 houses in the London borough of Camberwell (Dyos, 1961). These firms worked on restricted capital and built houses in anticipation of demand. Before the introduction of building regulations and without the constraints of restrictive covenants the builders increased their profits by maximising the number of dwellings on their particular plots of land. In many cities the builders maximised the number of dwellings on small plots building in a series of high-density terraces. And in many of the northern towns of England the high-density back-to-back form of house construction was a favoured method for increasing profits.

The building industry in Britain continues to be characterised by a multiplicity of small firms and a small number of large firms. The small firms in particular continue to operate with very little fixed capital and have a high failure rate. Although the small firms dominate in numbers, firms with over 1,200 operatives accounted for 21.5 per cent of output in 1965 and 24 per cent in 1973. It has been argued that size distribution of firms reflects the unstable nature of demand which causes alternating periods of expansion and contraction which militates against the concentration of firms into larger units which, in turn, prevents the exploitation of economies of scale and rapid improvements in productivity through the use of new technology. This means that housing is expensive in relation to the purchasing power of wages and that building firms lack large reserves of capital to finance their activities. Both these characteristics make the building industry very dependent on external sources of finance.

On the one hand, since very few households can afford to purchase housing outright, the building industry is dependent on the range of finance institutions which lend money for house purchase. These financial institutions maintain an effective demand for housing which allows builders to sell their houses and make a profit. On the other hand, since the construction of houses implies a large capital outlay, this means that the building industry is dependent on external sources to finance its activities. This heavy reliance on external financing makes the building industry, and hence the supply of new housing, very sensitive to conditions in the money market. This can be seen, at a general level, in the existence of building cycles, in which

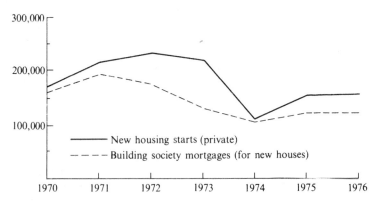

FIGURE 6.4 *Mortgage lending and housing starts in England and Wales*

the production of housing follows a roller coaster pattern with high and low points every twenty years, which are partly due to the changing availability of credit facilities to builders and consumers. More specifically, the crucial role of external sources of finance in stimulating or depressing the private housebuilding sector is clearly illustrated in Figure 6.4, which shows the relationship between building society mortgages and private housing starts in the period 1970 to 1976.

The aim of builders and developers is to make a profit on their activities. The criterion of profitability is the guiding principle in understanding the activities of builders and developers. From a range of profitable developments the one most likely to occur is the one which maximises the profits of the builders and developers. This can be most clearly seen in the choice between residential and non-residential development. Table 6.1 gives an indication of the different revenue properties of various types of land use. The implications of these figures are obvious – in the urban land market the most profitable form of development is the construction of offices. Since offices rely on centrality, the owners and developers of central land sites will therefore tend to promote office development. This process has been well documented in London and Brighton (Ambrose and Colenutt, 1975). It has also been argued that the profitable nature of office development has diverted building firms from housebuilding to office construction. Although numerous other factors have to be taken into consideration it is not accidental that during the peak year of the 'office boom' in 1974 the number of public and private housing completions had fallen to 269,000 units; the corresponding figure for 1968 was 414,000.

TABLE 6.1 *The relationship between land use and revenue in British cities*

Land use	Gross annual revenue over 1000 sq ft of site* (£)
housing (private renting)	400
factories/warehouses	1000
shops	3000
offices (provincial cities)	16,000
offices (central London)	60,000

* Including allowances for differences in plot ratio.
(Source: Ambrose, 1976)

Although the profit motive is the guiding principle to the activities of builders and developers, it is useful to distinguish between small, medium and large builders, for they differ in their modes of operations and in the constraints they experience. There is evidence that the small builder operates over a restricted geographical area where he has specialised local knowledge. The small-scale builders operate on restricted capital; they cannot afford to keep large land banks and unlike the larger firms they cannot afford speculative land dealings and hence tend to buy small blocks of land which have already been granted planning permission. In general, their activities are restricted to the construction of expensive housing on infill sites since this offers the greatest rate of return. The small builders studied by Harloe *et al.* (1974) operated in particular areas of London, employing less than twenty people and producing approximately eight to twenty houses per year. These houses were mainly of the more expensive, detached variety, built on small infill sites in 'good' areas and aimed at the higher-income established owner-occupiers.

At the other extreme are the large builders. Such companies starting more than 1,000 houses per annum, are often subsidiaries of a parent company and increasingly the largest companies have become interlinked with financial institutions which are extending their interests in the general direction of property and land. Because of their size and/or their institutional connections these large builder–developers have access to a wide range of capital sources which allows them to buy large parcels of land and maintain land banks. However, in order to raise finance from the stock market or from institutional connections the large builder–developer has to present an image of growth and prosperity if investors' confidence is not to be undermined. To maintain dividend repayments and a high turnover of capital implies the construction of housing for the mass market. In order to ensure an effective demand for their housing the large builder–developers very often seek arrangements with building societies to guarantee the availability of mortgages.

To reduce overhead costs and increase profits the large builder–developer tends to favour the construction of mass-designed housing on large sites. Since the large sites are usually found on the periphery of the city, and given the activities of the small builders in the central city, those middle- and low-income households who seek new housing are therefore faced with increasing length and time of journey to work and, in the absence of public transport, a heavy reliance on private forms of transport.

The medium-sized builders, as the name implies, occupy a position between these two extremes; in some ways their position is peculiarly difficult. They usually hold no land banks but, through a network of contacts with local solicitors and estate agents, they may be able to locate sites on which they can take out options to build. Financially their position may be delicate. Harloe *et al.* (1974) suggest that they typically lack the firmer financial basis of the largest companies and, although they need to grow, they cannot afford risky ventures or speculative activities.

We have already noted that the general effect of land policies and planning since the 1947 Act has been to push up land prices. This effect has been transmitted through to the consumers through the intermediary of the builder–developer. The small-scale builder–developers have continued to build the more expensive houses for higher-income households at the same low densities and have added the increment in land costs as an extra mark-up, while some builder–developers switched markets and concentrated on the more lucrative upper price range; as Hall *et al.* (1973, vol. 2, ch. 12) have noted, this reduced the effective choice of the households only able to afford the cheaper end of the owner-occupier market. But, in order to continue building houses for the mass market the larger-scale builder–developers have had to find ways of absorbing the extra land costs to avoid pricing their products out of the market. Typically they have responded by building smaller houses of poorer quality and at greater densities than before the war:

> If it were not for their greenfield sites, many of the 850 square feet bungaloid developments in exurbia could easily be confused with being the equivalent of late nineteenth century industrialised slums with their poor architecture, repetitive and unimaginative designs and totally inadequate space standards for a consumer society about to enter the last quarter of the twentieth century (Hall *et al.*, 1973, vol. 2, p. 401).

Consumption

In this section we will consider the role of those agents who are involved as intermediaries in the consumption of housing. Since the selling price of housing is far in excess of most households' annual income or level of saving, financial institutions and landlords act as intermediaries, enabling the builder–developers to recover their investment and households to finance the consumption of housing over an extended time period. Financial institutions in the owner-occupied sector finance not only a flow of housing services but also the purchase of certain property rights.

FINANCIAL INSTITUTIONS AND OWNER-OCCUPATION

Owner-occupation has been actively encouraged by successive governments especially since the 1950s. In 1954 there were 3.36 million owner-occupied dwellings comprising 26 per cent of the total housing stock. In 1976 the number of owner-occupied dwellings had risen to 10.7 million constituting 52 per cent of the total housing stock. This increase in home ownership has been based on the channelling of funds to house purchasers by financial institutions. The main institutions are the building societies, local authorities, banks and insurance companies. Table 6.2 shows the relative importance of each of these institutions as a source of funds for house purchase.

TABLE 6.2 *Loans for house purchase in Great Britain in 1973*

	Building societies	Local authorities	Insurance companies	Banks	Total
£m	3447	406	261	290	4404
%	78.3	9.2	5.9	6.6	100.0

(Source: DOE, 1977a, ch. 7)

THE BUILDING SOCIETIES

The building societies are the main source of funds for house purchase and they constitute one of the major financial institutions in contemporary Britain. In 1973 they held 50 per cent of national personal savings and by 1977 their total assets reached £30.4 billion. Unlike the other large institutions, the assets of building societies are totally tied up in the housing market. Building societies, as Table 6.3 shows, have evolved from a large number of small concerns to the increasing dominance of a few large societies.

Building societies operate in a non-profitmaking way by attracting deposits from investors and lending the money to house purchasers. Their ability to attract deposits depends upon their competitive position in the money market. Figure 6.5 indicates the close relationship between the relative interest rates offered by the societies (the difference between the building societies' rate of interest and the rate an investor could obtain elsewhere in the money market) and the inflow of funds. It is clear that the flow of funds is very sensitive to changes in relative interest rates and this sensitivity is due to the nature of the funds invested. It has been estimated that in 1974 at least one-third of all shares and deposits were in holdings of £5,000 or more, and the proportion of building society deposits held by large

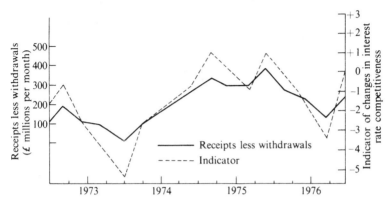

FIGURE 6.5 *Relative interest rates and building society receipts (Source: DOE, 1977a)*

investors was growing (DOE, 1977a). These larger investors are particularly sensitive to relative interest rates in the money market.

The flow of funds associated with relative interest rates has important consequences on the net lending of the societies. When the societies offer favourable rates of return, deposits are attracted and more loans are made available for house purchase. Conversely, when the societies' rates are uncompetitive, deposits are withdrawn and there is a reduction in the amount of loans for house purchase. This reduction in mortgage availability has three main effects. In the first place, since there is a decline in the effective demand for housing, builder–developers respond by building less housing. If the response time of builder–developers is long this means that when more mortgages do become available there are few new houses and the pressure of demand can lead to house price increases. In the second place, if other sources of finance are unavailable, some households will be unable to enter the owner-occupier sector. Finally, the reduction of funds will cause some societies to reappraise formerly marginal cases. It will become apparent that this reappraisal will primarily affect lower-income households and other households wishing to purchase older property in the inner city.

The building societies operate under constraints imposed upon them by the state of the money market. In order to guarantee the security of depositors' investment, the societies operate a risk-avoidance policy which, when translated into criteria for granting loans, has important consequences for certain types of property and for certain types of households. We will consider the policies of building societies with respect to (a) the distribution of mortgages between different types of households; (b) the distribution of mortgages between different types of property; (c) the distribution of mortgages with respect to different residential areas.

(a)   The distribution of mortgages between households
To avoid foreclosure, a costly and time-consuming business which societies try to avoid at all costs, building societies lend to households having little likelihood of future non-payment. The household characteristics which concern them are the absolute level of income and the stability of income. The societies operate an income-related loan scheme and, although it varies between societies, and often between the branches of any one society, the standard relationship is for the maximum mortgage loan to be two to three times the annual income of the head of household. In some cases the second income in a household may be taken partly into account.

TABLE 6.3

A   *Building society structure*

	1890	1961	1971	1972
Number of societies	2579	706	467	456

(Source: Revell, 1974)

B   *Percentage of total building society assets held by the larger societies*

	1901	1971
Largest society	15.8	18.6
Largest 2 societies	28.5	33.0
Largest 5 societies	46.0	50.4

(Source: Revell, 1974)

Of course, households can exercise a certain choice in that they need not take up the maximum mortgages. Ball and Kirwan found in their study of the Bristol housing market that 57 per cent of house purchasers interviewed claimed that they had borrowed as little as possible (Ball and Kirwan, 1975). However, the choices open to lower-income households are much more constrained in that they may need the maximum possible mortgage proportional to their income to stand a chance of entering the owner-occupier market even through the purchase of the cheapest houses.

In so far as building societies take into account income, security of income, and general creditworthiness, their lending policies are biased against low-income households and households headed by manual workers (Barbolet, 1969). Although manual workers can achieve relatively high incomes at the early stages of their working careers, they have less chance of increasing their income through time. Non-manual workers, in comparison, tend to have greater job security and are more likely to have an incremental pay structure. The biases in mortgage allocation have been highlighted in a series of studies (e.g. Boddy, 1976a; S. Duncan, 1976) and are illustrated in Table 6.4, which shows mortgage allocations by the Nationwide Building Society classified by the socio-economic group of the recipients.

TABLE 6.4 *Mortgage allocations by socio-economic group*
Nationwide Building Society: 1974

	% of first time* buyers	GB average proportion in SEGs**
Professional workers (SEGs 1,2,3,4)	24.4	22.2
Clerical, sale workers, (SEGs 5,6)	25.2	17.0
Skilled manual workers (SEGs 8,9,12)	25.3	37.4
Unskilled manual workers (SEGs 7,10,11)	10.5	20.7
Other	14.6	7.7

(Sources: * Nationwide Occasional Bulletin 1974, p.124; ** Household Composition Summary Tables, 1971 census, HMSO)

(b) The distribution of mortgages to different types of property
Concern for the security of their loans also biases the societies away from older property and 'non-standard' dwellings such as multi-occupied houses and converted flats. The ideal type of property from the building society viewpoint is the post-1945, semi-detached or detached house in the suburbs. It is assumed that houses in these areas will steadily increase in value and there will be no problem in realising the initial price in the event of foreclosure.

Figures for 1976 illustrate this pattern of lending. In that year 61 per cent of mortgages went to property built since 1945, 18 per cent to property built between 1919 and 1939, and 20 per cent to pre-1919 property. Many of the pre-1919 properties were large and substantial houses and only 4 per cent of mortgages actually went to pre-1919 properties which sold for under £6,000 in 1975. This under-representation of building society loans at the cheaper end of the market can be illustrated in another way. In 1975 10.9 per cent of all sales of second-hand houses were for sums below £5,000 but only 3.4 per cent of mortgage advances were for such properties (DOE, 1977a, ch. 7).

(c) The building societies and the inner city
The lending policies applied by the societies to allocate funds to household categories and housing types intersect to produce a distinctive spatial pattern to the flow of funds within the city. These policies lubricate the suburbanisation process by directing funds towards new housing on the expanding urban fringe where mortgages are more readily available through quota arrangements with developers. At the other end of the scale, policies which exclude many lower-income households and older, cheaper properties restrict the flow of funds to inner city areas. This pattern is illustrated in Figure 6.6, which shows the distribution of building society and local authority mortgages in Newcastle in 1974 (Boddy, 1976a). Building society mortgages were concentrated on new estates of middle- and lower-income housing on the periphery of the city and in certain stable areas of older property within the city, largely inhabited by middle-class and upper-class professionals.

The trickle of funds to inner city areas could be regarded as the natural result of the operation of lending rules applied to individual family circumstances and property characteristics. However, there is much evidence to indicate that societies adopt even more explicitly spatial policies by excluding certain inner city areas from consideration on the grounds of more general environmental characteristics, a practice that has been termed 'redlining' (e.g. C. Lambert, 1976; Karn, 1976; P. Williams 1978b). The Chief General Manager of the Nationwide Building Society has explained that societies 'are reluctant to lend on properties which may be acceptable in themselves, if the environment in which the houses are situated is declining and the values of the properties are therefore likely to depreciate' (quoted in P. Williams, 1978b, p. 25).

In many cases only a vaguely defined mental map exists in the minds of the local building society managers, but in some cases areas where mortgages will not be granted have been explicitly delimited. For example, Boddy's map of mortgage finance in Newcastle (Figure 6.6) shows areas defined as 'unsuitable for loan security' by branch managers, and evidence for other cities such as Leicester, Birmingham and Leeds has been brought together by Weir (1976) and P. Williams (1978b). A study of mortgage lending in inner

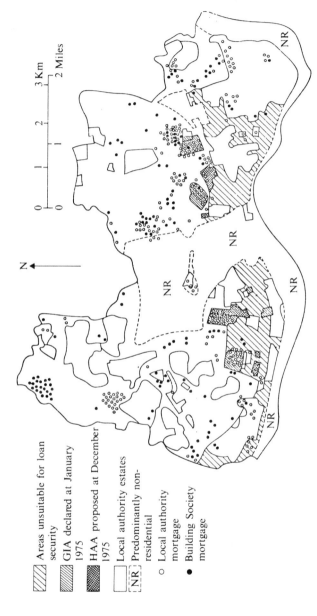

Areas unsuitable for loan security

GIA declared at January 1975

HAA proposed at December 1975

Local authority estates

NR Predominantly non-residential

○ Local authority mortgage

● Building Society mortgage

FIGURE 6.6 *The pattern of mortgage finance in Newcastle (From Boddy, 1976a)*

Birmingham, for example, found that three managers out of ten interviewed had marked off areas on a map and rarely looked at properties within those areas, and even when loans were considered, the societies' surveyors gave lower valuations for houses in redlined areas than outside, and mortgage offers covered around 70–75 per cent of the valuation rather than the more normal 80–85 per cent (Weir, 1976).

In a number of cases where redlining has been reported it appears that racial factors have played a part. Interviews with managers have revealed that the movement of a coloured population into an area is considered to be a sign of neighbourhood instability, with the possibility of growing multi-occupation and declining property values.

As long as building societies dominate the funding of home-ownership, and as long as demand for mortgages tends to exceed supply, inner city areas are likely to be considered as marginal areas for investment. This risk-avoidance policy, although seemingly logical to each society concerned with the security of investors' money, leads to some damaging consequences.

First, it may lead to the undermining of local authority policies to revive inner city residential areas, policies which have become particularly important with the swing away from clearance towards improvement. In Birmingham many of the city's General Improvement Areas and Housing Action Areas are excluded from consideration by at least one society, and evidence from other cities suggests that lending in General Improvement Areas is considered only when these areas seem to be substantially improving. However, the improvement of these areas may in many cases be conditional on an adequate flow of mortgage funds in the first place.

Second, the desire for home-ownership as an escape from rented accommodation, coupled with the difficulty of getting a building society mortgage on cheaper houses, has forced many households in redlined areas to borrow money at unfavourable rates from other institutions. In the Saltley area of Birmingham, for example, 50 per cent of loans for house purchase came from clearing banks between 1972 and 1974; 14 per cent came from fringe banks, finance companies or money lenders (Karn, 1976). The latter group act as lenders of last resort and are thus in a position to charge very high interest rates for short-period loans. The Birmingham Inner Area Study found cases of Asian families in Small Heath paying between 14 per cent and 22 per cent interest for home loans when building society rates were 10 to 11 per cent (DOE, 1977b).

Third, the overall effect of the societies' policies is often to create or increase the very uncertainty about property values that makes them reluctant to lend in the first place. The withdrawal of funds throws the area open to fringe financiers and speculative landlords and may hasten the transition to multi-occupation and declining property maintenance.

Despite the above comments, the building societies cannot be regarded as the major cause of inner city decline. The forces which have initiated the run-down of the inner city are rooted in wider changes in the economy which result in a redistribution of investment and jobs away from central areas. Nevertheless, building society lending practices contribute to the downward spiral, once started, by reinforcing the processes of housing and environmental decay that are initiated by rising unemployment and falling real incomes.

In some favoured inner city areas the downward spiral may be reversed and a change in building society lending practice may reinforce a process of gentrification and rising property values. For example, in the Islington area of inner London building societies were reluctant to lend in what was a poor and declining working-class area throughout much of the 1950s and 1960s (P. Williams, 1976). However, the increasing demand by middle-class commuters for houses nearer to the central business area, the active intervention of estate agents and developers, and a switch of local authority policy away from redevelopment towards improvement, seems to have combined to trigger a change in building society practice in the 1960s. The increasing availability of mortgages fuelled the upward movement in property values and resulted in the displacement of lower-income tenants and owner-occupiers by newer, more affluent groups.

In conclusion, the practices of building societies do impose constraints on the choices of households with regard to the age, price and location of property. It is clear, however, that these constraints operate most rigorously on lower-income groups and lower-income areas and are less of a problem for higher-income households and households wishing to purchase new homes built by large developers in the suburbs. The activities of the societies are in turn constrained by the activities of other agents in the housing and financial systems. It is these constraints that are partly transmitted to the consumer through the intermediary of the societies' rules and practices. Although they are a part of a web of interacting and mutually constraining agents, the societies still possess an important measure of autonomy in the way in which they interpret their constraints. This is shown by variations that exist among building societies and the changes in attitudes that periodically occur with respect to lending in particular areas and with respect to particular types of property.

OTHER INSTITUTIONS INVOLVED IN FINANCING
OWNER-OCCUPATION

We have concentrated on the lending criteria of the building societies because they are the single most important institution involved in mortgage lending. The other institutions, although subsidiary to the societies in terms of amount of mortgages, are not without interest, since they tend to operate in different parts of the housing market.

Since a government circular of 1965, the *local authorities* have been directed by central government to lend mortgages to those households who might not qualify for a building society mortgage. In general, local authorities with their less stringent rules than building societies have provided mortgages for lower-income households purchasing property at the lower end of the housing market. However, the local authorities do not enable all households to become owner-occupiers; Ball and Kirwan (1975) found that the lowest-income households, including single person and elderly households, failed to reach the, albeit lower than building societies', entry requirements of the local authority mortgage scheme. The main problem with the local authority mortgage scheme has been the fluctuation in net lending. Because the scheme is under the direct control of central government it has been periodically cut back in times of restrictions on public expenditure. This was most sharply demonstrated in 1975 when the mortgage scheme expenditure in that year was cut to half the 1974 expenditure. The relative success of the local authority mortgage scheme has caused many societies to leave the funding of house purchase in the older inner city areas entirely to the local authorities with consequent detrimental effects when the expenditure of the local authority mortgage scheme is periodically reduced.

Insurance companies and clearing banks are mainly involved in the upper end of the housing market. Generally speaking, insurance companies act as secondary mortgage lenders providing second mortgages, topping up loans and endowment policies which are used in conjunction with mortgage endowment policies. The banks' involvement in the mortgage sphere is mainly restricted to bridging loans, enabling households to buy one house before selling their present dwelling, preferential loans to bank employees and mortgage loans to favoured customers who have substantial business with the bank. As the previously quoted example of Saltley has shown, the banks sometimes provide mortgages for the lower end of the market where the lack of building society finance enables banks to charge high interest rates.

At the lower end of the market are the *finance companies*, which range from subsidiaries of the major merchant banks to small, back-street moneylenders. Their loan conditions are short term with relatively high interest charges, sometimes involving punitive repayment clauses. They can be seen as lenders of the last resort, lending money to house purchasers unable to obtain building society finance. They are most active in the inner city areas starved of building society finance. It has been argued that they have been extensively used by immigrant groups purchasing the older property in the inner city (Karn, 1976; Rex and Moore, 1967). The high interest rates charged by these finance houses can lead to a decline in housing quality, as some owners will take in lodgers to help meet the repayments and/or will have very little money to spend on house repairs. This over-crowding and lack of improvement can lead to a further decline in the housing quality of inner city areas.

THE PRIVATE RENTED SECTOR: THE ROLE OF LANDLORDS

Renting from a private landlord is the major alternative to those households who cannot enter, or prefer not to enter, the owner-occupier and public housing sectors. In a general sense, landlords can be defined as those capital investors who have invested in housing. Although good evidence is certainly scarce, what evidence there is suggests that the term 'landlord' does not cover an undifferentiated category of agents with similar goals and resources.

It appears that the typical landlord is a small-scale landlord. Cullingworth (1963) found in a study of Lancaster in 1960 that 524 out of a sample of 853 landlords owned only one property. In a sample of landlords in England, Greve (1965) found that 80 per cent had fewer than five tenancies and 40 per cent had only one. A more recent survey of London has estimated that in 1968 34 per cent of landlords owned one tenancy, 54 per cent between two and nine and only 5 per cent owned more than ten (DOE, 1977a, ch. 9). However, the small landlord is not necessarily the most important in terms of the organisation of the market. Although they are a small percentage of the total number of landlords, large landlords and property companies own a large proportion of the private rented stock. In Lancaster those landlords who had more than ten properties owned between them just over a third of all privately rented dwellings and in Edinburgh, Elliot and McCrone (1975) found that while only 2 per cent of landlords were property companies, they owned between them a quarter of all rented properties.

Large property companies owning thousands of properties do not have the same attitudes towards property, or the same goals, as small owner-occupier landlords with one or two properties. The property companies are profit-maximisers with a definite investment policy and a professional management of property. In Edinburgh the three largest companies owned 7,000 properties and were themselves subsidiaries tied into a network of estate agents, finance companies and property development interests. In some cases owning and renting properties may even be incidental to a wider market strategy. One of the large property companies studied by Harloe *et al.* (1974) in London was more concerned with the increase in the asset value of flats; if rents could be pushed up, asset values could be increased and large sums borrowed on the security of the building could be invested elsewhere.

For the small-scale landlord the situation is often quite different. Many are 'involuntary' landlords in the sense that they have acquired property through inheritance; 40 per cent of Greve's sample had acquired property in this fashion. For some, renting off part of their house is a supplement to their income. For immigrants, property ownership may be a symbol of status, of 'having arrived'. For the elderly, owning a few houses is a source of security, however small the return. It cannot be denied that there are many small-scale landlords who are just as much profit-maximisers as the largest property company; it is simply the case that other goals may often have priority.

An examination of the effects of landlords' actions on access to this sector of the housing market needs to be prefaced by a few remarks on the background to the decline of the private rented sector. The contraction of this sector, in both absolute and relative terms, which has been occurring ever since 1918, has been most marked since the end of the Second World War (see Table 6.5). In absolute terms this decline reflects a response by landlords to changes in the relative rates of return provided by the ownership of rented property compared with alternative forms of investment. Eversley (1975) has noted that investment in rented property was assured of an 8 per cent return on

TABLE 6.5 *Number of privately rented dwellings in England and Wales, 1914–75*

	Dwellings (millions)	Percentage of total housing stock
1914	7.1	89.8
1938	6.6	57.8
1960	4.6	31.5
1971	3.3	19.3
1975	2.9	16.1

(Source: DOE, 1977a, p.38)

investment before 1914 which was almost double the return on gilt-edged securities. In 1970, by contrast, landlords could only obtain an estimated 6 per cent return on investment in rented accommodation compared to 9 per cent on long-dated securities. The low profitability of investment in rented accommodation has been exacerbated by constraints imposed on the landlord to set rent levels. The first Act to control rent increases was passed in 1915 and despite two periods of rent decontrol, from 1923 to 1939 and from 1957 to 1964, rent controls of varying degrees of severity have been in operation ever since. At the present time the power to set rent levels for all but the most expensive property is in the hands of the Rent Officer. The 'fair rent' fixed by the Rent Officer is the likely market rent assuming no scarcity value. The fixing of fair rents applies to cases where the Rent Officer has received an application from the tenant or from the landlord, but when tenants are unaware of their rights, rents set by the landlord may be higher than the fair rent level.

The net effect of the relatively low profitability of private renting has been the reduction of the private rented stock, as landlords have endeavoured to sell their properties in order to invest capital in more lucrative investments. Another effect has been to restrict the construction of new housing specifically for private renting. If a developer has a plot of ground subject to planning permission, the most profitable course of action dictates either commercial development and/or the construction of owner-occupier housing. The lack of new building has meant that housing in the private rented sector is older and hence of lower quality than housing in the other two tenure categories. This feature is clearly shown in Table 6.6.

TABLE 6.6 *Housing quality by tenure category in England and Wales, 1976*

	Owner-occupied	Public housing	Privately rented and others
unfit dwellings (%)	3.0	1.0	16.0
dwellings lacking one or more basic amenities (%)	5.0	6.0	26.0
dwellings built before 1914 (%)	30.0	3.7	68.5

(Source: DOE, 1977a. pp. 1, 38, 56)

In relative terms the declining importance of the private rented sector reflects the increasing importance of owner-occupation and public housing. These developments now mean that the private rented sector provides housing for three major groups: young couples saving for a first house or waiting to obtain a council house; single people and other transient households who have high mobility and who do not want the ties and responsibilities that are associated with owner-occupation; lower-income households who would prefer alternative accommodation but have little chance of saving for a house, of obtaining a mortgage or of getting on an overcrowded council house waiting list. The first two groups are in the private rented sector largely by choice, but the last group are effectively trapped because they are excluded from the alternatives. The privately rented areas of the city act as reception areas for different groups, trapping some and providing short-stay accommodation for others.

Landlords are faced with a particular pattern of demand from particular types of households on the one hand and a network of financial and governmental constraints on the other. How have they responded? And what are the effects of their responses?

One response has been to sell off their properties either to property developers or to owner-occupiers. Between 1938 and 1975 2.6 million dwellings were sold by landlords to owner-occupiers and *ceteris paribus* this trend is unlikely to diminish. This reduction of supply combined with constant, or in some cities rising, demand has sharpened competition in the rented sector to the detriment of the lower-income households who may be outbid by the higher-income transient households. However, selling to owner-occupiers or to property developers is not a course of action which is open to all landlords. It may be difficult to gain vacant possession, and not all rented property is located on sites suitable for redevelopment. Furthermore, only certain favoured inner city areas will be attractive to potential owner-occupiers and to the building societies which provide the mortgages. An example of one such favoured area is the case of Islington, cited earlier, where the increasing demand for houses for middle-class owner-occupation has been encouraging landlords to sell their rented property from the 1960s onwards (P. Williams, 1976). Up to 90 per cent of the properties sold by estate agents in this area were sales of formerly rented property to owner-occupiers. In the buoyant property market of the early 1970s this process spread to many inner city boroughs of London, with landlords and property companies converting and upgrading low-quality rented accommodation, often with the aid of improvement grants. However, in many cities, such as Liverpool, such gentrification has hardly registered in inner-city housing markets.

Another response has been for landlords to concentrate on the segments of the market that offer the highest returns. Large landlords and property companies often adopt allocation rules that select higher-income, childless, professional households who can pay higher rents and cause fewer management problems. This is less of an option for the small landlord with rundown inner city houses, but even here there has been a significant switch to letting out to students whose combined incomes provide a higher rent than low-income families and whose temporary residence ensures the opportunity for regular rises in rents. Given the excess of demand over supply, even the smallest-scale landlord with the poorest property can afford to exclude low-income households. This switch to higher-income, short-stay households has been paralleled by the switch from unfurnished to furnished accommodation. The change in emphasis from unfurnished to furnished is also partly due to the legislative framework before 1974, and since then to the different rates of return afforded by these two categories of private renting. Before the 1974 Act tenants in furnished accommodation were not afforded security of tenure. Many landlords simply transformed their unfurnished accommodation into furnished accommodation with the addition of some furniture and thereby avoided the risk of having sitting tenants. Although the 1974 Act extended security of tenure to furnished tenants it still seems that landlords can make more money by converting unfurnished units into furnished units. The capital expenditure may be low and the rents, even when fixed by the Rent Officer, are much higher. One further response of landlords has been to reduce maintenance and improvement expenditure. The reduction of such expenditure allows profitability to be maintained in the face of low fixed rents and rising repair costs. This response has become more marked as repair costs have continued to rise. In 1975 repair costs increased by 85 per cent, but registered rents increased by only 40 per cent. The explicit policy of landlords to reduce maintenance expenditure, and evidence of the other responses, has been noted in a recent survey of landlords in Bristol (Short, 1979).

The direct consequences of these landlords' responses are a decline in the quality of some privately rented accommodation and increased difficulties for those households who are effectively trapped in the private rented sector.

Exchange

Finally, we come to the process of exchange. This term covers the buying and selling of houses within the owner-occupier and private rented sectors and the transference of dwellings between sectors. There are a number of agents who orchestrate these exchanges –

estate agents, solicitors, surveyors and valuers. We will concentrate here on the role of estate agents.

Estate agents help sellers to sell houses by providing information to buyers. They may also arrange mortgages for prospective purchasers, value houses before they are put on the market and manage rented property for landlords. In the past little consideration has been given to their activities and it has been assumed that their role has been largely passive. In fact the influence of estate agents on the housing market can be perceived as a continuum ranging from passive co-ordination to active manipulation of market processes. Two topics will be considered here: the agents' role in matching households to housing, and the implications this has for the residential structure of the city; and the agents' wider interconnections with other agents and organisations in the housing market.

Estate agents play an important role in providing information to households searching for a house to buy or a flat to rent. Cullingworth (1965) found that 46 per cent of households owning or buying houses found their accommodation through an estate agent. However, the importance of estate agents may not be uniform throughout all parts of the housing market. Short (1977) found that estate agents were more likely to be used by higher-income households while lower-income households were more likely to use informal sources of information such as personal contact.

It is probable that certain broad choices have already been taken by households before estate agents are approached. Owner-occupiers estimate the maximum amount they can afford given their income and mortgage constraints, and then begin a search for housing opportunities often within a sector extending outwards from their present location. This sectorial bias reflects dependency on existing schools and job locations and a desire to retain contacts with friends or relatives (Ball and Kirwan, 1975, ch. 10). In order to cut down the high costs of search, households consult the agents likely to have property on their books within the sector of preference.

Where households *can* live is primarily determined by their income and credit rating, but estate agents play the subsidiary role of directing households' attention towards areas commensurate with their means, and discouraging them from higher- or lower-income areas. In so doing they tend to reinforce existing socio-economic patterns. However, there are a number of market situations where estate agents can take on a much more positive role.

Such a situation exists when there are ethnic sub-markets. Estate agents can exercise some control over the flow of housing information to discourage black households from moving into white areas, and vice versa. Discriminatory practices have been widely reported in the

United States but have not been so extensively studied in Britain. Burney (1967, ch. 2) has suggested that estate agents do guide black purchasers away from certain neighbourhoods, if necessary by providing false information, and Hatch (1973) found some agents in Bristol steering black households from white neighbourhoods even when no discriminatory instructions were given by the vendor. Whether estate agents in this respect are acting as autonomous agents or whether they are simply reflecting the prejudices of the local population is a contentious issue. Whatever the precise factors, the effect is that estate agents do help to structure housing choices and play a part in maintaining ethnic residential segregation.

Estate agents may also play a more positive role in areas ripe for gentrification. Since estate agents make their money from the commissions earned in selling houses they have a vested interest in encouraging a faster turnover in the housing market and an escalation of prices. Both these things happen when an area gentrifies. In the Islington case already discussed in other contexts, P. Williams (1976) found estate agents working closely with building societies to encourage a transformation from low-cost private renting to higher-priced owner-occupation in the area. Agents encouraged building society managers to lend in the area, advised owners of rented property to sell to incoming owner-occupiers, advertised property in predominantly middle-class papers to encourage gentrification, and participated with property companies in purchasing, renovating and converting houses for re-sale. Williams concludes; 'through their role as advisers to landlords, building societies and property companies, estate agents are in an important position with regard to the generation of change' (1976, p. 80).

The close interconnections between estate agents and other agents in the housing market is also illustrated in the quite different context of the Tyne-Wear housing market. Figure 6.7 shows the network of local contacts between building societies, property companies, solicitors and estate agents that has been pieced together by the local Community Development Project (CDP, 1976a). The four local building societies had thirty directors, including five solicitors, two estate agents, two builders and five accountants. Five of the thirteen local agencies for building society funds were held by 'estate agents or legal partnerships which either include a building society director or close relative of building society director' (CDP, 1976a, p. 51). There are similarily close connections with property development companies. Such connections are important to estate agents in maintaining their hold over the business of property management and property sales.

We have now completed a survey of the main agents in the British

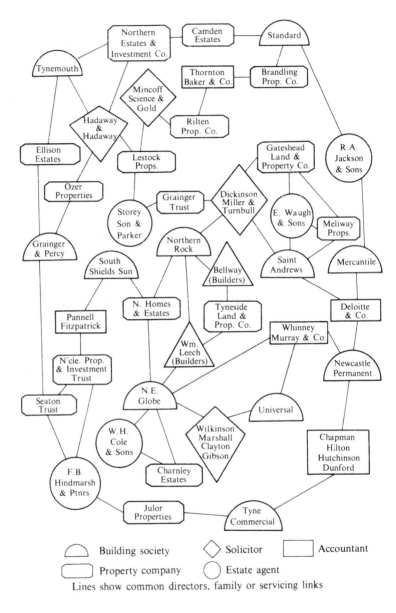

FIGURE 6.7 *The nexus of housing agents in Tyne and Wear (Source: CDP, 1976a)*

housing market and described some of their interconnections in the system of production, consumption and exchange. We have analysed these agents in terms of the roles they adopt in the market, the goals they are seeking to attain, the constraint imposed upon them by other agents and the effects of their behaviour on household choice and residential structure. The survey is by no means complete, but other agents, such as housing associations, largely fulfil a subsidiary role, and their actions are moulded by the decisions of the principal agents that we have described. However, it is important to see the British housing system in some form of international perspective. To do this we will describe the interaction between the agents involved in the housing market of the United States.

Agents in the US housing market: comparisons with Britain

The framework of production, consumption and exchange is broadly applicable to most housing markets which are based on private enterprise, although the level and form of government intervention varies from country to country and the processes of production, consumption and exchange are handled by different configurations of agents in different countries. We will illustrate some of these differences with some examples from the US housing market. The aim is not to give a comprehensive picture but simply to draw out some of the more interesting comparative aspects.

THE LEGISLATIVE AND PLANNING BACKGROUND

In the United States, government housing policy has been largely concerned with encouraging the construction of housing for home-ownership. Unlike Britain, public housing is relatively unimportant; until 1968 public housing constituted less than 2 per cent of the housing stock, and even with increased federal subsidies the public housing sector still does not exceed 5 per cent of the housing stock. To encourage home-ownership the federal authorities have created and maintained an effective demand for owner-occupied housing through the creation of Federal Housing Administration (FHA), the servicing of the secondary mortgage market and the introduction of various measures which make owner-occupation an attractive proposition. The FHA has underwritten the lending of mortgages by transferring the risk from the lenders, the various financial institutions, to the government by insuring the loans and by promising to pay any losses incurred in the event of foreclosure. This scheme has encouraged the production of housing, since it ensures builder–developers of a market. The FHA was partly responsible for lifting the US economy from the depression of the 1930s, and through the multiplier effects of house construction and the construction of associated infrastructure it has continued to increase aggregate demand in the US economy.

A significant feature of the US planning system is that planning and land use controls are two separate functions. Planners, as in Britain, are involved in constructing master plans for the proposed structure of cities and have been specifically involved in designing transportation and renewal schemes, but, unlike the situation in Britain, they do not have control over land use. The power to decide land use is invested in the local zoning boards, which are under the control of local political parties and community groups. Zoning has been used as a means of protecting property rights and as a positive aid to residential development. It has also been argued that zoning regulations have been explicitly used to maintain racial and social segregation (see Gottdiener, 1977).

In comparison to British land use controls, US zoning regulations have allowed a much freer rein to private enterprise, encouraging the wider spread of low-density suburban housing and the more pronounced decentralisation of cities. Nevertheless, although important differences between the land use controls in the two countries can be identified, the differences should not be exaggerated. Clawson and Hall (1973) have compared the land use control pattern in the two countries since the war and have concluded that the two systems, 'seem to have produced results that are alike . . . these similarities in part reflect deep social and economic forces that would operate whatever the system of planning controls' (Clawson and Hall 1973, p. 193).

PRODUCTION

The comparative lack of land use controls in the US has meant that there has been a steady supply of land for residential development and a corresponding reduction in the power of landowners to increase land prices. Builder–developers have therefore not come under pressure from rising land costs to reduce standards and increase densities. In spite of higher labour and raw material costs, building costs per square foot were lower in the US than Britain in 1969, a reflection of more effective mass-production techniques and of lower land costs. Land costs were 4.5 per cent of total building costs in the

US in 1969 compared to 23 per cent in south-east England (Hall *et al.*, 1973, vol. 2, p. 190).

The laxer controls on suburban expansions have not produced the upward pressure on land prices that has been experienced in Britain, but because of the greater possibility for buying agricultural land and getting it rezoned for residential development, land speculation had been a common feature in the US. Land speculation is so profitable that in many cases groups of investors have emerged as specialised speculators in real estate and their activities have influenced the location and character of subsequent residential development.

The US building industry also shows the pattern of many small builders and a small number of larger builder–developers who dominate the overall output. And, as in Britain, a similar pattern of small, medium and large builder–developers with similar goals, constraints and operations can be identified. In addition, Eichler and Kaplan (1967) have drawn attention to the increasing importance of large construction companies in creating, building and marketing new communities. They suggest that the merchant builder, simply concerned with building houses, is gradually being replaced by the larger community developers who develop, build and sell a total environment of houses, shops and recreational facilities for the middle-income (and especially the upper-income) households seeking a suburban residence.

The logic of profitability applies equally to North American builders as to their British counterparts. The goal of maximising profits in the North American context has meant that *ceteris paribus* housing will mainly be built to cater for the demands of the wealthier households. This was evident in the renewal programme of some US cities between 1949 and 1965. The 1949 Housing Act enabled the federal authorities to channel subsidies through the city authorities to make it profitable for the private redevelopment of 'blighted' inner city areas. When the slums were cleared the builder–developers built luxury dwellings and a few middle-income schemes. Gans (1972, p. 83) points out that these new dwellings were well outside the reach of the former low-income residents.

CONSUMPTION

On the consumption side there are some interesting contrasts between the two countries, particularly with regard to the type of financial institutions which fund house purchase. Compared to Britain, the financial market for house purchase is a Gordian knot composed of a multiplicity of institutions bound with many threads of federal and state legislation. Table 6.7 shows the kind of institutions and their relative importance. Only the bare outlines will be described here; a more detailed analysis is available in Starr (1975).

TABLE 6.7 *Sources of housing loans in the US*

	1965 $ (billions)	%	1975 $ (billions)	%
Savings and loans associations	94	44	224	46
Commercial banks	30	14	77	16
Mutual savings banks	30	14	50	10
Life insurance companies	30	14	18	4
Government agencies	6	3	66	13
Other	23	11	56	11

(Source: DOE, 1977a, Table VII)

The savings and loan associations (S and Ls) are the biggest single source of mortgage credit. They are the third largest financial institution in the US, after the commercial banks and life insurance companies, but unlike these institutions they invest the majority of their assets in residential mortgages. These associations attract small-scale deposits and operate on a non-profitmaking basis. Commercial banks are the second largest source of mortgages. Despite their importance, mortgage portfolios constitute only a small proportion of total assets, and loans generally go to upper-income households. Commercial banks can usually find more profitable forms of long-term investment than home loans. The mutual savings banks, which only operate in some eighteen states, are also non-profitmaking institutions, but they have been waning in importance as savers have found more attractive rates of return elsewhere. Finally, the insurance companies, like the banks, devote only a small percentage of their investments to mortgage finance since higher returns can be obtained in real estate, government bonds and a range of other investment opportunities.

These private institutions are backed up by several public and semi-public agencies that release funds to them in an attempt to stabilise the flow of mortgages to borrowers as interest rates change in the economy. For example, the Federal Home Loan Bank System and the Federal Home Loan Mortgage Association support the S and Ls, and the Federal National Mortgage Association deals primarily with the commercial banks and insurance companies.

Mortgage loans to households are based on the same kind of risk-aversion strategies as in Britain with mortgages being closely geared to the borrowers' incomes. The range of financial institutions and the variety in the types of mortgages makes it difficult to define an average income:mortgage ratio but in general, lenders require households' annual incomes to exceed five to six times the annual mortgage repayments. In terms of overall access to the owner-occupied sector, the high initial deposits required, until recently, by the institutions precluded lower-income households from owner-occupation. Although the FHA introduced the use of low-deposit mortgage schemes, the initial FHA schemes were explicitly used to promote home-ownership amongst the middle-income groups. In 1970, while 50 per cent of all US households were earning less that $10,000, the respective figure for households with the initial FHA insured mortgages was only 32.5 per cent.

One of the most widely publicised effects of financial institutions on housing opportunities has been their implicit and often explicit discrimination against low-income black households. Black households were frequently denied access to credit for house purchase except for house purchase in predominantly black neighbourhoods. This discrimination was maintained by racial zoning and restrictive covenants. Abrams (1965) further maintains that the early federal housing subsidies were administered in a fashion that encouraged the containment of low-income black households in central city ghettoes. These households were trapped in the run-down inner city areas as industry and job opportunities were relocating and growing in the suburban areas.

The racial riots which rocked the major cities in the mid-1960s forced the government to use the FHA to insure mortgages for low-income households. Under the 235 programme, introduced in 1968, the federal government insured no deposit loans for the purchase of cheaper properties. Although this scheme did widen the housing opportunities of low-income, and especially low-income black, households it was often misused by property speculators. Boyer (1976) vividly describes the process in Detroit where property speculators would sell off dilapidated property at inflated prices to low-income households with FHA insured loans. Many households could not afford the high maintenance costs and many of the dwellings were subsequently abandoned.

The clearest illustration of the interrelationship between the financial structure of the housing market and its spatial structure is presented by Harvey (1975a) in his analysis of the Baltimore housing market. The data for 1970 – see Figure 6.8 and Table 6.8 – clearly show that the different financial institutions were responsible for mortgages in different price ranges with small-scale state-chartered S

TABLE 6.8 *Housing submarkets in Baltimore, 1970*

	Inner city	Ethnic	Hampden	West Baltimore	South Baltimore	High turnover	Middle income	Upper income
% Transactions by source of funds*								
Cash	65.7	39.9	40.4	30.6	28.3	19.1	20.8	19.4
Private	15.0	—	—	12.5	—	—	—	—
Federal S and L	—	—	18.2	12.1	22.7	13.6	29.8	23.5
State S and L	12.0	43.2	26.3	11.7	13.4	14.9	17.0	10.5
Mortgage bank	—	—	—	22.3	13.4	32.8	—	—
Community bank	—	—	—	—	—	—	—	—
Savings bank	—	—	—	—	—	—	—	21.1
% FHA insured	2.9	2.6	14.1	25.8	22.7	38.2	17.7	11.9
Average sale price ($)	3,498	6,372	7,059	8,664	8,751	9,902	12,760	27,413

* Figures of less than 10% are not recorded.
This table is reprinted from 'The political economy of urbanization in advanced capitalist societies: the case of the United States', by David Harvey, in *The Social Economy of Cities*, Gary Gappert and Harold M. Rose (eds), volume 9, Urban Affairs Annual Review, © 1975, p. 142 by permission of the publisher, Sage Publications Inc. (Beverly Hills/London).

and Ls catering for the lower end of the market and the savings banks servicing the upper end. These different institutions served different geographical areas and acted to form distinctive housing submarkets. Table 6.8 shows that the financial institutions operate a minimum lending policy in the inner city area of Baltimore. In the areas defined as 'Inner City', housing transactions are predominantly in the form of cash payments. The institutions lend money for house purchase in residential areas where there is little likelihood of deterioration in property values. Translated into spatial terms this aversion to risk leads to a minimum lending, or redlining, policy towards certain inner city areas. In response to the social unrest of the 1960s, the FHA was forced to intervene in order to insure mortgages for the purchase of older property in the inner city. However, as Harvey notes, the FHA had to 'draw the line' somewhere in administering the programme. In Baltimore, and in other cities (see Dingemans *et al.*, 1978, for a case study of Sacramento), this line became the division between

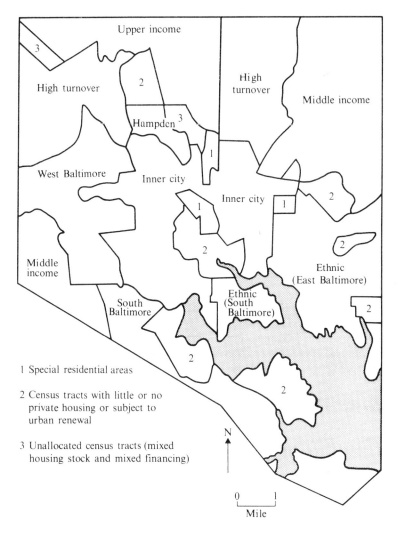

Upper income

High turnover

High turnover

Middle income

Hampden

West Baltimore

Inner city

Inner city

Middle income

Ethnic (East Baltimore)

South Baltimore

Ethnic (South Baltimore)

1 Special residential areas

2 Census tracts with little or no private housing or subject to urban renewal

3 Unallocated census tracts (mixed housing stock and mixed financing)

N

0   1
Mile

FIGURE 6.8 *Housing submarkets in Baltimore (This figure is reprinted from 'The political economy of urbanisation in advanced capitalist societies: the case of the United States', by David Harvey, in* The Social Economy of Cities, *Gary Gappert and Harold M. Rose (eds), volume 9, Urban Affairs Annual Review,* © *1975, p. 142, by permission of the publisher, Sage Publications Inc. (Beverly Hills/London))*

cash transactions and credit finance. Within the redlined area households find it difficult to obtain funds for house purchase and landlords are forced to reduce maintenance expenditure in order to recoup the high initial cost of purchase. This leads to the deterioration of housing quality and in this respect the policies of the institutions and the FHA become self-fulfilling prophecies. They refuse to invest in an area because they fear it is deteriorating and by their reduction of credit facilities to the area they create the conditions which lead to further deterioration. The institutions not only read the market, they also write large sections of the dialogue.

In the same article Harvey also traces some of the repercussions of changing lending policies on the boundaries between submarkets. For example, the introduction of the FHA 221(d) programmes in the 1960s, which insured mortgages for the purchase of dwellings below $18,000 with little or no downpayment, increased the effective housing demand of low-income black households. Estate agents (termed 'realtors' in North America) could therefore direct such households into the white middle-income areas. Such blockbusting tactics resulted in 'blow out' as white middle-income families, putatively threatened by the further encroachment of low-income black families, sold up and left for more distant suburbs. This process was lubricated by the activities of mortgage banks and estate agents eager to cash in on the increases in trade associated with such high turnover. Underlying these boundary shifts and submarket changes are changes in job opportunities, wage rates, etc., but all these forces are registered and given coherence in the housing market through the intermediacy of the financial institutions and their lending policies.

There are also some interesting comparisons to be drawn between Britain and America with respect to the private rented sector and the behaviour of landlords. The private rented sector is relatively more important in the American housing system (it comprises 30 per cent of the stock) than in Britain, and correspondingly more information is available on landlords and landlord behaviour.

A significant feature in inner city areas in recent years has been the abandonment of private rented property. For example, Stegman (1972) reported 4,000 vacant and abandoned units in Baltimore, and Sternlieb and Burchell (1973) estimated that 8 per cent of Newark's total housing stock had been abandoned. Abandonment of property seems to be one response by landlords to high costs of finance, low rent levels, and mounting maintenance costs.

Harvey and Chatterjee (1974) concluded that professional landlords expected a 20 per cent return on the estimated value of their fixed capital assets, thought 15 per cent normal, and would accept returns of between 11 and 12 per cent. In inner city areas where mortgage facilities were available the landlord could purchase a property with a small downpayment and manage the property so that rent covered mortgage repayments. If, on the other hand, mortgage finance was not available because the area had been 'redlined', landlords had to pay cash for their property and attempt to extract higher rents to offset the larger initial outlay. Abandonment could result when landlords were unable to make an acceptable return even by doubling up tenants and cutting back on maintenance expenditure.

This process illustrates the importance of mortgage 'redlining' in creating the climate for disinvestment, deterioration, and ultimately abandonment. It also highlights the hierarchical nature of decision-making by agents in the housing market. The financial institutions compete in the money market to attract deposits. To be competitive they have to ensure the security of investments and competitive rates of return. They refuse to lend in certain areas of the city because such investment is neither secure nor lucrative. Within this decision-making environment of restricted credit, landlords try to maximise profits. At the end of this sequence of constraints the most dis-advantaged households, trapped in inner city areas, are presented with very few housing options.

EXCHANGE

In the process of exchange of housing, estate agents play a more important role in US cities than they do in Britain. Discriminatory practices have been widely reported in the US for many years (see Drake and Cayton, 1962). In fact, the policy of discouraging black households from moving into white residential areas was once explicitly stated in article 34 of the Code of Ethics of the National Association of Real Estate Boards, 'A realtor should never be instrumental in introducing into a neighbourhood a character of property or occupancy, members of any race or nationality or individual whose presence will be detrimental to property values in the neighbourhood.'

Estate agents have also played a prominent gate-keeping role in preventing lower-income households from moving into higher-status residential areas. Palmer (1955) found that in New Haven estate agents were very effective in controlling who bought houses where, and were successful in maintaining the status of an area by dis-couraging lower-status buyers through providing false information or by giving warnings of future unhappiness. One agent was reported by Palmer to have said: 'People often try to get into higher class areas than they'll be accepted in. We just don't show them any houses in those areas. If they insist . . . we try to talk them out of it one way or another.' Estate agents have also been active in some cities in increasing the turnover of households by 'block-busting'. This involves selling houses in white areas to black families, encouraging a white exodus to more distant suburbs. By concentrating on certain areas this gives the estate agents the possibility of buying houses cheaply from anxious whites and selling them with a considerable mark-up to incoming black families, in addition to the extra business and commission associated with high levels of turnover.

CONCLUSIONS

The comparison of the British and US housing systems reveals a similar configuration of agents with similar goals and constraints and also some marked contrasts. The lower level of government intervention in the US is an important background factor. The greater range of financial institutions involved in the housing market creates a greater differentiation into housing submarkets than is apparent in Britain. The phenomenon of abandonment of private rented property is, as yet, only found on any large scale in the inner areas of US cities. Estate agents seem more important as agents of change, or enforcers of residential segregation, in the US housing market than in the British.

More importantly, it is hopefully apparent from the previous discussion that an analysis of the different agents involved in the housing market provides a useful and revealing way of exploring the functioning of different housing systems and their effects on household choices, household constraints and residential structure.

Chapter 7

Public policy, local government and urban housing markets

A framework for analysis

In this chapter we turn to the institutions of local government and the impacts of public policy on urban housing markets. In many ways this poses more complex problems than the study of institutions and agents in the private housing sector. Local authorities have a variety of goals and objectives and intervene in housing markets through interrelated policies that have a great range of effects on the housing opportunities of many different groups. They often command immense resources compared to some private institutions, and they are subject to a wider range of influences and constraints. Understanding the decision-making process behind public policy is a complicated task.

To organise the discussion, the framework of analysis shown in Figure 7.1 has been adopted. National economic conditions set the general context of policy-making and directly influence the state of the local economy. Central government policies are filtered through the local government system and find expression in a particular mix of local policy outputs that impinge upon the local housing market. Changes in the housing market in turn affect the local economy (e.g. through changes in labour availability) and social class relations (e.g. through changes in residential segregation, property values or differential access to new housing opportunities). Finally, the changes in the housing market may feed back into the local government system through official monitoring and evaluation or through the intermediary of various pressure groups acting to reinforce or change existing policies. There are also feedback effects from the local to the national level as local authorities collectively attempt to influence the direction of central government policies.

The diagram by no means captures the full complexity of the situation but it does serve to identify and link together a number of key themes. These can be categorised as follows

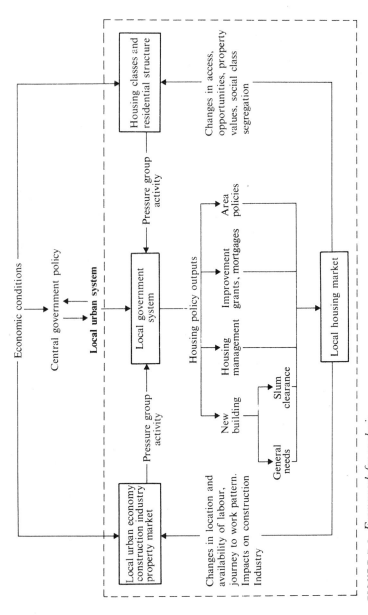

FIGURE 7.1 *Framework for analysis*

1 The national policy framework
2 Local housing market conditions
3 Policy outputs and their impacts
4 Local political processes and housing policy decisions.
We will use information about the British housing system to illustrate these categories and then go on to make some selected international comparisons in a later section.

The national policy framework

This is clearly of great importance today in all advanced capitalist countries. Central government policy sets the framework for local government policy by specifying the forms of intervention that are open to local governments and by establishing priorities between different policy options. This can be clearly seen in the evolution of British housing policy.

Policy development in Britain since the end of the First World War can be divided into fairly distinct phases. The inter-war period (1918 to 1939) began with an ambitious public housing programme (1918–21) to meet general needs in the context of a depressed private market. In spite of a short-lived attempt to return to a private-market solution to Britain's housing problems in 1922–3, public building for general needs continued until the early 1930s. A slum clearance and re-development programme was added in 1930 to supplement the general needs programme, but, following economic crisis, public expenditure cuts and the restoration of market conditions favourable to private housebuilding, public investment was cut back and concentrated on meeting special needs (slum clearance, housing large families, etc.).

The inter-war policy cycle was largely repeated following the Second World War in the period 1945 to 1964 (Figure 7.2). A phase of public housing construction to meet general needs gave way to a revival of private housebuilding for owner-occupation in the mid 1950s and the concentration of a reduced level of public investment on slum clearance, redevelopment and other special needs.

The parallel with the inter-war policy cycle largely ends in the 1960s. The situation in the 1960s, with interest rates, costs and subsidies all rising steeply was quite different to the 1930s when interest rates were low, costs were falling and subsidies could be cut. From 1964 onwards there is evidence of a convergence of thinking between the parties on certain aspects of housing policy, a widening of the range of policy measures, and a groping towards some form of comprehensive housing policy. The Labour party began to re-examine its commitment to council housing and both parties began to put increasing reliance on policies of housing improvement and an expansion of housing associations to provide an alternative to the main forms of tenure. Nevertheless controversies continued over what to do about the continuing decline of the private rented sector, over sales of council houses, and increasingly over the most equitable distribution of housing subsidies between the public and private sectors. Significantly, the search for a comprehensive policy has eluded both parties, partly because of the very intractability of the problem, partly because of the deepening economic crisis and the fluctuations of public expenditure.

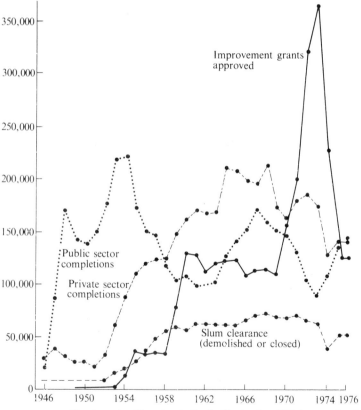

FIGURE 7.2 *Components of housing policy in England and Wales, 1946–76*

Historical studies of British housing policies have tended to stress a wide variety of economic, political and social forces in accounting for the major policy developments. Murie, Niner and Watson (1976) point out that government housing policies have been severely affected by general economic conditions (changes in interest rates, for example), and, although party political factors play a part, housing policy gives the impression that it 'has developed in a haphazard fashion and in response to particular crises' (Murie *et al.*, 1976, pp. 241–42). Heidenheimer, Heclo and Adams (1975) note the importance of certain socio-economic trends in guiding the main outlines of housing policies. Party ideologies have played an important part, but although the parties have articulated quite different viewpoints on housing their public rhetoric has often not been matched by their practices when in office. 'Neither party's programs have been a pure reflection of party ideology on housing' (Heidenheimer *et al.*, 1975, p. 80). Finally, a number of authors point out that policies must be implemented through local government systems which vary in political outlook and administrative efficiency. There are endless

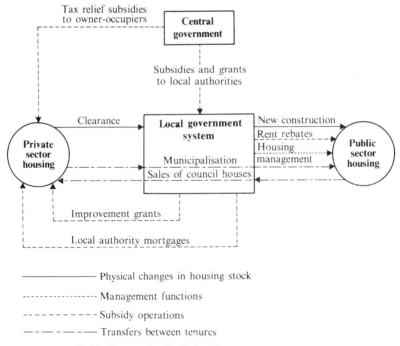

FIGURE 7.3 *Public intervention in the housing system*

possibilities for conflict which further undermine the possibility of a clear-cut national policy on housing.

Housing policies have also been influenced by the wider context of planning at the urban and regional levels. The importance of the 1947 planning system on post-war urban development has already been referred to in chapter 6. Containment, the growing separation of home and workplace, and the inflation of land and property prices have also had their impacts on local government housing policies (Hall *et al.*, 1973). Containment policies have encouraged the re-development of inner city areas at high densities. Higher density building and rising land values have pushed up housing costs and put an increasing financial burden on many urban governments. Restricted opportunities for outmigration have favoured the more affluent and mobile workers and may have contributed towards social polarisation and the creation of lower-income 'housing traps' in certain inner city areas (Coursey, 1977). The revision of many of these planning policies brought about by the priority now being attached to 'inner city' regeneration will work its way through to affect housing policies in quite different ways over the next decade. The interaction of planning policies and housing policies is therefore a vital dimension in understanding and explaining housing policy developments.

Whatever the precise causal explanation, the present pattern of public intervention in housing represents the end result of a long and complex history. Figure 7.3 summarises the main forms of intervention operating in the mid-1970s. The local government system is shown here as an intermediary between the central government and the local private and public housing stock. It intervenes most directly and visibly in the housing system by demolition and new construction, but other less obvious forms of intervention are cumulatively of considerable importance. Management policies have important impacts on the social structure of the public housing stock. Property is transferred from the private sector to the public (municipalisation) and vice versa (council house sales). Local authorities also intervene indirectly through subsidies and loans to private owners (improvement grants and mortgages) and council tenants (rent rebates) and these interventions have further repercussions on local housing systems.

The degree of local autonomy varies from policy area to policy area. The Department of the Environment exercises close controls over housing standards and costs, but local authorities have considerable discretion over the definition of local housing needs, management practices, improvement grant policies, declaration of Housing Action Areas, mortgage lending, etc. (see Murie, Niner and Watson, 1976, chapter 8, for a review). This makes it necessary to give individual attention to these different policy areas when we come to look at the urban policy making processes.

Local housing market conditions

The local government response to central government policy takes place within a specific urban environment. Certain general environmental characteristics such as income distribution and class structure are important in that they affect the income base for public expenditure and shape attitudes towards government intervention. However, it is the structure of the local housing market that is of particular importance in the present context. Variations in local housing market conditions lead to distinctive local patterns of housing problems and needs, reflecting factors such as city size, age, growth and the interaction between sub-markets and the history of past policy interventions. The distinctive nature of local housing problems obviously makes some central government initiatives relevant to the local authority and others less so.

There have been few attempts at systematic comparisons between local housing markets in Britain. A recent paper by Harrison and Webber (1977) is useful in at least giving some idea of the major sources of variation observable in the 1970s. The authors used forty 1971 census indicators to compare 457 local authorities, and identified through cluster analysis six distinctive types of stress area. These were named respectively: overcrowding/large families (towns in Scotland and parts of the North region), multi-occupancy in London, overcrowding among transient single-person households (certain inner London boroughs), overcrowding among immigrant owner-occupiers (many inner city immigrant areas), poor quality, older, owner-occupied terraced housing lacking basic amenities (South Wales, West Yorkshire, North-East, Manchester), small proportions of owner-occupiers (many inner city areas with extensive council redevelopment). Each of these areas was associated with different combinations of stress variables.

Although this is only one example it suffices to emphasise the point that the local housing problems facing local authorities will vary markedly from area to area.

Policy outputs and their impacts

It is convenient at this point to turn to housing policy outputs at the local level before looking at the interaction of local political processes and central government policy that lies behind these outputs. Taking Britain as an example once again, we will look at different areas of policy and trace their impacts on urban structure and the housing opportunities open to different groups in the housing market.

The different phases of housing policy since the war, with their changing emphases and priorities, have left a substantial mark on the structure of most major British cities. As an example, Figure 7.4 shows the extent of the areas in Birmingham directly affected by council estate building, redevelopment, and area improvement since the war. The map gives some idea of the spatial scale of intervention but captures only some of the impacts. In addition, management policies affect the socio-spatial patterns to be found within estates and redeveloped areas, and estate building, redevelopment and area improvement all set off complex chains of reaction in the private housing market.

The overall effect of public intervention on this scale will be to open up opportunities for some groups and restrict them for others. Housing policy will first provide access to housing of certain types and quality in certain locations. Second, it will modify access to various public facilities and employment opportunities. Third, it will re-distribute positive and negative externalities (behaviour, status and property value externalities). The end result will be a complex pattern of costs and benefits affecting a cross spectrum of housing classes. For convenience in exposition we will explore some of the ramifications of housing policy by considering different areas of policy in turn, although they are obviously interrelated in their effects.

(I) PUBLIC HOUSING: CONSTRUCTION AND MANAGEMENT

The spatial impacts of public housing construction
The large volume of public housing constructed since 1919 through the redevelopment of inner city areas and the building of new sub-urban estates has had a considerable impact on the spatial structure of the city and the physical structure of the housing stock. The effect of over fifty years of public housing construction is illustrated by Figure 7.5, which shows the main areas of public housing in two typical provincial cities, Bristol and Nottingham. Such housing is not homogeneous; it varies in style, quality and layout according to the

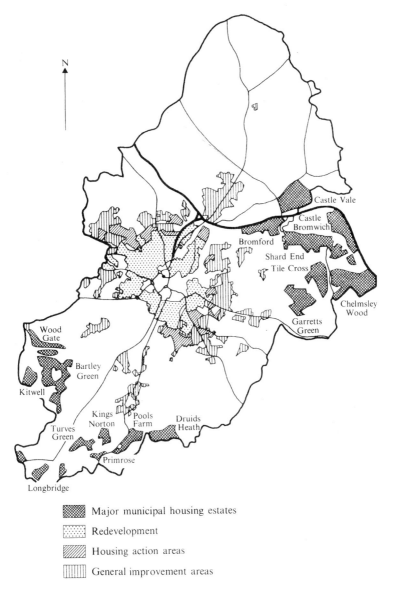

N

Castle Vale

Castle
Bromwich

Bromford

Shard End

Tile Cross

Chelmsley
Wood

Garretts
Green

Wood
Gate

Bartley
Green

Kitwell

Kings
Norton

Pools
Farm

Druids
Heath

Turves
Green

Primrose

Longbridge

▓ Major municipal housing estates

Redevelopment

▨ Housing action areas

▥ General improvement areas

FIGURE 7.4 *Aspects of public intervention: Birmingham in the 1970s*
(Source: Joyce, 1977)

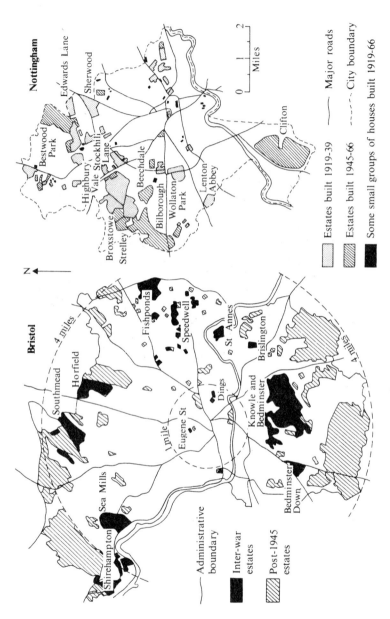

Nottingham

Edwards Lane
Sherwood
Bestwood Park
Highbury Vale Stockhill Lane
Broxstowe
Strelley
Bilborough
Beechdale
Wollaton Park
Lenton Abbey
Clifton

Estates built 1919-39
Estates built 1945-66
Some small groups of houses built 1919-66
—— Major roads
---- City boundary

0   1   2
Miles

Bristol

N ←

Southmead
Horfield
Sea Mills
Shirehampton
Fishponds
Speedwell
St Annes
Brislington
Dings
Eugene St
1 mile
Knowle and Bedminster
Bedminster Down

4 miles

—— Administrative boundary
Inter-war estates
Post-1945 estates

FIGURE 7.5 *Public housing areas in Bristol and Nottingham (Source: Thomas, 1966)*

policy phase under which it was built and the functions it has performed.

J. Jennings (1971) has described some of the variations in design that marked the different phases of inter-war building, variations that are still evident today in the structure of residential areas. The houses built in the emergency conditions following the First World War under the 1919 'Addison' Act were built to high standards to meet general needs. They were typically laid out as garden suburbs of low-density, semi-detached housing on the periphery of existing built-up areas. The largest inter-war estates were usually built under the 1923 and 1924 'Chamberlain' and 'Wheatley' Acts. Although they were also built for general needs, a less generous subsidy system, greater financial stringency and less idealism about the role of public housing combined to produce more monotonous estates with lower housing quality and a greater use of terraces. The swing to slum-clearance programmes in the 1930s added a new band of estates to the periphery of many cities, although they were often indistinguishable from the estates built under the 1923 and 1924 Acts. A change in the subsidy system in 1930 encouraged some local authorities to build high-rise flats for rehousing, but this was usually on a small scale (Ravetz, 1974). Different local authorities responded to these Acts with different degrees of enthusiasm. Jennings illustrates the considerable inter-urban variations during the different policy phases. County boroughs in some regions achieved much higher output rates than others, but the areas of highest output shifted under the different Acts.

The way these shifts in policy were registered at the local level is illustrated in Figure 7.6, which shows the distribution of houses built on Bristol estates under the various inter-war Acts. The Addison Act houses were built in three garden suburbs on land available immediately after the war. The Wheatley and Chamberlain Act houses, of more uniform design and layout, were widely distributed on new and existing estates. The poorer quality slum clearance houses of the 1930s were once more spatially concentrated, over 70 per cent being built on one already large estate. In spite of more than forty years of subsequent development and improvement, many of the differences between and within estates are still visible today and significantly affect housing management policies.

In the five years following the Second World War there was a return to something like the idealism and enthusiasm that had launched the Addison Act building programme. Building for general needs was re-established, high building standards were enforced and low-density suburban estates were quickly laid out as neighbourhood units. However, starting in 1951, minimum standards were reduced,

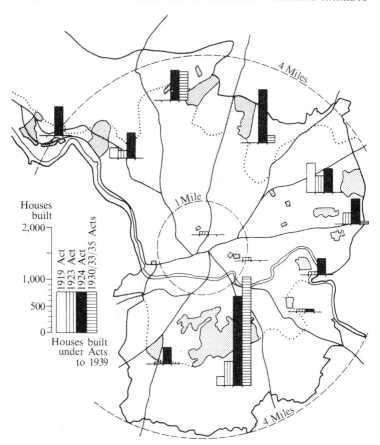

FIGURE 7.6 *The spatial impacts of changing public policy: public housing in Bristol, 1919 to 1939*

smaller and more economical houses constructed and savings made on landscaping and communal facilities. Some cities came to rely more on 'non-traditional' systems-built designs launched by major contractors (CDP, 1976b). Again the shifts in quality and system style still show up in the internal structure of many post-war estates (Burnett, 1978).

The 1950s were marked by the swing towards redevelopment and many cities embarked upon ambitious slum clearance schemes in inner city areas at the same time as their overall public building programmes began to decline. For many large cities slum clearance was the major concern right down to the late 1960s although there were considerable variations between cities in the impacts of these clearance drives. Two examples illustrate the spatial scale of the larger redevelopment programmes. In Birmingham (Figure 7.4) two phases of post-war redevelopment resulted in the demolition of nearly 60,000 houses by the beginning of 1974 (see Sutcliffe and Smith, 1974, and Stedman and Wood, 1965, for details). In Liverpool more than 10,000 houses had been cleared by 1965 and a new accelerated programme was launched aimed at clearing 33,000 by 1971. Figure 7.7 shows the situation in 1972; policy changes since then have removed large areas from the clearance programme and scheduled them for improvement.

The cycle of growth and decline of clearance and redevelopment in the 1950s and 1960s overlapped with a cycle of development of high-rise building which has also strongly marked the physical and spatial structure of many British cities. New subsidy systems were introduced in 1956 to encourage local authorities to redevelop central areas at higher densities. There was a gradual increase in multi-storey construction from 1953 to 1961, a sharp increase from 1961 to 1966, and a marked decline after 1966 when the subsidy system was once more modified (Cooney, 1974; McCutcheon, 1975). At the peak of building in 1966 contracts for more than 44,000 dwellings were approved in flats of five storeys or more. Again inter-city variations were significant during these phases. By 1971, in the ten largest county boroughs outside London the percentage of the local authority stock in flats varied from 13 per cent in Teesside to 44 per cent in Liverpool (Gittus, 1976).

Redevelopment programmes and high-rise construction are still continuing in some cities on a more limited scale, but the most recent trends have been away from redevelopment towards the improvement of the remaining older housing, and away from tower block construction towards new forms of high-density, low-rise construction.

It is apparent from this brief historical sketch that a typical English city will have varied public housing, with the style, quality, size and location of its houses and estates reflecting different phases of national policy and its own local responses to those policies. Liverpool represents a classic example with almost every policy shift being reflected in the physical and spatial structure of the city (DOE, 1977c). The inner city council estates represent a great variety of conditions and styles. There are 1930s tenements arranged in barrack-like squares, regimented blocks of 1950s three-storey walk-up flats, high-rise tower blocks from the 1960s and newer two- and three-storey blocks of terraced houses built at higher densities around open squares. Together these estates housed 55,000 people in 1971. Although the outer council estates have a certain basic similarity and

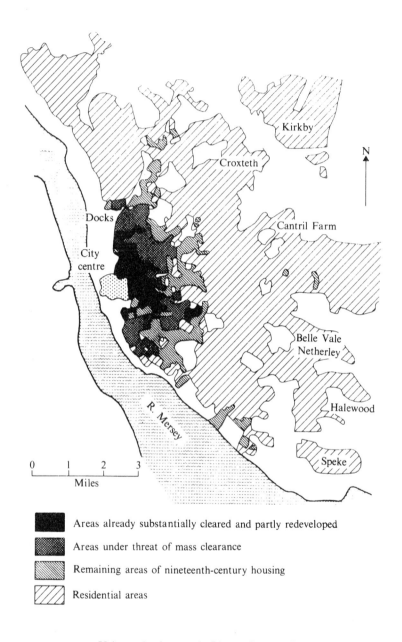

Kirkby

Croxteth

Docks

City
centre

Cantril Farm

Belle Vale
Netherley

Halewood

R. Mersey

0   1   2   3
Miles

Speke

N

Areas already substantially cleared and partly redeveloped

Areas under threat of mass clearance

Remaining areas of nineteenth-century housing

Residential areas

FIGURE 7.7 *Urban redevelopment in Liverpool, 1972 (Source: Stones, 1972)*

are clearly distinguishable from private housing developments, internal variation is also significant. The oldest estates are the inter-war garden suburbs, almost entirely semi-detached houses and short terraces. The next wave of estates built in the 1950s included a mixture of semi-detached houses and walk-up flats and the most recent developments have a higher proportion of flats and tower blocks. Altogether these outer estates provided homes for 200,000 people in 1971.

Management policies and socio-spatial patterns
All major local authorities in urban areas are faced with a demand that usually far exceeds the available supply, so management policies must be developed to regulate access to, and allocation of, public dwelling units. The physical nature of the stock (its size and location, etc.) to some extent determines the kinds of household units that can be allocated certain units but there is a wide area of choice open to any local authority in deciding how it matches demand and supply. The policies adopted in matching households to dwellings are the means by which distinctive socio-spatial patterns are maintained within the public housing sector.

As a framework for discussion the following sets of rules and priorities can be distinguished.
1 Eligibility rules and priorities – these are designed to determine which groups are to be offered the chance of a council house by regulating access to the waiting list.
2 Allocation rules and priorities – these are designed to order the waiting list applicants into priority categories and allocate households to houses and locations as they become available.
3 Transfer rules and priorities – these are designed to allow movement by households already within the public housing stock seeking to change houses to match their needs and preferences to space and accessibility.

The precise formulation and application of these rules has varied over the different phases of policy outlined earlier. At times, in the 1930s and 1950s, for example, the rules have been narrowly defined to restrict access mainly to slum clearance families or households with special needs. At other times the rules have been relaxed to allow entry of a much wider range of social groups with varying housing needs. General guidance has been offered to local authorities at each stage through the wording of Housing Acts backed up by circulars and special reports such as those of the Housing Management Sub-Committee of the Central Housing Advisory Committee (CHAC).

It is useful at this point to illustrate the characteristics of the council house population as it exists today as the historical result of the operation of these policies. Tables 7.1 and 7.2 show household type

TABLE 7.1 *Household types by tenure, 1971*

Household types	Local authority and new towns population (%)	All tenures (%)
Individual under 60	4	5
Small adult household	11	14
Small families	18	22
Large families	17	12
Large adult household (children over 16)	21	18
Older small household	15	17
Individual aged 60+	14	12
	100	100

TABLE 7.2 *Occupation of head of household by tenure type, 1971*

Occupational category	Local authority and new towns (%)	All tenures (%)
Professional occupations, employers, managers	5	18
Intermediate and junior non-manual	12	20
Skilled manual and own-account non-professional	40	33
Semi-skilled manual and personal services	28	19
Unskilled manual	12	6
	100	100

Source: DOE (1977a)

and occupational classifications for the local authority population in 1971 compared to the population as a whole in England and Wales. It is evident that the access and allocation rules operate as filters to favour selectively some groups at the expense of others. Larger families and elderly individuals appear to have a definite advantage when it comes to access to council housing and the rules also operate in favour of skilled and semi-skilled manual workers. These are aggregate figures, however, and within the broad guidelines laid down by the government different local authorities have had and continue to have considerable freedom to put together different versions of these general rules in different combinations to shape the characteristics of their local council house populations.

Redevelopment and rehousing policies

Redevelopment is something of a special case when it comes to a consideration of access and allocation rules and priorities. Families in clearance areas have generally been awarded high priority status for housing allocation, although, as the 1969 CHAC survey discovered, local authorities carrying out redevelopment since the 1950s have had differing rehousing obligations under different statutes of the 1957 Act and have had a significant degree of latitude in interpreting these obligations (CHAC, 1969).

The extent of redevelopment and rehousing in the late 1950s and 1960s has already been noted in physical and spatial terms. It is now time to look at the socio-spatial effects. In 1958 160,000 people were moved from clearance areas, a figure which reached a peak of 189,000 in 1968. Numerous case studies have been written documenting the impacts of large-scale clearance on the social structure of inner city areas and the effects of allocation policies on the relocation of families. Jennings's study of the effects of redeveloping the Barton Hill area of Bristol between 1953 and 1955 is a good example from the earlier stages of post-war redevelopment (H. Jennings, 1962). The Barton Hill area was a long-established working-class community when surveys showed that more than 38 per cent of the houses were unfit, with a larger percentage on the borderline. Jennings traced the movements of the 407 households displaced by the first phase of clearance. The location of the local authority's housing stock meant that a large proportion of these households had to move long distances to outlying suburban estates. Eventually 171 moved to adjacent areas, 74 to inner area council estates and 158 were displaced to the outer estates on the southern fringe of the city. Allocation policies operated geographically to separate different age groups in the original community. Older people were relocated as far as possible near to Barton Hill, but 48 per cent of the couples under forty went to the distant estates. It is significant that half of those moved to the outlying estates applied for transfers within a very short period on the grounds of distance from relatives and lack of accessibility to workplace. The dislike for the high-rise blocks which replaced the cleared terraced houses also prevented most families from returning to Barton Hill even when they were offered first refusal for the new units.

A second example, this time from the early 1960s, is the classic study of slum clearance in St Mary's, Oldham, carried out by the Ministry of Housing and Local Government (MHLG, 1970). The area included over 2,400 people living in 947 houses, the vast majority of which were declared unfit. Figure 7.8 shows the spatial redistribution of population that resulted from clearance and rehousing. More than 90 per cent of families were rehoused by the council, 3 per cent became owner-occupiers and about 7 per cent became private tenants (before clearance 27 per cent had been owner-occupiers and the rest largely private renters). The council accepted a general obligation to rehouse all those who wished to become tenants, including lodgers in private households, but choices open to people were

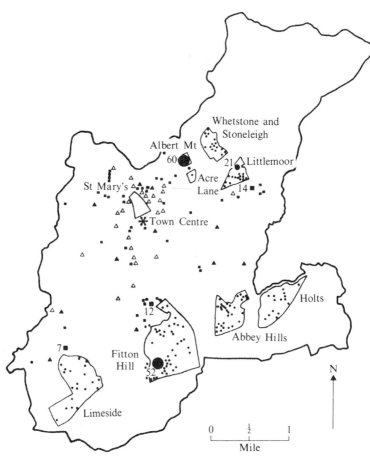

FIGURE 7.8 *The relocation of residents during redevelopment in Oldham (After MHLG, 1970)*

heavily constrained by the availability of houses. The 10,600 houses owned by the council were largely located on peripheral council estates, yet most of the families wished to be relocated as near the centre as possible. Up to four houses were offered, sequentially and not simultaneously, to families and a family could not generally go back and accept a house previously rejected. In general those who rehoused themselves did so within about a mile of the original area, those rehoused by the council had to move to quite different environments 2–3 miles away.

These examples have illustrated some of the impacts of the management of redevelopment on population redistribution and a number of other studies confirm the general picture for the 1950s and 1960s (e.g. Muchnick, 1970). Although slum clearance programmes have now been much reduced important variations are still apparent in the management of the redevelopment process in different cities. A study by English, Madigan and Norman (1976) which compared the redevelopment programmes of five large local authorities between 1970 and 1971 has revealed continuing differences in allocation policies in terms of the number of choices offered to clearance families, the eligibility of certain residents to be considered for a council house after clearance, the priorities accorded to certain groups and the grading systems operated to match prospective tenants to houses and neighbourhoods of varying quality.

Access and allocation policies – waiting lists and transfers
The problem of rehousing slum-clearance families is only part of the broader problem of the management of the public housing stock. In recent years the bulk of day-to-day problems have related to the operation of rules governing access to the general waiting list, the ordering of waiting-list applicants into priority groups, the allocation of families from the waiting list to suitable houses and the handling of transfers within the council's housing stock. All these rules and priorities interact to shape the nature and location of the council house population.

Niner's study of the housing policies of six local authorities in the West Midlands reveals the kinds of variations that exist between local authorities and the complex interrelationships between access, allocation and transfer policies (Niner, 1975). All the authorities required some form of residential qualification for access to the waiting list and some also applied other criteria such as age, marital status and specific forms of housing need. Allocations from the differing waiting lists tended to accord first priority to clearance, followed by transfers and general needs. However, clearance needs nowhere absorbed more than 16 per cent of lettings and the bulk of allocations of new lettings (excluding transfers and exchanges) went to waiting-list applicants. These applicants were in turn ordered into priority ranking either through date-ordering of their applications or through the award of points measuring various aspects of housing need such as the degree of overcrowding. However, the fact that the different authorities gave differing weights to different aspects of need implied that a family in identical housing conditions could be put into different categories of priority by different authorities. It is an interesting fact that in spite of these differences in formal allocation systems the actual pattern of allocation made did not vary greatly between authorities and the same kinds of groups were selectively favoured in each case (in particular, families who were living in lodgings or in overcrowded conditions). This may have reflected the similar nature of the authorities' housing stocks or the willingness of certain types of families in need to accept almost any offer that came available.

The pattern of transfer allocations was somewhat different. Local authorities were allocating between 27 per cent and 40 per cent of their lettings to families seeking transfers. The demand for transfers generally reflected changes of state in the typical family cycle with young growing families trying to move to larger accommodation and small elderly households seeking flats and maisonettes. The pattern of allocations actually made tended to reflect this pattern of demand fairly closely, although there were also varying emphases among the authorities on meeting special medical needs or reducing over-crowding.

These rules and priorities interact in complex ways. A completed transfer opens up a vacancy that can be filled by another transfer, opening up whole chains of movement within the stock. Certain chains can end in a vacancy for a flat or maisonette that becomes available for certain types of family from the waiting list, a process that is selective of certain categories of household type and need. The kinds of needs that can be favoured depend in turn on the eligibility rules that govern access to the list in the first place. Demand for access is in turn related to demographic structure, housing aspirations and preferences, and knowledge and perception of the opportunities available. There is therefore a complex interconnection between the nature of the stock, its vacancy pattern and local housing demands through the intermediary of the management procedures of the local authority. It is not surprising, as Niner claims, that in many cases the final outcomes may not accord closely with clear, rational intentions.

Grading tenants
Local authorities have used and continue to use a variety of systems to grade tenants in order to match households to houses and areas

according to 'suitability'. These grading systems have been applied to slum-clearance and waiting-list families.

Studies of redevelopment in the 1950s and 1960s do not lay much emphasis on grading, probably because it was of less significance when the great majority of lettings on estates were going to slum-clearance families. With a much reduced clearance programme, the matching of clearance families to 'suitable' houses and neighbourhoods seems to have assumed greater importance. All the authorities studied by English, Madigan and Norman (1976) sent round housing visitors to interview clearance families, partly to inform them of their rights and ask for their preferences, and partly to gather information about their family circumstances and the state of repair of their homes. This last information was often summarised in a system of family grades from A to C or a verbal grading from 'Good' to 'Poor'. The gradings were then taken into account by the housing department staff making the actual allocations, a poor or low grading usually precluding the offer of a more recent or post-war council house.

The 1969 CHAC Report confirmed the general prevalence of grading for waiting-list families as well as slum-clearance families. The Report found considerable variations in the grading systems, with local authorities managing a highly varied stock tending to grade much more finely than those with a relatively undifferentiated stock. The Report commented that many authorities took a moralistic attitude towards their applicants, distinguishing the 'undesirable' tenants from the 'desirable' tenants who received the best offers. As a precise example, Gray (1976a) found a significant correlation between the grades awarded to tenants by housing visitors in Hull and the quality of property actually offered, measured in terms of age and gross rateable value.

The problem estate

Access, allocation and transfer policies interact to shape distinctive socio-spatial patterns and chains of mobility within the council house sector (see Thomas, 1966, and Bird, 1976, for examples drawn from Nottingham, London and Newcastle). However, the forces leading to the internal differentiation of council housing have as their extreme expression the creation of 'problem estates', regarded as dumping grounds for problem families or as the end of the line when it comes to housing opportunities in the council sector. Their presence indicates the complex relationships between the physical structure of the housing stock and management policies.

In some cases the image of an estate as a 'problem estate' may go back to the origins of the estate and may be difficult to change in spite of deliberate policies. For example, Jevons and Madge (1946) noted the distinctive partitioning of the huge Knowle and Bedminster estate in Bristol in the 1930s according to the age, quality and origin of the housing. The slum-clearance section of the estate had the highest concentration of the poorest families, the families with the largest numbers of children and the highest unemployment rates on the estate. The recent large-scale influx of these clearance families had created a certain tension within the estate with tenants in surrounding areas requesting transfers on the grounds of dissatisfaction with their neighbours. The origins of the estate and the characteristics of its initial population established a definite image that proved difficult to change. In 1964 the local authority attempted to upgrade the area by transferring families with fewer problems from other estates. However, most tenants resisted moving to the area even if it meant a longer wait for alternative accommodation, and Tucker (1966), studying the area in 1966, still found people in the eastern end of the estate strongly condemning the housing conditions and family behaviour found in the western part.

It is also apparent that in some cases an estate may have deteriorated into problem-area status only years after it was built. Both Corina (1976) and Shenton (1976) have looked at the gradual deterioration of the Abbeyhills estate in Oldham and attempted to disentangle its causes. The estate was built in 1934, but downgrading seems to have come about largely in the last ten years or so. Older residents, many anxious to leave, felt the decline had set in with the movement of problem families onto the estate, and no less than 30 per cent of the tenants had applied for transfers to other estates on the grounds of dissatisfaction with neighbours or the poor state of the environment. Whatever the origins of this deterioration (deliberate policy or the unforeseen side effects of other policies) the decline has become a self-fulfilling prophecy. The image of a 'residual area' (Shenton's term) or a 'temporary transit camp' (Corina's term) once established cannot easily be displaced by a change of allocation policy. 'Better tenants' refuse to accept transfers to the estate and the diminishing number of better tenants on the estate become more and more anxious to move out as their neighbours and relations transfer to other areas. Dispersing the problem families to other estates may provoke opposition by tenants already living on those estates who may ask for transfers and set up chains of movement that create the problem afresh in the new area. Both authors conclude that the housing department now attempts to practise liberal allocation policies, but the constraints imposed by lack of finance for maintenance and the momentum behind the forces of social segregation result in the continuance of discriminatory practices.

Finally, it is worth noting that in some cases problem estates may evolve as the result of labelling that may have little relation to the social reality of the estate. Damer (1974), in seeking the origins of the bad reputation of 'Wine Alley', a 1930s estate in Glasgow, discovered little evidence of a deliberate dumping policy by the local authority. The estate had certainly been built for slum-clearance families rather than the 'decent poor' but perhaps more significantly the label of a problem estate had been applied very early on by the surrounding population living in slum conditions who resented the movement of slum families from other parts of the city into houses they felt should have been reserved for their own, very real needs. What started as a conflict over scarce housing resources rapidly became through labelling a self-fulfilling prophecy.

Council house sales
It is important to remember that the council house stock need not grow cumulatively or remain fixed. A number of authorities have transferred houses back to the private sector through the sales of council houses. In the peak year of 1972 over 60,000 houses were sold to tenants. As Niner (1975) and Murie (1975 and 1977) have pointed out, sales are selective in terms of tenants and houses. Those who buy are generally distinguished from the general run of tenants by their higher wages, greater skills and their length of tenancy. The houses that are in greatest demand are semi-detached houses with gardens on the more peripheral and environmentally better estates. For cities that have fostered selling schemes (a relatively small number) such a pattern of sales can have important consequences for management flexibility in the long term by reducing the variety as well as the size of the stock available for letting.

(II) HOUSING IMPROVEMENT

Housing improvement has become a major component of housing policy since the 1969 Housing Act. The impacts of improvement have not been so visually striking as clearance and redevelopment. Nevertheless, in many areas housing improvement has had widespread effects on local housing markets, bringing important advantages to some groups and disadvantages to others.

The 1969 Act introduced higher levels of grants and the concept of the General Improvement Area where individual home improvement would be backed by environmental improvements carried out by the local authority. The increased emphasis on improvement in 1969 reflected a combination of factors (see Pepper, 1971; T. Duncan,

1973; Roberts, 1976). The redevelopment programmes of the 1960s were meeting increased local opposition because of their scale and their organisation. National House Condition Surveys revealed a massive problem of deteriorated but not yet unfit housing that needed substantial repairs rather than clearance. Underlying the technical and administrative arguments over the relative advantages of improvement and redevelopment was an emerging economic crisis and a concern to control public expenditure. As a result the early 1970s saw a reduction in new council building and redevelopment and a redistribution of expenditure towards the improvement of the existing stock.

Following the 1969 Act there was a rapid increase in voluntary grant take-up. However, this take-up was highly differential, favouring particular tenures, particular social groups and particular areas (see Expenditure Committee, 1973, for a thorough review and a mass of evidence). In general, grants went to better-off owner-occupiers living in areas peripheral to the poorest housing areas. Take-up by landlords was generally low, although the poorest conditions were in the private rented sector. Take-up was also low in areas dominated by small, low-income, elderly households. These patterns have been documented in a number of case studies. Kirwan and Martin (1972) found a low propensity to improve by elderly households in the older cotton towns of north-east Lancashire where population was falling and the pressure of demand on the housing market was low. S. S. Duncan (1974) found that grants in Huddersfield went mainly to owner-occupiers in 'decent working class' areas rather than to private rented or twilight areas with the poorest conditions. Similar findings are reported for Bristol by Bassett and Hauser (1976) and Bassett and Short (1978).

In certain favoured submarkets a high grant take-up produced more dramatic social changes through fuelling a 'gentrification' process. This was particularly apparent in certain parts of inner London, where landlords and property companies were able to upgrade poorer quality private rented property with grants and sell it off to owner-occupiers anxious to move back into inner London from more distant commuting areas. This process is documented by Hamnett (1973) and in a scathing report by Counter Information Services (CIS, undated). The net effect was often to displace working-class tenants, contract the supply of low-cost housing for rent, and fuel an already buoyant property market.

General Improvement Area policies were not successful in substantially modifying this pattern of take-up. A thorough review of GIA policies by Roberts (1976) concluded that GIAs had made a pitifully small contribution to national improvement programmes.

Central government policy was imprecise and full of paradoxes and contradictions. Local authorities, left largely to their own devices in the implementation of GIA policies, gave differing weight to objectives in their declaration of areas for treatment. Some stressed housing obsolescence, some stressed social goals, some environmental goals and some planning goals. GIAs were declared in a variety of submarket situations but the majority avoided 'difficult' areas where local authorities felt success would be problematical. Duncan's case study of Huddersfield (S. S. Duncan, 1974) confirms this pattern. The eight GIAs under consideration avoided areas with large numbers of immigrants and old people and concentrated aid on owner-occupier areas with a reasonable potential for upgrading. The pattern of GIA declarations reinforced the broad city wide pattern of selective grant take-up.

The 1974 Housing Act added the concept of the Housing Action Area to the local authority's improvement armoury. These were designed to fill the gaps left by previous improvement policies by allowing local authorities to intervene in a more positive manner in areas of housing stress, the kinds of areas which had previously fallen between redevelopment and GIA status. It is too soon to come to any definite conclusions on the effectiveness of HAAs, but a review by Paris (1977a) suggests that the pace of declarations does not match the scale of the problem in inner city areas and that the rate of take-up within HAAs, particularly by landlords, has been disappointingly low. The choice of areas to be declared as HAAs has also been questioned, in some cases the ranking of areas for treatment has been somewhat arbitrary and not justified by statistical analysis (Dennis, 1978).

In spite of disappointing progress to date the impacts of improvement are likely to become cumulatively more important over the next decade, particularly in inner city areas. The Birmingham case has already been illustrated in Figure 7.4. In 1976 there were already twenty-three HAAs in the pipeline covering 14,000 dwellings and seventy GIAs covering more than 60,000 dwellings, together with a number of residual clearance areas (Paris, 1977b). Although progress has been slow in these areas, the spread of improvement zones has brought the local authority into a more interventionist role with respect to a larger and larger proportion of the city's housing stock. This appears to be a trend apparent in most major British cities (although not necessarily on the Birmingham scale) with important implications for the future.

(III) OTHER FORMS OF INTERVENTION

We have explored some of the impacts of public intervention in two main policy areas. Local authorities can also intervene in other more restricted ways. One of the most important of these secondary policies concerns mortgage lending. Local authority mortgage lending has varied between 3.8 and 17.8 per cent of total UK mortgage advances since 1960, with peaks in the periods1960–5 and 1970–5. Since 1971 local authorities have been encouraged to lend to certain categories of borrowers so that they act theoretically as the lenders of last resort. Local authority funds have certainly been concentrated in inner city areas in many cases and have done something to correct the spatial biases of building society lending practices (see for example Duncan's study of Huddersfield, S. S. Duncan, 1976). However, funds have generally been inadequate to offset the negative effects of redlining by the building societies and in practice funds have not gone to the groups in greatest need. Authorities have also varied widely in the way they have operated their lending schemes.

Harloe, Issacharoff and Minns (1974) have compared the lending practices of two London boroughs and the GLC in the early 1970s. Lambeth, an inner city borough, operated with fairly restrictive lending rules, while Sutton, an outer London borough, and the GLC, adopted more liberal rules. Nevertheless, all three schemes favoured skilled and semi-skilled manual workers and white-collar workers at the expense of unskilled workers. In effect the authorities did not operate as lenders of last resort, a role which was left to the finance houses and secondary banks. Karn (1976) has presented similar evidence of the selectivity of local authority schemes in Birmingham. In spite of government intentions a significant gap remains in the housing market such that those buying on lowest incomes get the worst property and because of their reliance on loans from finance houses they pay more for it.

This by no means exhausts the range of local authority interventions in housing markets. Many authorities have been involved in municipalisation of private rented accommodation and many now operate in partnership with housing associations, although these policies often operate as part of broader improvement policies. Much less information is currently available on the impacts of these policies.

(IV) CONCLUSIONS

In reality, the different forms of intervention that we have separately described interact to mould the housing opportunities of a large section of the population. This interaction is particularly strong in inner city areas which may be affected simultaneously by clearance and redevelopment programmes, improvement programmes, municipalisation and mortgage lending policies. Public investment in new housing directly benefits certain groups in clearance areas or on the general waiting list or on the transfer list from existing property. Area improvement policies provide grants of different value to different areas of the inner city and offer different incentives to groups within those areas. Mortgage lending policies may reinforce improvement processes by facilitating the inflow of young, first-time buyers or work against such processes. These policies interact to produce a complex interplay of secondary repercussions in the market. Redevelopment or improvement produces many positive and negative externality effects within and between neighbourhoods. Property values may rise or fall and relative price changes may accelerate tenure changes and the closing off of certain opportunities, particularly for private tenants. The lack of co-ordination between policies may produce many side effects unforeseen by the policy-makers. It is not surprising that it has proved very difficult to arrive at any overall balance sheet of advantages or disadvantages to different groups or housing classes, although there would probably be general agreement that private tenants in inner city areas have experienced the greatest disadvantages.

Political processes and housing policy decisions

The local political system provides the crucial connecting links between central government policies, local housing problems and local housing policy outputs. The term political system is used in a wide sense to encompass interest-group activities and formal government processes. A number of questions immediately present themselves relevant to policy-making in general and housing policy in particular. Which housing needs actually find expression in the decision-making arena? How are policy decisions actually made and what determines the success or failure of different policy initiatives? What are the major factors explaining variations in housing policy between local government systems? How do the conflicts generated by housing policy feed back into the political system and with what effects? There is a well-developed literature dealing with these kinds of questions from a number of different perspectives. It is worth briefly exploring some of these perspectives to identify the main themes and concepts that provide a focus for current research on local political systems and policy-making. We will look briefly at theories of urban power structures and urban managerialism and then look at their application to the study of housing policy in Britain.

THEORETICAL PERSPECTIVES ON LOCAL POLITICAL SYSTEMS

Urban power structures and decision-making

We have already referred to the study of locational conflict in Chapter 5 in terms of a critique of neo-classical and ecological approaches. According to this perspective the social geography of the city can be seen as the outcome of a power struggle between various interest groups. Given the wide range of spatial impacts that result from public housing policies, the locational conflict approach seems particularly relevant to the study of the political processes behind the making of housing policies. The locational conflict approach can, however, be viewed as the socio-spatial dimension of a wider body of theories and concepts dealing with urban power structures and decision-making. We will briefly review this wider field to identify the concepts that are most relevant to the question of housing policy-making.

Much of the work on urban power structures and decision-making has been American in origin and has developed out of a protracted debate, going on since the early 1950s, over pluralist, elitist and neo-elitist theories.

According to the classical *elitist* position, urban power structures are pyramidal in form with a small, cohesive and self-conscious elite at the top effectively controlling the main outlines of urban policy in their own interests. Members of the elite owe their position to wealth, social status or crucial business position. The politicians and officers who implement policy are largely drawn from lower levels in the pyramid and the mass of voters have minimal influence on the direction of policy.

According to the alternative *pluralist* position, urban society is characterised by a large number of competing interest groups. Government is the focal point of group pressure and policy tends to reflect a temporary consensus resulting from bargaining and the formation of shifting coalitions between groups. Interest groups tend to specialise in policy areas of particular concern to themselves and no one interest group has power over all policy areas. Interest groups are usually run by small groups of activists who could be termed elites of a sort, but these are relatively open elites. The power structure has the appearance of a large number of separate pyramids rather than one single pyramid with a cohesive elite at the top. (There are actually many variants of the pluralist position: see Parry, 1969, for a review.)

Historically, the differences between the elitist and pluralist positions have been entwined with differences in methodology, with elitists tending to identify power-holders by general reputation (the 'reputational approach'), and pluralists preferring to examine the influence exerted by the participants in selected policy decisions, (the 'decision-making approach'). However, the 'decision-making approach' has been criticised from a position that has been called *neo-elitist*. The keystone of this approach is the idea of 'non decision-making' (Bachrach and Baratz, 1962 and 1963). The neo-elitists point out that the pluralists base their analysis of power structures on the study of the participants in key issues in the urban community. These issues are often the most dramatic and public issues where pluralist power relations are most likely to be evident. However, this approach ignores the fact that power can be exercised by elites to confine the scope of decision-making to those relatively safe issues that do not threaten the real power of the elites. Behind the apparent pluralism of the visible decision-making process can lie the exercise of power by elites to exclude a wide range of issues from the policy arena. The study of non decision-making is therefore just as important as the study of decision-making.

These arguments have recently been extended by Lukes (1974) in a brief but valuable review of the whole debate. The pluralist view, Lukes argues, is essentially a one-dimensional view of power. It focuses on the behaviour of actors in decision-making situations where the issues are such that there are observable conflicts over different subjective interests and policy preferences. The neo-elitist view can be characterised as a two-dimensional view of power. It embraces both concepts of decision-making and non decision-making and represents a qualified critique of the behavioural perspective underlying the pluralist approach. It assumes that non decisions are identifiable and leave their traces at the behavioural level in terms of grievances and conflicts. Lukes then suggests a three-dimensional view of power that incorporates a more thorough-going critique of the behavioural focus. This view takes into account the possibility that power may be exerted by elites even when there is no visible sign of conflict. A consensus may be established by ideological means if, for example, the elite controls the educational and communicative apparatuses, so that rulers may make the ruled have wants appropriate to their own legitimation. This implies that subordinate groups may be held by a 'false consciousness' that blinds them to their true interests and obscures the forms of elite control. The three-dimensional view of power thus incorporates a dimension that takes

us a long way from the early focus on actors and individual preferences and interest-group conflicts. In fact it takes us to the frontiers of
a Marxian analysis of ideology and class power, themes that we will
take up in a later part of the book.

Elitist, pluralist and neo-elitist approaches have been presented
here as if they were mutually exclusive. This need not be the case. In
fact, elitist, pluralist and neo-elitist concepts may turn out to be
relevant to different policy areas at the same time, rather than aspects
of mutually exclusive theories. For example, Kantor's comparative
study of educational policy-making in London boroughs suggests that
when class-wide interests are at stake and policy involves a significant
redistribution of resources, then decision-making is characterised by
elite conflict management (Kantor, 1976). When policy issues cut
across class cleavages, many specialist interest groups are involved,
and the redistributional consequences are not clear, then decision-
making takes the form of a pluralistic bargaining process leading to
incremental change rather than definite policy shifts. This has
implications for the study of a wide range of local policies.

Finally, it is worth noting the recent trend towards comparative
studies of urban government in which the distribution of power is
linked to a wider range of community characteristics. It can be
regarded partly as a development of the power structure debate to
encompass a more systematic comparison of different communities
and partly as an attempt to break out of the confines of that tradition
to incorporate new factors, pose new questions and test different
hypotheses (Dye, 1975; T. Clark, 1972). In particular, it does not
assume that in every case power structures are crucial determinants
of policy outputs.

The basic structure of the approach is very simple. It is an attempt
to trace the interrelationships between the environmental characteristics of communities, their political characteristics and various forms
of policy outputs. Community characteristics typically include
measures of class and ethnic status, poverty levels, industrial
structure, city size and age. Policy outputs include a wide range of
decisions on education, housing, social services, etc. with output
measured in terms of enactment or non-enactment of a given policy or
in terms of levels of expenditure. The intervening political variables
include measures of the centralisation or decentralisation of power
relevant to the power structure debate and also a wider range of
variables relating to such factors as the formal structure of government, degrees of party competition and levels of bureaucractic
organisation and professionalism. Typically the analysis uses correlation and regression techniques to trace the interconnections
between the different sets of variables in an effort to find the major

determinants of policy variations between cities. This approach has generated a vast literature in the United States and Europe. A rough generalisation of the findings is that straightforward measures of socio-economic or environmental structure are often sufficient to explain *levels* of policy outputs unless the policy involves substantial redistributive effects – in which case political variables have a great explanatory power.

Urban managerialism

The theories and concepts generated by the power structure debate, although generally valuable, are very much related to the pattern of dispersed power characteristic of American cities where powerful interest groups outside the formal structure of local government often exert a dominating influence on decision-making. In European cities more power seems to reside in the formal structures of local government and the managerialist perspective outlined in Chapter 5 is particularly relevant to the study of the well-developed bureaucratic structures of urban government.

The broad overlap between the urban managerialist perspective and the power structure debate can be seen in Pahl's four 'ideal types' of local government systems (Pahl, 1975).

(a) *The pure managerialist model* assumes that access to local resources and facilities is controlled by the professional officers of the authority who share a common ideology and shape policy through the manipulation of the elected representatives.

(b) *The statist model* assumes that access to local resources and facilities is largely the result of national government policy and local managers and representatives have little room for manoeuvre.

(c) *The control-by-capitalists model* assumes that resources are allocated primarily to serve the interests of private capitalists. Resources may be allocated to public housing, for example, if there is difficulty maintaining a supply of local labour, but public services are generally seen as a 'luxury' and locations and facilities are generally allocated according to the principles of private profit-making.

(d) *The pluralist model* assumes that resource allocation reflects a permanent tension 'between national bureaucracies, committed to obtaining and distributing larger resources (following partly their own internal logic of growth), and the interests of private capital' manifested through pressures from private industry and the political party representing the dominant class (Pahl, 1975, p. 271). This tension is reproduced at the local level once funds are allocated between the competing authorities.

These different ideal types give different weight to the role of urban managers. At one level these types are appropriate to urban government in different countries; at another level they may be appropriate to different cities within a given country.

Power structures, managerialism and housing policy
The theories and concepts we have outlined here have general relevance to the study of local political systems and policy-making. However, in the context of housing policy we are dealing with a specific problem area and the following points should be noted. First, the pattern of interests and the distribution of power centering on this problem area need not be the same as that for other problem areas even within the same political system. We have noted that many housing policies involve a specific area externality effects that give them a distinctive character in terms of locational conflicts compared to many other local government outputs. Second, elitist, pluralist and neo-elitist concepts may all turn out to be relevant to the study of housing policy depending upon the scale of redistributional impacts generated by particular policies. Political or economic elites may control the shaping of policies that involve class-wide interests and a significant redistributive effect (e.g. expanding public housing programmes). Pluralistic bargaining may be involved in the shaping of policies without obvious class-wide effects or clear redistributional consequences (e.g. area improvement policies). Third, a focus on managerial control will be most appropriate in those local systems characterised by powerful bureaucratic structures, a high level of public intervention in local housing markets, and a well-developed system of professionalised housing management. Finally, it would seem likely that the processes of 'non decision-making' with respect to housing policy would operate most strongly to the detriment of minority groups in local political systems dominated by elite political control and powerful bureaucracies involved in the allocation of scarce resources.

We shall look at the general applicability of some of these theories and concepts by focusing on local housing policies in Britain. We begin with some general observation on urban politics in Britain to set the scene.

(II) POLITICAL PROCESSES AND LOCAL HOUSING POLICY IN BRITAIN

Local politics in Britain – general
In reviewing research on local government in Britain, Rhodes has commented that until the late 1960s 'The politics of local government

was a lost world' (Rhodes, 1975, p. 39). There has been a significant increase in research since then but large areas of local government organisation, behaviour and practice remain unexplored.

The discussion of American ideas and concepts drawn from the community power debate has played an important part in the recent revival of interest in the study of urban political systems in Britain. Admittedly, the straightforward application of elitist and pluralist concepts and methodologies has been limited and the few comparative studies have generally confirmed the inapplicability of the concepts in their simpler form (Miller, 1958a and 1958b; Clements, 1969). However, the more general debate on the relevance of these concepts to the British context has had the effect of throwing the distinctive structures of British urban politics into sharp relief and has led to the posing of new kinds of questions for research.

In reviewing the lessons to be learnt from the American research Newton has drawn out some of the important differences between the British and American urban systems (Newton, 1974 and 1975). There are, first, important differences in the formal structure of government. American local government tends to be fragmented, with a multiplicity of administrative and political units and weak central-government control. Local councils tend to be relatively weak and there are many competing centres of power. By contrast, British local government is much less fragmented, is much more uniform in structure, and is much more under central government control. Councils are the main centres of power and decision-making and are a logical starting point for the study of urban policy. There is also a long-established tradition of powerful bureaucracies backed by training in a variety of professions (town planning, housing management, etc.). Second, there are important differences in party organisation and interest-group representation. American cities are often characterised by many forms of social cleavage along the lines of class, race, ethnicity, neighbourhood and religion. The local party system is often weak or non-existent and politicians respond to a shifting pattern of interest-group activities and coalitions. Britain has a more homogeneous population and there is a simpler but stronger cleavage along class lines. The major parties are powerfully represented at the urban level (in the larger cities at least), broadly coincide with major class divisions, and provide the main focus for what interest-group activity does take place. It at least appears, Newton suggests, that urban government in Britain is 'hierarchical, closed and elitist' (Newton, 1974, p. 71).

The distinctive nature of British urban political systems has been reflected in recent British studies which have developed some of the concepts drawn from the community power debate as well as shifted the focus towards problems more relevant to the British context. Of particular interest are the studies by Elkins (1974), Dearlove (1973) and Saunders (1975) on various London boroughs, Hampton's study of Sheffield (Hampton, 1970) and Newton's study of Birmingham (Newton, 1976). (There are also valuable general reviews by Rhodes (1975), Jones (1975), Gyford (1976) and Darke and Walker (1977).) Many studies have dealt with the kind of situation, common among the major British cities, where party politics has been strongly developed, and where one party has typically enjoyed an extended period of one-party rule. Dearlove has argued that in this kind of situation strong local government systems function in a relatively passive environment and are subject to weak environmental pressures. The focus of the analysis should be switched to the internal structures of party political and administrative organisations which allow only the selective import of information and influence from outside groups. Saunders terms this selective openness the 'routinisation of bias'. In this kind of context it is often more accurate to refer to the policy-*maintenance* process rather than the policy-*making* process.

The major themes that run through these and related case studies may be briefly categorised as follows. First, there is an interest in party organisation, party ideology and the roles and perceptions of councillors. There are obviously important differences between the major parties but there are also important differences within these parties in terms of 'leftness' and 'rightness', in the degree of elite control and in party discipline. These factors interact with the roles adopted by councillors, their perception of local problems and their openness to different sources of outside information.

Second, there is an interest in the balance of power between administrators and representatives and the relative power of different departments within the government system. In the British system, with its well-developed committee and departmental structures, the relationships between chief officers and committee chairmen assume considerable importance. When party ideology is not well developed and party discipline is weak, political conflict may take the form of interdepartmental and intercommittee conflicts in which differing professional ideologies play an important part.

Third, there is the interest in the role of pressure groups in urban areas and their relative influence on the policy-making process. Dearlove, Newton and Saunders all identify certain 'non decision-making processes' that operate to exclude certain groups, and the issues that they represent, from the decision-making arena. Although there may often be a very large number of identifiable interest groups this does not imply that the decision-making process is pluralistic.

There seems to be a definite relationship between a pressure group's resources, its style and its influence. As Newton points out, well-established interest groups interested in incremental change may be quite successful in their dealings with council leaders and officers (Newton, 1976). They are labelled as 'helpful' or 'co-operative' groups if their aims broadly coincide with council policy. Smaller interest groups with fewer resources more concerned with fundamental changes in local authority policy are likely to be more strident in tone and more publicity conscious. They are often quickly labelled as 'unhelpful groups' and their policy proposals are looked upon with suspicion. This situation often leads to a further escalation of demands and deepening suspicion on the part of councillors and officers. When a councillor's success at the polls is largely dependent on the party label and party support there is little to be gained from breaking party discipline to champion such ephemeral local causes. Unless the pressure group can find representation within the party apparatus, exclusion can often be effectively practised.

These characteristics of urban political systems vary considerably from city to city, but the identification of distinctive configurations of elements has not as yet proceeded very far. Some attempts at constructing typologies of local authority structures have been made by Jones (1975), M. Hill (1972) and Brown, Vile and Whitmore (1972), but these classifications tend to be one-sided or overgeneralised.

This lack of a well-developed body of comparative studies of urban political systems and policy-making in general makes it more difficult to situate housing policy-making within a wider context. When we look at housing we are looking at a particular policy area and a particular subsystem where the configuration of elements relevant to decision-making may differ from the configurations in other policy areas. Information on housing policy is thinner, more selective and less comparable than information on the system as a whole. In what follows we can attempt only some very loose and preliminary generalisations. It is useful to begin at a very general level by looking at some of the findings from comparative studies of British cities.

Comparative studies of housing policy
The various reports by the Committee on the Management of Local Government (published in 1967) provide a wealth of information on many of the differences in the formal organisation and functioning of local government systems. The part of the report dealing with housing administration (CMLG, 1967, chapter 13) emphasises the volume and complexity of business handled by housing committees. Many items (rent policy, housing allocation, direct works, etc.) are politically sensitive, which partly accounts for the high standing of

housing committees in the committee hierarchy of local government. Housing matters are also, however, the concern of other committees, and on the officer side housing managers share responsibility with a number of other officers and their departments (planning officers and finance officers, for example). The report brings out variations in the delegation of authority to officers, and variations in the relative importance of housing managers compared to other officers. Much of this material is valuable but not specific enough to take us far in an understanding of the wider forces at work shaping committee decisions.

The comparative or 'systems' approach, which we have already referred to in general terms, does attempt to establish the broader interrelationships between environmental variables, political-system characteristics and policy outputs. An increasing number of policy studies have adopted this approach in the British context in the 1970s and a considerable debate has revolved around the question of the relative weight of political variables and socio-economic variables in determining policy outputs (see Newton and Sharp, 1977, and Alt, 1977, for useful reviews of the general field). In the specific area of housing policy the findings are ambiguous.

One of the best of the earlier studies in this tradition is Boaden's analysis of a variety of policy outputs in the county boroughs (Boaden, 1971). Boaden's model attempts to link outputs to various measures of needs, dispositions and resources. In the case of housing, needs are measured by physical characteristics of the housing stock and social characteristics of the population. Disposition is measured by the party composition of the council, public mobilisation (voting turnout) and officer disposition (administrative structure). Resources are measured in terms of local rates and central government subsidies. These measures are then used to try and explain the percentage of new housing in the boroughs built by the local authorities between 1945 and 1958. The statistical findings indicate that physical and social need, local resources and Labour party control are all important factors, but the influence of political mobilisation and officer disposition is not clear.

A somewhat different approach has been adopted by Nicholson and Topham (1971) in attempting to relate a broad range of variables to capital expenditure on housing by the county boroughs. Their analysis concludes that housing need factors are the major determinants of capital expenditure and that political variables are of little significance. These findings may reflect the greater central government control over capital expenditure than revenue expenditure. Their analysis also includes only two political variables out of thirty-seven and it is not clear that they are measuring the relevant political factors.

Finally, Pinch (1978) has adopted the comparative approach at the intra-urban level in attempting to explain variations in housing construction and renovation rates between the London boroughs between 1966 and 1971. In this study measures of need and resources appear of far less significance than the simple political variable measuring Labour party control. This conclusion challenges the earlier findings (Minns, 1974) that political variables were relatively unimportant in the London context.

These examples do not cover the entire field of research in this field but the amassing of detail from studies at different spatial scales, over different time periods, and using different sets of variables does not make the picture much clearer at the present time. On balance, it seems political control is important for certain policy outputs, but analysis at this level of aggregation is bedevilled by the problems of accurately measuring the appropriate political and administrative characteristics. Moreover this approach does not tell us anything about the processes of policy-making. Accordingly, we will now turn to look in more detail at the richer field of case studies of individual cities to see if a more detailed picture can be built up.

Case study approaches: housing policy in general
Case studies of the making and implementation of housing policies vary greatly in depth and quality. The studies refer to towns of varying sizes with different housing problems and different political and administrative characteristics. Some studies look at the broad sweep of housing policy over the whole post-war period; others concentrate on the development of particular policy components (e.g. renewal) during specific short-term phases of central government policy. Some studies only concentrate on specific actors in particular decision-making processes (e.g. residents' groups in urban redevelopment programmes). As a result it is difficult to make systematic comparisons between studies, and what follows is selective of certain themes and tentative in its conclusions. We shall look first at broad surveys of general housing policies and then at studies of particular policy areas over more limited time periods. To provide a loose framework we will look at the empirical material under the broad headings suggested in our introductory survey – the role of party control and ideology; the role of administrative power and professional ideologies; the influence of pressure groups and housing conflict. These political factors, of course, only operate within the constraints imposed by central government policies and local housing conditions, and we shall draw out these influences when they are important.

A good introduction is provided by the case studies compiled by

National Community Development Project workers and published as part of a general review of public housing policies since the First World War (CDP, Informations and Intelligence Unit, 1976b). The review is written from a viewpoint critical of recent housing policy developments, but a great deal of empirical detail has been assembled on the historical development of policy in Batley, Coventry, Newcastle, Newham (London), North Shields, Paisley and Southwark (London). We shall concentrate on the post-1945 period.

The importance of central government policy in shaping local policy developments comes out strongly in most of the case histories. In each case local policies followed the same general pattern. A period of council house building for general needs lasted from 1945 to some point in the mid-1950s and was followed by a switch to an emphasis on slum clearance and redevelopment, often associated with system-built, multi-storey flats. From the late 1960s redevelopment began to give way to improvement, and housing policy became increasingly diversified to include local authority support for house purchase and housing association activities. However, although these broad policy shifts are registered in each urban area they are registered to differing degrees and a great deal of local variation remains to be explained by local factors.

It is apparent from the studies that local environmental factors have varied greatly and have imposed varying demands and constraints on local policies. Local labour-market conditions, local housing-market conditions, and differences in resources and land constraints have all had varying impacts on the different towns. The towns vary from a small, relatively poor community such as Batley to a prosperous, rapidly expanding (until recently) community such as Coventry. The latter has experienced much greater demand for new housebuilding to accommodate an expanding industrial and commercial base than the former but has had a better financial base and fewer land constraints. The inner London boroughs, on the other hand, have been mainly preoccupied with the redevelopment of existing housing and have been strongly affected by land shortages.

A considerable amount of attention has been paid in these studies to the role of party control and party ideology in shaping the local policy response to the twin influences of central government policy and local needs. The conclusions are perhaps more ambiguous than one might expect. The towns cover a wide spectrum of party political control, from safe Labour councils (Newham), through highly marginal systems (Newcastle) to safe Conservative/Independent councils such as North Shields. In general, local Labour parties have been in favour of more public housing and Conservative parties less. However, the picture is not so clear-cut in every case. For example, the temporary loss of control by Labour in Batley between 1967 and 1972, in Coventry between 1967 and 1972 and in Newcastle between 1967 and 1974 was variously associated with cutback in capital expenditure on public housing, rent rises and the sale of land to private enterprise by incoming Conservative/Independent councils. However, in some cases the preceding Labour councils, faced by mounting housing costs and deficits on the housing revenue account, had already taken some steps in these directions. Conservative councils in power after the 1969 Housing Act often eagerly embraced the new policies on improvement and responded enthusiastically to the government's encouragement of housing associations. The return of Labour councils in the early 1970s often did not result in any really significant policy changes. In Newcastle and Batley, for example, although Labour re-established council building programmes, many features of the Conservative policies remained.

A certain convergence in party housing policies since the late 1960s has resulted in a diminishing ideological content in many local debates. Local Labour parties have often toned down their commitment to an expansion of public housing. Several of the studies refer to 'disorientation' and 'confusion' among local Labour parties on the broad aims of housing policy. However, these trends are made more complex by divisions within local Labour parties on certain housing issues. The Newcastle study, for example, notes a division between those with a 'gut socialist' commitment to council housebuilding and those with a less ideological, more pragmatic approach. This is not a simple 'left-right' division; it tends to differentiate older party stalwarts from younger representatives from the professions. In the past this division has been further complicated by the role of certain dominant personalities such as T. Dan Smith, the party leader of the 1960s, whose grandiose vision of a revitalised Newcastle included a commitment to high-rise redevelopment.

Another source of variation in local housing policies is provided by the varying influence of administrative departments and officials. The Coventry study refers to the 'hegemonic power' of the Architecture and Planning Department in the overall planning of the city and its influence in the setting of redevelopment priorities. In Newcastle, too, the Planning Department was the dominant department from the early 1960s onwards and the Planning Officer was awarded Chief Officer status long before the Housing Manager. Housing management was classified as a low-level administrative function and many housing policies were subordinated to the comprehensive plans drawn up by the Planning Department. In other cases (Newham and Southwark, for example) Housing Departments appear to have played a much more dominant role. The dominant role of certain

departments often accords an important position of power to their
Chief Officers. However, what is not clear is the extent to which this
importance reflects the priorities established by the ruling parties and
the relative power of different committee chairmen. The extent to
which leading officials, specific departments and professional
ideologies exercise an *independent* influence on decision-making is not
clearly established (by its very nature the problem is a difficult one to
explore).

Finally, there is the question of pressure-group activities and their
influence on housing policy. This is another difficult area to explore
because by their nature many forms of pressure are hidden from the
public gaze. The opposition by small private builders to Direct
Labour Organisations is a theme that runs through many of these
studies. Local authorities were particularly pressured by large,
national building companies in the 1960s to adopt different types of
system building once government subsidies were restructured to
encourage multi-storey redevelopment. By contrast, the local
councils experienced little in the way of significant pressure from
residents' groups. There was scattered opposition to redevelopment
in the late 1960s where local councils had placed great emphasis on
high-rise flats, but opposition by council tenants only developed on
any scale when various councils (Labour and Conservative) had to
implement the 1972 Housing Finance Act with its threat of rent
increases. The last few years seems to have seen a more widespread
community activism, perhaps taking advantage of the new requirements for participation in the drawing up of plans. However, none of
the case studies is able to report much in the way of significant success
by any of these residents' groups, and local housing policies appear to
have unfolded with remarkably little direct pressure by the local
consumers of housing.

The broad patterns revealed by the CDP reports find general
confirmation in the work of Newton (1976) on Birmingham. Newton
is mainly concerned with the political structure of Birmingham in the
1970s but he does include a brief historical sketch of housing policy
since the war as part of his analysis. He concludes that 'when the
separate performances of all the leading actors on the local stage have
been weighed and appraised, it appears that the leading part in the
city's housing drama has often been played by central government on
the one hand, and by general economic conditions on the other'
(Newton, 1976, p. 200). Nevertheless, 'there is some evidence to
suggest . . . that the local apparatus of elections, pressure groups and
parties can be used to influence housing policy within the limits set by
national government and by national economic circumstances' (ibid.,
p. 202).

Newton's analysis indicates that housing issues are rated very highly by councillors in terms of their effects on local elections (although this is not borne out by the evidence on the electorate's voting habits) and councillors are bombarded by their constituents with a constant stream of questions and complaints. Yet Newton's interview surveys with councillors reveal a remarkable lack of understanding of the dynamics of housing markets and a tendency to offer naive and simplistic solutions to highly complex problems.

One of Newton's main objectives in his book is to explore the officer-councillor relationship to see how far policy-making is becoming subject to 'the dictatorship of the official'. His general conclusion is that this trend has been overemphasised; the influence and experience of long-serving committee chairmen often serves as a powerful counterweight to the professional expertise of the officials. This general conclusion appears to apply in the housing field also. The Chief Architect and Engineer seems to have exerted considerable influence in the city until the early 1960s, but Newton suggests that since then the controlling Labour group has taken more of the initiative into its own hands. 'So far as one can judge from this flimsy evidence, conflicts between officers and elected representatives have not always resulted in the victory of the officers, especially in recent years' (ibid., p. 200).

Newton also provides some valuable information on pressure-group activity over housing issues. He identifies no less than 159 voluntary organisations concerned with housing in some way or another. Builders, building employees, professional groups, civic societies, owner-occupiers and council tenants all seem to be represented, although the power and resources that these groups can command varies greatly. The evidence of 'social' pluralism does not necessarily imply 'political' pluralism. Furthermore, certain groups – private renters and the coloured population – tend to be outside the pressure group system with no effective representation. Certain interests find little expression in the political arena.

Finally, the study by Harloe, Issacharoff and Minns (1974) of housing policy in two London boroughs (Lambeth and Sutton) and the Greater London Council provides additional useful information on the themes we have been developing here, although this study concentrates on a more restricted period, from 1967 to 1972. The authors adopt a more structured framework for their enquiry than is evident in the previous studies we have mentioned. Drawing upon some of Pahl's work, they focus on the interrelationships between the territorial distribution of needs, policies and resources. The different local authorities are assumed to have certain policy aims – a function of party ideology, a particular perception of local housing needs, and the distribution of power within the local authority. Each local authority operates in a system of constraints imposed by land, finance, the nature of local problems and the policies of other housing organisations (including other local authorities). The interaction between constraints and aims results in a particular spatial pattern of housing opportunities, favouring some groups at the expense of others.

Perhaps because of the shorter time period of the analysis the influence of central government comes out less strongly in this study than the influence of local market conditions and constraints. All three authorities were Conservative controlled for most of the study period but their policies differed considerably. Lambeth adopted a more interventionist policy not normally associated with a Conservative council, combining new council building with improvement, mortgage-lending and the encouragement of housing associations. Housing was given a high priority and an attempt was made to co-ordinate the activities of a wide range of housing agencies, public and private. This priority was reflected in the establishment of a powerful housing directorate and in close ties between the Chairman of the Housing Committee, the Housing Manager and the Leader of the Council. Sutton, on the other hand, gave low priority to housing, concentrated on the encouragement of owner-occupation and sought to keep down the proportion of council housing in the borough. The Housing Department had much less power, and the Housing Manager even lost Chief Officer status for a while.

These differences in policy largely reflected the different nature of the housing problems that the two boroughs faced and the kinds of constraints imposed on their activities. Lambeth, an inner London borough, had major problems of overcrowding, poor housing and long waiting lists which were much less evident in the outer borough of Sutton. Nevertheless, local problems were not automatically translated into policy. The Conservatives came to power in Lambeth in 1968 committed to a reversal of Labour's interventionist policies and the encouragement of private enterprise. The Housing Manager seems to have played a significant part in ensuring continuity in policy through his advocacy of higher levels of public building and redevelopment.

Lambeth's policies were also more severely constrained than those of Sutton by shortages of land and finance. These constraints often operated to shape policy outputs that undermined major policy aims. The shortage of land forced the council to look for maximum housing gain in its redevelopment programme. This meant avoiding areas of multi-occupancy and concentrating on lower-density areas where the population was older and families smaller. The end result was the loss by out-migration and council nominations to outer borough council estates of the younger, skilled and often more affluent families. This displacement of certain housing groups undermined the council's policy of achieving 'social balance' and put a greater burden on rate subsidies.

A particularly valuable aspect of this study is the exploration of the interactions between local government and various private housing agents such as building societies, landlords and estate agents. Lambeth, for example, attempted to co-ordinate the activities of these different agents with their own patterns of ideologies, aims and constraints, in order to achieve some kind of comprehensive attack on local problems. This was generally unsuccessful and the interactions between local government policies and the actions of different private agents also produced a pattern of unwanted side-effects. Tight controls on the quality of private rented accommodation led to a decrease in the amount offered, and shortages of local authority mortgage funds provided a profitable market for the often unscrupulous finance houses to help purchasers at exorbitant interest rates.

The studies that we have briefly reviewed here at least indicate some of the main factors at work in shaping local policies, although only in a fairly general and imprecise way. We can gain some further insight by exploring particular policy areas. Given our emphasis on spatial impacts, the subject of redevelopment and improvement policies is a particularly fruitful one to explore.

Studies of particular policy areas – urban renewal and community action
A large proportion of the studies of policy-making in particular policy areas concentrated on the interrelated themes of urban renewal and community action. Many of the better-documented studies refer to the 1960s when redevelopment was in full swing and community opposition was only just beginning. Most of the studies adopt a critical stance, emphasising the strong interlock between councillors and leading officials in pushing through redevelopment policies with scant regard for the feelings of those affected. As a result these studies have more to say about the role of professional ideologies and 'non decision-making' than the more general studies we have already referred to. Dearlove's description of strong political and professional organisations operating in an environment of weak pressure group activity, allowing only a selective flow of information congruent with established policies, seems particularly appropriate in the case of urban redevelopment. Nevertheless, there is often evidence of conflict, but conflict *within* the governmental

structure – a kind of interdepartmental conflict that Hill has called 'administrative politics' (M. Hill, 1972).

One of the best and most detailed studies is Muchnick's analysis of the making and implementation of Liverpool's redevelopment policy in the 1960s (Muchnick, 1970). The year 1966 marked the launching of a new renewal strategy and Muchnick focuses on the different actors involved: the politicians, the Housing Department, the Planning Department and the Department of the Medical Officer of Health. The enormous scale of Liverpool's post-war housing problems made housing a number-one political and administrative priority and gave great power to the Housing Department. The Medical Officer of Health, using criteria of unfitness and fitness, demarcated zones for potential clearance, but the Housing Department programmed the actual clearance and redevelopment, concentrating on areas where conveniently sized sites could be put together to get a good housing return. This often meant including many fit houses in clearance schemes and it also meant giving a low priority to the redevelopment of areas designated for non-housing purposes (schools, parks, etc.). As a result new housing tended to be widely scattered throughout the inner city. This emphasis on maximising housing output at the expense of more comprehensive redevelopment was supported by the politicians. There were more votes in meeting high housing targets, and the scattered nature of redevelopment meant that many councillors could point to visible results in their own wards. Only the Planning Department favoured a comprehensive plan for redeveloping area by area with a full range of school and recreational facilities. The possible threat that this posed for the goal of maximum housing output brought the Planning Department into conflict with the much more powerful Housing Department, and its coalition of interests.

The new housing strategy was the result of the initiative of the Labour leadership, which brought in an outside agency to make recommendations. In spite of some opposition by the Housing Department, which saw its powers being curtailed and its programming functions undermined, a modified form of the plan was accepted in 1966 which envisaged an accelerated rate of clearance, more comprehensive redevelopment, higher levels of improvement and changes in allocation policies. The way in which the plan was actually implemented, however, reflected once more the balance of influence and power within the governmental structure.

The rehabilitation component received little encouragement. The Planning Department was in favour of improvement zones round the renewal areas, but the Housing Department saw improvement as expensive of staff and money for little return; the Medical Officer of Health had staff shortages and could not survey the large number of houses involved; and the politicians saw new housing as a more visible sign of success. Similarly, no consensus could be established on the comprehensive redevelopment component. This was championed by the Planning Department, but the concept posed a threat to the autonomy of other departments and the goal of maximising the output of new houses. The Planning Department attempted to exert some pressure for comprehensive redevelopment by encouraging the demands of community councils then springing up in some of the potential clearance areas (with the support of Community Workers employed by yet another department, the Education Department). This indirect pressure ran up against the stone wall of indifference erected by the Housing Department to this form of community involvement in its complex programming problems.

Given the distribution of power within the governmental structure, the close interlock between the interests of the Housing Department and the politicians, and the lack of political representation for those actually moved by the redevelopment programme, it is not surprising that the new strategy unfolded very much as before with a strong emphasis on maximum housing gain and an emphasis on physical renewal.

Muchnick's study of Liverpool in the 1960s can be compared in many respects with Gower Davies's study of renewal in Newcastle (Davies, 1972) and Dennis's study of Sunderland (Dennis, 1970), but there are important differences in emphasis. Gower Davies places considerable stress on the way in which an 'ideology of planning' pervaded the policy-making process in the city, with disastrous consequences for the renewal of the Rye Hill area of the inner city. Planners, according to Gower Davies, are 'evangelistic bureaucrats' with a professional self-conception that protects them from opposition to their often grandiose and ill-conceived plans. Their claim to the 'comprehensive' viewpoint and their role as the 'guardians of the future' enables them to dismiss attacks as representing merely short-term sectional interests. Gower Davies sees this ideology personified in the work of Newcastle's Chief Planning Officer whose views on the reconstruction of Newcastle coincided closely with those of his political supporter, T. Dan Smith, the Labour leader. Impelled by this ideology, the planning process in Newcastle produced unfortunate consequences for Rye Hill. A twilight area in the early 1960s, it was designated as an area of comprehensive revitalisation to the highest environmental and housing standards. The insistence on the simultaneous treatment led to long delays, the boarding up of houses, the spread of blight and the flight of many sections of the community. Gower Davies claims that, after nine years of planning, Rye Hill had only seven fully modernised houses to show for all the effort and debate.

Gower Davies could be criticised for throwing too much weight in his analysis on an assumed universalistic planning ideology. It could be argued that the dominance of the Planning Department and the dynamic role of the Chief Planning Officer reflected the political context peculiar to Newcastle in the early 1960s, in particular the leading role played by the Labour leader in committing the party to large-scale comprehensive planning embracing housing as a major priority (see Elliot, 1975, for the general background). Other cities at this time, with a different party political structure and a different distribution of departmental power, were operating more flexible and successful comprehensive improvement and renewal strategies (see Pepper, 1971, on the Leeds case).

The broader political context is even less apparent in Dennis's study of redevelopment in Sunderland. Dennis is concerned to explain the continuance of the slum-clearance drive in an inner city area in the face of the facts that a substantial minority of the residents did not wish to be relocated and were satisfied with their existing accommodation. Again the role of an ideology of planning and the force of bureaucratic inertia are put forward as the main explanations, although Sunderland's planners do not appear to have expressed the same grandiose sentiments that Gower was able to illustrate in the Newcastle case.

A theme that comes out strongly in these and related studies is the low level of public participation in policy-making. In the majority of cases there is either (a) no organised resistance or (b) resistance is successfully blocked. Where plans are successfully challenged by residents (case (c)) this appears to reflect the presence of a powerful middle-class element in the community. We will briefly review examples of each kind of situation.

(a) Protest unorganised – Muchnick (1970), Dennis (1970), Elkins (1974), Batley (1972), and J. Lambert (1975) all provide examples and explanations for the lack of organised protest even where there is a great deal of individual opposition to the proposals. For Muchnick, it is a gap in the political process that explains the powerlessness of those affected. During much of the 1960s there was no formal mechanism whereby residents of clearance areas could register their views with the appropriate departments involved, and their local councillors, themselves dependent on Housing Depart-

ment expertise and information, were less concerned to represent the views of voters who would soon be transferred to other wards and constituencies. Relocation became more of a political issue only when it threatened the voting base of some inner city councillors and upset the political equilibrium. Only then were some councillors prepared to attack the Housing Department's expertise. Dennis, on the other hand, explains the public apathy and sense of helplessness he found in Sunderland clearance areas in terms of the passiveness of working-class families and the self-fulfilling nature of the slum-clearance process. The designation of a zone for clearance at some time in the distant future poses only a vague threat but drives out many of the more active or affluent families and accelerates the process of planning blight. Eventually the area may become so run down that the remaining residents see redevelopment as a positive relief.

Batley explains non-participation in terms of the lack of local organisations prepared to take up political issues on the one hand and the values and goals of the various agents which encourage a negative response on the other. Councillors often see themselves as representing the interests of the city as a whole and are suspicious of local groups. Planners can adopt a 'comprehensive' view that serves to override local interests. Housing architects produce plans reflecting national yardsticks and professional standards that leave little room for negotiation. For housing managers participation is a threat to the complex tasks of programming relocation.

Lambert also refers to the diversity of agents involved, but he places more emphasis on the divisions within the local community that makes co-ordinated action difficult. Renewal areas often contain a variety of 'housing classes' in diverse housing situations. Some are owners, some tenants; some are in redevelopment zones, some are not; some are in acquired houses, some are awaiting decisions; some are dependent on the council for rehousing; and some have a wider range of opportunities open to them.

Elkins perhaps offers the most wide-ranging interpretation, although his lofty theoretical edifice is built on only two, slight, case studies. Elkins refers to widespread attitudes of deference on the part of the voting public in Britain towards councillors and planners. This supports the holistic viewpoint that planners assume as guardians of the interest of the community as a whole. It also enables councillors to detach themselves from local interests, particularly when electoral success depends upon the party label rather than the direct representation of neighbourhood demands. Party structures, planning ideology and traditions of deference interact to sustain a hierarchical political structure which makes decisions in relative secrecy, releases little information, and is unresponsive to pressures from small, territorial groups.

(b) Protest blocked – In some cases a combination of local circumstances resulted even in the 1960s in some form of residents' organisation and efforts to resist or change the renewal strategy. Gower Davies (1972), Dennis (1972) and Dunleavy (1977) give examples where such resistance was blocked or largely ignored. Gower Davies explains how a Rye Hill Advisory Committee was set up (partly at his own instigation) to defend community interests. Tracing the history of its negotiations with the council and its officers, he concludes that both sides felt the exercise was a failure. The Committee felt that the major policy decisions had already been made and no substantial concessions were forthcoming. The officials felt that the Committee was obsessed with details and blind to the totality of the plan. The councillors were reluctant to give away any significant power over decision-making. Changes in the overall plan were forthcoming largely in response to pressures from outside the area – the government's refusal of a Compulsory Purchase Order and a change of party political control on the Council.

Dennis's second study of a residents' organisation in Sunderland gives a similar picture of a strong council and a resistant bureaucracy, although in this case most of the blame for the failure of participation is placed on the Planning Department which effectively controlled the flow of information to residents and to Committees in such a way as to preserve the basic structure of the plan.

The Beckton protest in the London borough of Newham analysed by Dunleavy provides an especially clear example of protest suppression. An organised protest group sprang into being after the collapse of the multi-storey block of flats at Ronan Point in 1968. Residents of adjacent clearance areas awaiting rehousing petitioned against rehousing in similar system-built flats. The Labour-controlled council had based its whole housing strategy on system-built multi-storey flats and a major contract was outstanding with a national building firm. In spite of criticisms at a government inquiry and an escalation in protest activity on the part of residents the council rode out the storm, made no significant concessions, and the protest collapsed. Relations with the protestors were handled almost entirely by the housing chairman, the chief officers and the Labour group leaders, all of whom were committed to a continuation of the building contracts. The Beckton organisation was dismissed as a small minority of trouble-makers, particularly after the group attempted to enlist Conservative support after they had failed to gain the backing of Labour backbenchers. By ignoring the organisation and denying it legitimacy the leading officials and councillors were able to practise 'non decision-making' and exclude the protest from the decision-making arena.

(c) Protest partly successful – Where redevelopment plans were successfully challenged, this seems to have reflected the presence of a vocal and organised middle-class in the local area. A well-documented example is provided by Ferris's study of the Barnsbury area in London in the 1960s (Ferris, 1972). The Barnsbury area was 'going through a phase of rapid gentrification in the 1960s. Working-class tenants were moving out as landlords sold houses for incoming middle-class owner-occupiers. The Labour council, however, was still wedded to long-term redevelopment proposals dating back to the 1950s. An attempt to apply a Compulsory Purchase Order on part of the area in 1964 led to a vigorous and well-organised resistance on the part of the Barnsbury Association. Drawing upon the expertise of its members, who included planners, architects, lawyers and journalists, it drew up an alternative plan embodying the latest thinking on rehabilitation, traffic management and environmental planning. The implementation of many of the Association's ideas was aided by a Conservative election victory in 1968 and, although the obvious middle-class domination of the organisation provoked the later formation of a more working-class Barnsbury Action Group, the Association had considerable success in getting its ideas incorporated into public planning.

The studies we have discussed so far have largely referred to the 1960s, when redevelopment was the dominant housing policy in inner city areas and there were few formal mechanisms for participation by residents. Since the late 1960s there have been some important changes and developments that have ostensibly provided more opportunities for local groups to shape renewal policies. First, the 1968 Town and Country Planning Act and the 1969 Skeffington Report developed the framework for participation in planning, and the 1969 and 1974 Housing Acts extended these obligations to housing renewal policies. Second, the government's encouragement of area improvement from 1969 onwards provided local residents with an alternative with which to attack an authority's redevelopment proposals. Third, the 1970s saw the development of government programmes such as the Community Development Projects which were partly directed at the stimulation of community action in certain deprived inner city areas. The early 1970s certainly saw an upsurge in various forms of community activism, many centering on the redevelopment–improvement alternative. However, it is as yet difficult to discern any clear-cut pattern emerging beneath the welter of protest activities and participatory exercises.

Paris's study of the making and implementation of Birmingham's latest renewal policy (Paris, 1977a and 1977b) suggests a limited role for local groups in the making of overall city policy. The Labour council launched the new policy in 1973, phasing out comprehensive redevelopment and expanding GIAs and HAAs on a massive scale. The plan was a hurried response to a central government circular and reflected departmental submissions with little direct public input. Significantly, there was little party debate or party conflict over the issue. Given their stated beliefs, Paris argues, the Conservatives would have carried out the same basic policy if they had been in power.

The mass of community activity takes place at a much smaller spatial scale. In so far as much of it revolves around GIA or HAA designation (or non-designation) of areas, it tends to be defined by the nature and objectives of local government policies. For example, Roberts (1976) has documented the kinds of conflicts involved in the setting up of GIAs. Out of seventy-five GIAs studied twenty-four had residents' groups of one sort or another, but the majority had been set up with local authority assistance and they worked closely and co-operatively with councillors and officers. Serious conflicts were rare. A similar pattern may be emerging more generally; those groups adopting a more co-operative stance and pushing for the kinds of policies congenial to the local authority may well achieve significant, though limited, concessions (see Peaden, 1977, for a good example). At one extreme this can simply mean the co-option of local organisations by local government so that participation becomes simply a means for 'putting-across' local authority plans and ensuring local co-operation (see Mason, 1977). Nevertheless, there are examples of local residents' groups achieving effective political organisation and forcing a substantial change in policy. Holmes (1977), for example, has claimed considerable success for the activities of the North Islington Housing Rights Project in organising private tenants and pushing the local council into a more interventionist role at a time of public expenditure cuts. However, in many cases where significant successes have been recorded local groups have benefited from a considerable input by independent professionals (e.g. Shelter and various Community Development Project teams). It remains to be seen, therefore, whether the increased options for participation will bring about any significant or lasting redistribution of power within urban communities.

The determinants of housing management style

We have already discussed the complexities of housing management in our consideration of the impacts of various public policies. Our discussion there considered management as a technical problem of matching households to the housing stock and we paid particular attention to the physical and financial constraints on management practices. However, there is evidence that management systems also vary independently of these constraints and we now have to look at the wider political and ideological determinants of these practices.

The area of housing management has been an obvious area of inquiry for those adopting the managerialist perspective. Here, apparently, is a classic case of urban managers allocating scarce resources, structuring the housing opportunities of different social groups, and generating certain secondary patterns of inequality independent of the primary forces of the labour market. As Paris (1974) has emphasised, the growth of council housing, the decline of the private rented sector, large-scale redevelopment and a continuing gap between housing needs and public resources have placed considerable pressure on systems of housing allocation. Particularly for those in inner city areas the way of getting a home is 'via the bureaucratically-organised allocation structure of the City Housing Department' (Paris, 1974, p. 14).

Studies of housing management systems from the managerialist perspective have focused on the role of professional ideologies in determining practices. Gray (1976b) has broadly categorised some of the main elements of this ideology in terms of a stress on 'fairness' but strictness, the interests of the 'community' over the individual, education in home management and an attempt to produce 'good' and 'respectable' tenants. He suggests the origins of this ideology can be found in the values of nineteenth-century philanthropists and housing reformers.

English, Madigan and Norman (1976) have adopted a more sophisticated approach to professional ideologies that stresses the many-layered complexities of management organisations. They distinguish 'occupational ideologies' from 'operational stereotypes'. The former are sets of beliefs, factual claims and objectives which higher-level management staff use to justify their action to themselves, their competitors and their detractors. The latter describe the routine practices that guide the day-to-day work of the lower echelons. Their empirical analyses compare the 'operational styles' of five housing departments in terms of these dimensions, distinguishing varying emphases on property management, client service, and moralistic distinctions between the 'deserving' and 'undeserving' poor.

The broad criticisms that have been raised against the managerialist perspective can be raised here. Such an analysis (as Gray recognises) tends to treat the urban managers as independent variables in the urban system. The relationships between management systems and management ideologies on the one hand and the wider political system on the other remain largely unexplored. Gray has certainly pointed out that Labour and Conservative councils in Hull have operated the same basic management systems, but this simply pushes the search for determinants further back into a broader political and ideological context that structures managers' and politicians' attitudes towards the function of public housing. Some of these wider connections will be made when we come to look at Marxist approaches to housing.

Conclusions

We have concentrated in our survey on those policy themes which are reasonably documented with case studies. Fewer studies are available of other areas of decision-making although local party political controversy has also revolved around rent policies, council house sales and the use of direct labour departments. Nevertheless, even within the restricted areas of our survey it is difficult to arrive at many definite conclusions. There is obviously a gulf between the highly aggregated comparative studies, with their relatively crude measurements, and the mass of detailed case studies, which refer to different policy areas, time scales and spatial scales.

As a rough generalisation it could be argued that the post-war period up until the mid-1950s was dominated by controversies centering on new building and redevelopment. Party ideologies were reasonably well defined on many of these issues but within the broad policy frameworks laid down by party elites there was often plenty of room for professional manoeuvre and interdepartmental conflicts over the implementation of policy. The picture since the mid-1960s has become more confused and many factors have been changing simultaneously. Housing policy has become more complex, the ideological divisions between the major parties have become blurred on many issues, the local government system has been reorganised, public participation has been officially encouraged in some policy areas, long-term policy has become increasingly subject to economic crisis and the fluctuations of public expenditure, and 'locational conflicts' have increased.

Institutional structures and political processes – cross-national comparisons

Up to this point we have illustrated a broad approach to housing systems in terms of institutional structures, political processes and locational conflicts with material drawn from studies of the British housing system. We have attempted to show some of the inter-connections between national policies, local political systems, types of policy output and forms of housing conflict. The interconnections 'of these elements will, however, vary from social system to social system and we can illustrate some of the major sources of variation through some selected cross-national comparisons.

NATIONAL POLICY FRAMEWORKS

A number of studies have begun to emerge comparing the broad outline of housing policy for a wide range of countries (e.g. Heidenheimer, Heclo and Adams, 1975; Burns and Grebler, 1977). The conclusions are often pitched at a very high level of generality and stress the sheer variety of factors involved. Even amongst the advanced capitalist countries housing policy developments seem to reflect no overall rational public strategy, but are made up of *ad hoc*, internally contradictory measures that are responses to short-term crises, changes in party ideology and control, and shifting pressure-group activities. Perhaps of greater interest are the more detailed comparisons of pairs of countries which are able to explore the links between institutional structures and political processes in more depth. We will briefly refer to two studies comparing British public housing policy respectively to that of France and the United States.

We saw, earlier in this chapter, how housing policy has developed in Britain through a sequence of fairly clear-cut policy phases. These phases have usually been related to changes in party control. Class divisions have underlain the major tenure distinction between owner-occupation and public housing and have structured party political attitudes towards these tenures. As Duclaud-Williams (1978) has pointed out, this is not the pattern that underlies French housing policy. The institutional structure of housing provision is different. Subsidies for owner-occupiers are channelled through the Crédit Fonçier, a semi-public institution with no parallel in Britain. Public housing (about 15 per cent of the stock compared to 30 per cent in Britain) is provided through HLMs (Habitations à Loyer Modéré) which are run by specialist housing organisations and not by the local authorities. This institutional structure was largely established before 1950 and has remained relatively unchanged since. There has therefore been a continuity to French housing policy and a tradition of gradual, incremental change quite lacking in British policy. These differences can be traced back to differences in political structure and political traditions. Parties of the right and left in France have agreed on the importance of various forms of state intervention in economic management and social policy. No major political grouping has emerged to champion the liberal view of the non-interventionist state. As a result the public sector building programmes have not been the subject of right-wing hostility and have been protected as far as possible from economic crises. The fact that HLMs also build houses for sale, and the presence of various other intermediate forms of tenure (housing co-operatives, etc.), has also blurred any clear-cut relationship between tenure and social class.

The situation in the United States is different from Britain in other ways. Public housing here accounts for less than 2 per cent of the total housing stock. There is a strong tradition of non-intervention by the state and where public housing is provided it is largely provided through independent, federally appointed bodies that by-pass state and local government. Public housing also serves quite different functions to public housing in Britain. As Wolman (1975) points out, public housing in America is largely housing for the sub-working class – the poor, the blacks and the unemployed. If the politics of housing in Britain revolves around class, the politics of housing in America revolves around race.

HOUSING AND LOCAL POLITICAL PROCESSES

The form and intensity of housing conflicts at the local level are strongly related to the institutional structure of local government. In Britain, as we have seen, housing is a major responsibility of local government and the formal structures of local government are major sources of power and decision-making. It is significant that in France and the United States public housing provision by-passes the local government system and housing is not such a major issue in local politics.

More controversy has surrounded the issue of urban renewal in United States cities, but even here the nature of local political systems has tended to exclude the representation of minority interests through various processes of 'non decision-making'. Newton (1976) has argued that the weak and fragmented nature of local government systems, with their apparent openness to group pressure and influence, in fact works in favour of certain powerful interest groups representing the building, real estate, banking and property-development businesses. Newton re-examines the evidence in one of the classic texts of pluralism – Dahl's 'Who Governs?', a study of New Haven politics and policy making – and concludes that the evidence does not support Dahl's picture of a pluralistic power structure and bargaining politics. In the case of urban renewal the policy-making process was dominated by representatives of the local business elite, and minority-group interests were largely excluded. Comparing urban renewal in New Haven with urban renewal in other US cities in the 1950s and 1960s, Newton concludes 'New Haven's experience of urban renewal and housing problems is in no way unique among American cities where big business has invariably played a crucial role' (Newton, 1976, p. 51).

It is evident that differences in policy outputs in Britain and America are intertwined with differences in the formal structure of government and differences in the distribution of local power. This comes out clearly if one compares, for example, Muchnick's study of urban renewal in Liverpool in the 1960s with Hayes's study of renewal in Oakland over approximately the same time period (Muchnick, 1970; Hayes, 1972). In the former case policy outputs reflected the importance of national policy on the one hand and inter-departmental politics on the other. In the latter case policy outputs (the clearance of older, black housing areas for higher-cost rental units and new businesses) clearly reflected the power and influence of major industrial and financial corporate interests, which successfully sponsored and implemented much of the renewal programme.

HOUSING AND LOCATIONAL CONFLICTS

A number of recent studies have directly compared the forms of housing conflict at the neighbourhood level in Britain and the United States and attempted to explain the lower level of neighbourhood activism observable in Britain. Cox (1978) has pointed to the presence of a vigorous local political activity at the neighbourhood level in the United States, much of it concerned with the control of housing markets to local advantage through the enhancement of property values and neighbourhood characteristics. This is evidently much less the case in Britain where intensity of preference for co-residents is not so marked. Cox relates this difference to differences in national culture and jurisdictional organisation between the two countries. First, local government in Britain is subsidised to a much greater extent by central government so that there are fewer fiscal externalities from marked variations in local government spending between areas. Second, the organisation of school boundaries in Britain does not involve a strict relationship between residential area and neighbourhood school. In America the neighbourhood school concept leads to stronger preferences for certain types of co-residents. Third, public safety is much less significant as a basis for residential choice or locally based political action in Britain. In addition to these major factors there have also been differences in rates of suburbanisation and rates of inner city decline in the two countries. Cox concludes that 'the housing market in American cities has historically been much more sensitive to social class geography than has the housing market in British cities' (Cox, 1978, p. 104).

Cox's article is pitched at a fairly general level but Cox and Agnew (1974) and Agnew (1978) have provided some empirical details in the particular case of public housing provision. Cox and Agnew have documented the different locational patterns of public housing in British and United States cities. Public housing is heavily concentrated in inner city areas in the United States but more evenly distributed between central city and suburb in Britain. Nevertheless, there is less opposition to the location of public housing by private home-owners in Britain. Cox and Agnew suggest that this is due to the facts (a) that suburban council estates often pre-date private developments, (b) that the neighbourhood is less a source of social status in Britain than in America so that public housing is perceived as less of a threat, and (c) that British owner-occupiers are less interested in the exchange value of their property because they move less and the effects of public housing are already capitalised in property prices. In a later article Agnew (1978) provides some empirical data to support these arguments. A comparison of Leicester and Dayton reveals that British home-owners are indeed less concerned over the location of public housing in their neighbourhoods, and a comparison of sixty-nine United States and eighty-one English cities indicates that the site-selection process is much more often a source of conflict in the United States. Agnew relates these differences to different attitudes by home-owners to property as a source of profit and investment. Conflict is therefore related to the extent to which home-owners have been incorporated in the network of market relationships.

PART III

Marxist approaches to housing and residential structure

This section of the book involves a much more substantial change of perspective than the transition between Parts I and II. A Marxist approach involves a shift in the kind of questions that are posed for analysis as well as in concepts and methodology. It is impossible in a book of this kind to give a detailed exposition of Marxist theory and its many lines of development. However, it is necessary at least to sketch in some of the basic themes and concepts of Marxism to provide a basic vocabulary before analysing in later sections some of the varied attempts to apply Marxist theory to the field of housing. Without a general introduction the lines of enquiry discussed later may appear strange or arbitrary. We provide such an introduction in chapter 8. In chapter 9 we look at some of the criticisms that Marxists have mounted against the approaches to housing that we have dealt with elsewhere in the book, and we provide an overview of some of the main themes of an alternative Marxist approach to housing. In chapter 10 we look at the way these themes are inter-linked in the work of Castells and Harvey and, finally, in chapter 11 we pull out some major issues which are a source of controversy within the Marxist tradition for more detailed discussion.

Chapter 8

Marxist theory and Marxist method: an introduction

The elements of classical Marxism*

MARX'S METHOD

Marx's main intention, at least in his later writings, was to explain the causal mechanisms that generate the structures of different modes of production and the capitalist mode of production in particular. These causal mechanisms were explored in terms of the interactions between certain theoretical entities which were themselves not directly observable.

In focusing on the economic structure of society, Marx rejected any approach that pictured individuals with given needs and preferences interacting only through the anonymous mechanisms of buying and selling in the market place. For Marx human needs and preferences are historically contingent and cannot be given independently of the social and economic structure that shapes them. There are no objectively given economic laws that define relations between things (commodities, capital and labour, etc.) independently of the historically defined social relations that underly them. It follows that Marx's approach to political economy is sociological and historical, focusing on social relations and their changes over time.

---

* Marxist literature has now assumed major proportions. To avoid scattering the text with an indigestible mass of references it is worth referencing at this point some general works that the reader could profitably explore for a deeper understanding of Marxist theory. McLellan (1971) has edited a useful collection of Marx's basic texts with a commentary and Michael Evans (1975) has provided a good, balanced introduction to Marxist theory as a whole. Marx's economic theories are clearly outlined in Sweezy (1968) and explored more critically in Howard and King (1975) and Desai (1974). Fine (1975) also provides a short but useful introduction. Keat and Urry (1975) and Benton (1978) make clear the philosophical and methodological foundation of Marxism as a distinctive approach in the social sciences. Other works will be referenced at relevant points in the text.

Three specific features of Marx's method need stressing. First, Marx emphasised the distinction between social appearance and social reality. The classical economists, he argued, concentrated their analyses on the world of appearances, dealing only with the phenomenal forms of capitalist societies. But reality is deceptive and a true scientific approach should try to penetrate the world of phenomenal form to a deeper underlying reality. This penetration can only be achieved through the use of certain theoretical concepts (e.g. abstract labour and value) that can be used to explain the generation of phenomenal forms. The problem of the relation between appearance and reality is particularly acute in capitalist systems where underlying social relations between men appear to the superficial eye as relations between things governed by the objective laws of the market. Marx described this as a form of commodity fetishism.

Second, Marx adopts in his major work, *Capital*, a logical-historical method of analysis and exposition. Beginning with a series of simplifying assumptions, Marx constructs progressively more complex models showing logically and historically how the capitalist mode of production unfolded through successive stages. This does not imply a simple one-to-one correspondence between an historical order and a logical sequence of presentation. Certain features of the capitalist mode of production that are present from the beginning – such as agricultural production and groundrent – can only be explained adequately at a later stage in the logical-historical exposition. In *Capital* ground rent is only analysed after the main lines of evolution of the capitalist mode of production have already been explained.

Third, Marx's method is dialectical. In its simplest terms, this means that Marx focuses on the way in which social structures change and through change create the conditions for further change of a qualitative as well as quantitative nature. Social systems are marked by contradictory tendencies that create the conditions for their own supersession.

BASIC ELEMENTS OF HISTORICAL MATERIALISM

Marx gave one of the most complete expositions of his materialist approach to his 1859 Preface to 'A Contribution to the Critique of Political Economy'. The economic structure of a society, he argues, is the 'real foundation' on which arises a superstructure of legal, political and ideological forms. The economic structure is a definite mode of production which is constituted out of a totality of relations

of production, embracing particular forms of work relations and property relations. These relations of production correspond to definite stages in the organisation of the material forces of production (machinery, labour power, technical and scientific knowledge, etc.). The principal source of change from one social form to another is the contradiction between the forces of production and the relations of production. Through innovation and competition the forces of production tend to develop more rapidly than the relations of production, so that the relations of production (and property relations in particular) increasingly become fetters on the full development of the productive forces. The breaking of these fetters involves a period of revolutionary change, the recasting of the economic foundation of society, and ultimately a transformation of the whole immense superstructure. This pattern of change leads to a definite periodisation of history conceived as a succession of modes of production (although this does not imply that all countries must follow an inevitable and fixed progression).

This dynamic of social change is inseparably linked to a theory of class and class conflict. The history of societies is ultimately the history of class struggles. Class structures are rooted in the economic basis of society, so that the relations of production are ultimately class relations. At the simplest level of exposition Marx works with a dichotomous class model centering on the ownership or non-ownership of the means of production and the form of exploitation that this makes possible. Each mode of production is characterised by a dominant class owning the means of production and ruling through the wealth and power that such ownership entails. The contradictions between the forces and relations of production are ultimately expressed in class terms. The existing property relations buttress the position of the dominant class but are increasingly challenged by a rising class whose interests are tied closely to the fullest exploitation of the new productive forces. The contradiction between the forces and relations of production is expressed in political and ideological conflict between classes with the ultimate triumph of the rising class and the establishment of new property relation and political forms, and a new dominant ideology.

Marx looked at the transition between the feudal and capitalist modes of production in these terms. But the triumph of the bourgeoisie over the feudal landowners and the establishment of capitalist relations of production brought forth a new subordinate class, the industrial proletariat, whose interests conflict with the dominant class and whose future is tied to the fullest development of productive forces increasingly blocked by the rigidity of bourgeois property relations. The contradictions of capitalism can only be resolved through the revolutionary transition to a socialist mode of production.

The role of the state is closely related to the power of the dominant class. Marx did not write extensively on the state and even his mature conception is sketchy and simplistic. The key proposition is that the state is not a neutral organisation standing above society adjudicating between rival interests. Ultimately it is an instrument of class rule, serving to maintain the power of the dominant class and the subordination of other classes.

The exposition so far can only be regarded as a cursory summary of Marx's own simplified representation of his views. Such a representation can be found expressed in a number of key passages in Marx's voluminous writings, but he himself recognised the elements of oversimplification and his position is modified (and even contradicted) at various points in other texts. First, both Marx and Engels are at pains to point out that the relation between economic base and superstructure is not one of simple determination. The components of the superstructure have a relative autonomy and changes react back onto the economic structure. Nevertheless, in spite of this recognition of mutual interaction, the economic structure is ultimately dominant, conditioning the forms of mutual interaction and feedback. Second, certain passages (in *Grundrisse*, for example) invert the relationship between forces of production and relations of production, assigning primary importance to the latter in shaping the former. Third, in his analysis of contemporary society, Marx develops a more complex description of class structures than a simple dichotomous class model. In his writings on France (in *The Eighteenth Brumaire of Louis Bonaparte*, for example) he distinguishes a variety of classes, fractions of classes and class strata. This complexity partly reflects the overlapping of different modes of production within specified social formations (such as France in the mid-nineteenth century), partly divisions of interest within classes, and partly a range of secondary political and ideological factors.

Finally, Marx also accords the state a more complex role than simply an instrument of the dominant class. In *The Eighteenth Brumaire* the French state achieves a relative autonomy, reflecting the temporary equilibrium of class forces with no clear-cut domination by one class or fraction.

Such reformulations, shadings and revisions mean that the Marxist texts comprise a rich, ambiguous and sometimes confusing literature. There are three major reasons for this rich ambiguity. The first stems from Marx's relational view of reality and the way in which he accordingly uses his concepts (Ollman, 1971). Since a social system is an organic unity in which the parts mutually condition each other, it follows that particular objects can only be understood in terms of their relation to all other parts. In a sense each part contains the whole within itself. Marx uses his concepts in such a way as to try and open up, yet not destroy, such a unity. The definitions of the concepts change subtly throughout the texts in an attempt to capture the many facets of each entity. The concepts change according to the viewpoint of the observer and the particular range of interactions that are being highlighted at that point in the texts.

A second reason stems from the logical-historical method of analysis and exposition. The initial, simplified approach is gradually made more complex through the relaxation of assumptions as new concepts are added and new layers of interaction are explored. These succesive approximations to reality lead to re-appraisals of the initial, basic interactions.

A third factor must also be taken into account that is in many ways more serious. Many areas of ambiguity do genuinely reflect a lack of coherency in the texts. Marx's views developed over a lifetime of copious writing, and passages in his later works, when he had sloughed off his Hegelian heritage, seem to conflict with some of his earlier writings. Even a later and relatively finished work such as *Capital* does not present a coherent whole. The recent work of Cutler *et al.* (1977, 1978) has shown to good effect the contradictory nature of some of the analysis. Some of the implications of this inconsistency for Marxist approaches to specific areas such as housing will be drawn later.

THE ECONOMIC THEORY OF CAPITALISM

We have outlined some of the general concepts that run through Marx's work. It is also necessary to say something about the economic theories that increasingly preoccupied him in later years and which find their fullest expression in the three volumes of *Capital*.

The analysis of the capitalist mode of production in *Capital* rests on the labour theory of value which Marx uses to reveal the nature of exploitation in the system and the real sources of profit and capital accumulation. Marx assumes a dichotomous class structure in which a capitalist class owns the means of production and a proletarian class has only its labour power to sell. Labour power is a commodity and, like any commodity, its value is equal to the amount of socially necessary labour time required to produce (or reproduce) it. In the case of labour its value implies an historically determined bundle of goods and services necessary to ensure the survival of the worker and his family. The capitalist appears to purchase the worker's labour on the market in a straight exchange for wages. In reality he purchases labour power as a commodity which is free to use for a specified period of time, the working day. For part of that time the worker labours to create value equal to the value of the wage that he is paid. This is necessary labour time required to pay for the bundle of goods and services necessary to ensure the worker's survival. The rest of the working day is surplus labour time during which the worker creates value over and above that necessary to reproduce himself and which is appropriated by the capitalist as surplus value. This surplus value is the real source of profits and capital accumulation. On the surface the capital–labour relation appears as a simple exchange relationship in which wages are exchanged for their equivalent, and profit appears as the reward for the productivity of a thing called capital. The labour theory of value enables Marx to bring to light the class relations and class exploitation that lie beneath the world of appearances.

On this simple basis Marx builds up a logical-historical exposition of the development of the capitalist mode of production, exploring the mechanisms of capital accumulation and bringing in the concept of the reserve army of the unemployed to explain the tendency for wages to oscillate around a subsistence level. In Volume II of *Capital*, Marx pioneered the use of two- and three-sector models of the economy to explore the dynamics of the system and the conditions of equilibrium. In the third volume he brings landed property and groundrent into the picture and explores the division of surplus value between wage labourer, landowner and capitalist. At various stages further levels of complexity are added through a consideration of the role of banking capital and commercial capital, which appropriate part of surplus value through costs of circulation and interest.

The capitalist mode of production that is carefully and cumulatively laid bare in *Capital* is a structure riven by contradictory tendencies that create the conditions for its own supersession. These contradictory tendencies find expression in periodic crises that threaten the rate of profit, the mainspring of capital accumulation. In fact Marx has several theories of crisis scattered throughout various sections of *Capital*, although they are not incompatible with each other. They can be grouped under two main headings. First, there are crises associated with the tendency of the rate of profit to fall. Since the rate of profit is positively related to the rate of surplus value and inversely related to the organic composition of capital, this tendency can reflect either a fall in the rate of surplus value or a rise in the organic composition of capital as capital (machinery, etc.) is substituted for labour. Since the tendency for capitalists to substitute capital for labour to undercut other capitalists is a basic feature of the system, it follows that the basic processes of innovation, technological development and capital accumulation undermine the stability of the system. Second, there are realisation crises that reflect the difficulty of actually selling commodities when produced. Realisation crises are either crises of disproportionality (due to the unequal development of sectors) or underconsumption crises (due to the slower growth of workers' purchasing power relative to the capacity of capitalists to produce goods for sale).

This is not the place to go into further detail on these themes; additional detail will be brought in when it is relevant to housing themes in later sections. However, it is worth ending by returning briefly to the labour theory of value that underlies the text of *Capital* in order to emphasise the importance of what has been called 'the Transformation Problem'. Throughout Volumes I and II (and much of Volume III), Marx's analysis is based on values which are measured in units of socially necessary labour time. When Marx talks of profit rates or organic compositions of capital it is important to realise these are in value terms. But the value relations are not themselves directly observable. The day-to-day world of capitalist transactions is characterised by profit rates and capital-labour ratios which are measured in prices. Prices are only the phenomenal expression of the deeper, underlying value relations. What is the exact relation between the value domain and the price domain? This is the problem that Marx attacks in Volume III in seeking to establish definite mathematical relationships between values and prices. His solution is now recognised as being seriously flawed, but more sophisticated mathematical treatment shows that solutions can be found – values can be transformed into prices. However, the relationships are often complex, to such an extent that it is quite possible to conceive of situations where a declining rate of profit in value terms need not automatically imply a declining rate in price terms (Desai, 1974). Despite the tendency for some Marxists to push the transformation problem aside as a mere puzzle that has been conceptually solved, the distinction between prices and values remains an important problem with important implications for empirical analysis.

Marx and Engels on housing

Marx himself did not write very much on housing and what he wrote is not closely integrated into his broader theories of economic structure and social change. There are passing references in *Capital* to slums and urban redevelopment in nineteenth-century England and also some brief points on urban ground rent, but urban residential structure was not in fact one of his major theoretical preoccupations.

Engels wrote more and drew directly upon some of Marx's economic theory at several points. A number of recent authors have gone back to his early work on Manchester in the 1840s (Engels, 1958 edition) and noted how his description of concentric zones in the city has superficial similarities to the later concentric zone model of Burgess (J. Anderson, 1977; Harvey, 1973; Richardson, 1977). Yet the differences are also important. Engels closely related his concentric zones to an analysis of class structure. The industrialisation of Manchester involved a growing social separation of the classes and this was reflected in a growing spatial separation which stamped new patterns of residential differentiation on the old commercial city. Burgess's model of Chicago was based more on a description of the residential succession of ethnic and status groups. However, geographers have built upon the tradition of Burgess rather than Engels and this has been associated with the exclusion of a social class dimension in the Marxian sense and a preoccupation with individual household competition in anonymous market processes.

Engels addressed himself more directly to housing issues in his later work *On the Housing Question* (Engels, 1970 edition) where, in the course of much heavy-handed polemic against contemporary reformers, he makes a number of interesting and provocative points. *On the Housing Question* is partly an attack upon Proudhon who had argued that the worker/capitalist relationship was basically similar to the tenant/landlord relationship. Engels denies this, arguing that the housing problem is not directly the result of the exploitation of the worker, as a worker, by capitalists. The tenant/landlord relationship takes the form of an ordinary commodity transaction obeying the normal rules of the market. Rents reflect building and maintenance costs, land values and the state of supply and demand. The rent payment involves the transfer of already created value (wages) to the landlord; the transaction does not involve the exploitative creation of surplus value as does the worker/capitalist relationship.

On the Housing Question is also partly an attack on reformist support for home-ownership for the working class. Engels directs much of his fire against Sax who supported the building society movement as a means of encouraging home-ownership, giving workers economic independence and a stake in society, and ultimately promoting social stability. Engels argues that lowering housing costs would simply result in lower wages being paid by capitalists; home-ownership would tie workers more firmly to particular factories and employers and reduce their bargaining strength; and building societies were either speculative organisations or they catered primarily for the petty bourgeoisie. He could see no salvation for the working class in building societies or home-ownership.

To Engels it seemed clear that reformist solutions must ultimately fail. The housing problems of the great cities were inseparable from the whole process of capitalist industrialisation which drove a wedge between town and country, concentrated workers at the points of production without regard for adequate housing, paid them low wages and subjected them to periodic bouts of unemployment as cyclical crises alternately drained and replenished the reserve army of labour. The state as the instrument of the dominant class was incapable of solving the crisis. At best, slums were cleared for boulevards and public buildings, and the population of slum dwellers was simply displaced to other and perhaps less publicly visible areas.

Simply put, the housing problem was inseparable from the capitalist mode of production; it could only be solved by the abolition of that mode of production, the abolition of the big city and the ending of the separation of town and country.

Engels's writings contain the basis for several lines of enquiry on housing issues, but they are barely adequate as a starting point to explain many of the developments in housing policy and residential structures since his day. Engels's analysis draws only lightly on Marx's economic theories and his views on the state and the potential for reform within the system are fairly crude versions of Marx's views (although this is not to deny that Marx also expressed himself in such a way at certain times).

Developing a Marxist approach to housing: some problems

Developing a Marxist approach to housing is by no means an easy task. On the surface it appears basically a matter of taking the principles of historical materialism and certain elements of the economic theory of capitalism and applying them to a problem area barely touched upon by Marx or Engels. The problem is more complex than this, however, for several reasons. First, there are the ambiguities in the texts. Some of the basic principles of historical materialism are not at all clear and the economic theory has certain inconsistencies and important lacunae. For this reason it is not simply a matter of applying a clearly defined set of concepts in some automatic way to a new problem area, or simply extending general macro-economic models to a specific type of commodity production. There is a great need for a preliminary theoretical development involving an extension to certain basic concepts and a revision of others.

Second, there is the simple fact that capitalist systems in general and housing systems in particular have developed along paths only dimly foreseen by Marx writing in the mid-nineteenth century. In important areas of development Marx's theories provide only the sketchiest basis for theoretical development. This applies to some extent to the development of bourgeois, democratic, welfare-state systems in the twentieth century and their capacity for reform over wide areas of social policy, particularly in the housing sphere.

It is not as if later Marxists have not responded to the challenges posed by Marx's unfinished work and the new developments in capitalist systems. In fact we are faced with something of an embarrassment of riches. A hundred years of Marxist theory and practice have seen the development of many lines of enquiry as attention has shifted between economic, political and philosophical problems (see Perry Anderson, 1976, for a good, compact, historical review). Today Marxism presents itself as a rich and varied tradition, but a tradition riven by many controversies and points of disagreement, on even the most basic themes of value theory, class theory and the theory of the state. At the level of economic theory, for example, a rough distinction can be made between those who have defended the labour theory of value (the fundamentalists) and those who have been quite prepared to abandon it in favour of an alternative approach based on the work of Sraffa (the neo-Ricardians). (See Rowthorn, 1974, and Fine and Harris, 1976, for recent reviews.) Particular attention has also been paid in recent years to the theory of the state, and this has been an important arena for controversy; Jessop (1977) has recently distinguished six approaches that can be developed from the classic texts alone.

In conclusion, there are a variety of often conflicting theories within the Marxist tradition today that can be drawn upon to explore the area of housing problems and policies. In the next chapter, we begin the task of reviewing some of this recent work. The recent burgeoning of interest in the field, the rush of recent publications and research, and the exploratory nature of much of the writing means that our review can be at best an interim assessment.

Chapter 9

Marxist approaches to housing: an overview

Critiques of non-Marxist approaches to housing

It is a common feature of the development of any new approach that a great deal of effort is initially expended on the ground-clearing operation of surveying, reviewing and criticising existing lines of research. The development of a Marxist approach to housing has been no exception and it is useful to begin by noting some of the salient criticisms that have been levelled at the kinds of approaches we have already discussed.

THE CHICAGO SCHOOL AND THE ECOLOGICAL TRADITION

A number of Marxist writers have made passing criticisms of the Chicago school tradition but the most developed critique is probably that presented by Castells (1976a, 1976b and 1977a, Part II and Chapter 8). Castells criticises ecological approaches as part of a wide-ranging critique of urban sociology in general. The critique is based on the argument that a science must have a specific theoretical object (i.e. particular theoretical concepts) or a specific real object (i.e. a particular domain of reality). If a body of research work has neither then it exists only to perform certain ideological functions. Castells argues that this is precisely the case with urban sociology.

Castells identifies three themes around which urban sociology has attempted to constitute itself as a science. First, there is the theme of 'urbanism as a way of life', which found its classic exposition in the writings of Wirth. Second, there is the exploration of the links between social structure and spatial organisation, which began with Burgess. Third, there is the notion of cities as ecological systems. Castells rejects these themes as a basis for a science because they lack theoretical distinctiveness. The notion of an ecological system is not a specific urban theoretical object, it is rather an expression of a theory that applies to social structure as a whole. The concept of urbanism presents the cultural values of 'mass society' as if they were the products of the distinctive ecological form of the city. The work of Burgess explores the important problem of the interrelationships of spatial structure and social structure, but the concentric zone model in particular errs in presenting as a universal feature a social process peculiar to a particular stage in American capitalist development. Castells concludes that urban sociology has no specific theoretical object.

Castells also argues that urban sociology has no distinctive real object either. Nevertheless, he points to two types of problem that have been touched upon in the past that could be developed as real objects to provide the basis for a genuine science in the future. One of these concerns the social organisation of space, not conceived in traditional terms as the outcome of struggles and conflicts between actors, but as an expression of structural changes in the elements of the urban system. The second concerns the theme of collective consumption. Both of these problems will be explored in more detail later. For the moment the crucial point to be emphasised is the rejection of the work of the Chicago school as part of a broad critique of urban sociology as a whole in the light of a distinction between science and ideology.

NEO-CLASSICAL ECONOMICS AND URBAN RENT THEORY

The critique of neo-classical spatial equilibrium models and urban rent theory can be linked to the wider critique of neo-classical economics as a whole. The main elements of this broader attack can be summed up in three major lines of criticism (Rowthorn, 1974; Roweis and Scott, 1978).

First, neo-classical economics is individualist and subjectivist. It presents a society made up of individuals whose nature, preferences and tastes are assumed as given. Marxist critics argue that these characteristics are structured by broader social and economic processes peculiar to particular historical stages in the development of particular modes of production. An analysis of the mode of production is logically prior to an analysis of the mode of consumption.

Second, neo-classical economics concentrates narrowly on exchange. The only form of social relationship that assumes importance is that concerning the exchange of commodities in the market place.

Third, neo-classical economics suffers from naturalism. Economic processes appear to be relations between things. Production is presented as an asocial, technical process in which inputs of land, labour and capital are transformed into outputs. Marxist critics argue that it is essential to uncover the exploitative class relationships that underlie and structure the nature of the production process.

Rowthorn (1974) points to the ideological consequences that follow from an adoption of the neo-classical perspective. Apparently neutral assumptions lead to the picture of an inherently stable capitalist market system in which crises are temporary deviations from equilibrium due to frictions or market imperfections. Wages, profits and rents appear simply as the rewards to different factors of production proportional to their marginal productivities, and the relationships between capitalists, landlords and workers, although based on competition, are ultimately harmonious.

These general criticisms apply with particular force at the urban level in so far as spatial economic equilibrium models are based on the principles of neo-classical economics. A wide range of urban problems (congestion, decay, etc.) can be interpreted as deviations from an equilibrium position. Rent appears merely as a reward to a scarce factor of production and functions as an allocative device to secure an optimal pattern of land use. Class and property relations do not explicitly appear in the analysis.

There are superficial similarities between Marxist and 'institutionalist' criticisms of neo-classical economics in so far as both approaches condemn the unreality of its assumptions. The Marxist approach, however, takes its criticisms much further. The institutional approach focuses on the manipulation of land uses by institutions and land interested groupings with varying motives, ideologies and power. The Marxist approach argues that these organisations cannot be regarded simply as actors obeying some logic peculiar to themselves. Their behaviour is structured by the deeper, underlying logic of capital and its laws of accumulation and circulation in a specific mode of production. It is this logic that shapes the forms of ideology and the distribution of power.

HOUSING CLASSES AND URBAN MANAGERIALISM

The concepts of housing classes and urban managerialism are rooted in Weberian sociology and have often been attacked as part of a wider critique of this perspective. The concept of housing class is possible in terms of a Weberian perspective in which classes can arise in any market situation. The Marxist concept of class, as we have seen, is linked to the extraction of surplus value in the process of production. It follows that property ownership or tenure are by themselves an inadequate basis for class formation. The basic line of argument here stems from Engels who argued that the tenant/landlord relation is not equivalent to the worker/capitalist relation. Nevertheless, as we shall see later, there is some disagreement among Marxists on the exact relationships between conflicts in the housing field and the basic conflict between capital and labour.

Criticisms of the urban managerialist perspective have often been linked to a critique of Weberian or corporatist views of the state and the bureaucracy (Harloe, 1977). In Pahl's early formulation, as we have already noted, urban managers appear as independent variables in the urban system engaged in the allocation of scarce resources. Scarcity is taken for granted as a natural phenomenon and urban problems are interpretable in terms of managerial inefficiency or bureaucratic insensitivity. This position has been criticised both by Marxists and non-Marxists. In his more recent reformulations Pahl has begun to link his managerialist theories to a corporatist view of the state and has interpreted the role of urban managers in terms of mediation between the state and the private sector, each with its own system of allocating scarce resources (Pahl, 1977a). At one level this reformulation can be criticised for its ambiguity; for example, if the managers are part of the state how can they fulfil a mediating role? At a more general level Marxists reject the theory of a neutral bureaucracy and a corporatist state and emphasise the relationships between the role of the state and the interests of capital. However, as we shall see, there is considerable disagreement amongst Marxists on the precise relationship between state and capital and on the class position of the bureaucracy.

COMMUNITY POWER STRUCTURES AND URBAN POLITICS

Marxists have directed a number of attacks against the approach to urban power structures that has dominated much of the literature in urban politics. Castells (1977a, Chapter 11) has critically reviewed the field of urban politics and questioned some of the major underlying assumptions. He argues that theories of urban power structure have been largely based on the concepts of actors with different preferences and strategies attempting to maximise power and gains. Urban policy emerges as the result of a necessary compromise between conflicting aims. Such an approach either slips into a simple description of what happened in a particular decision-making process or becomes highly formalistic in making broad comparisons in terms of measures such as centralisation and decentralisation of power (e.g. as in the comparative approach). A Marxist approach, Castells suggests, looks at the positions that actors occupy as the supports of social structures and examines the processes at work within the structures that define the contradictory relations between the actors/supports. Furthermore, power is defined not at the level of individual actors but at the level of class in terms of the capacity of one class to realise its objective interests at the expense of others. It is evident that a Marxist approach to the making of housing policy involves a major shift of perspective and a search for determinants at a different level in the social structure than the approaches we discussed in chapter 7.

Having roughly indicated some of the main lines of criticism directed against non-Marxist approaches, we must now begin to unravel the distinctive theories of Marxist approaches. We will start with a broad overview to see what kind of questions and problems are posed within a Marxist framework.

Basic questions and problem areas

From the broad principles outlined in chapter 8, it can be argued that the housing system is interconnected with the wider social system in the following important ways. First, housing is a commodity and a source of surplus value for certain forms of capital. Second, housing is part of the necessary consumption of workers and as such is an aspect of the reproduction of labour power. Third, the forms in which housing is provided are interlinked with the reproduction of the social relations of capitalism. Fourth, in so far as it is embedded in a system of contradictory forces, the housing system will be an arena for social class conflicts and a locus for various forms of state intervention. We will consider some of these aspects in turn.

HOUSING AS A COMMODITY

As a commodity, housing is the vehicle for the production of surplus value and a means of capital accumulation for a particular sector of industrial capital (building industrial capital). However, housing is a commodity with peculiar features and requires the mediation of other forms of capital if profits are to be realised.

The production, realisation and consumption of housing can be looked at from the point of view of the interconnection of circuits of different forms of specialised capitals. Marx distinguished industrial capital, commercial capital and interest-bearing capital in the general process of commodity production, realisation and consumption (see G. Thompson, 1977, for a clear summary), and a number of authors have attempted to extend this analysis to the specific field of housing (Topalov, 1973; Lamarche, 1976; Boddy, 1980).

The process of producing the commodity housing can be viewed as a circuit of production in the following way.

$$M - C \left\{ \begin{array}{l} MP \\ \\ ... \, P \, ... \quad C' - M' \\ \\ LP \end{array} \right.$$

The capitalist producer (the builder–developer) lays out money M, to purchase commodities C (labour power LP and means of production MP), which are combined in a production process to produce the final commodity C' (the prime signifying that the commodity embodies surplus value). The commodity is sold for M', realising the surplus value as profit which can be consumed by the builder–developer or reinvested to begin a new circuit of commodity production. This is the standard form of the circuit of commodity production, but in the case of housing the successful completion of the circuit presents certain problems.

First, the period of production from C to C' is particularly long, extending over many months, and the process of production involves a number of specialised skills and types of labour that have to be co-ordinated with a flow of materials. This must take place on site in conditions far removed from normal factory production where authority relations can be established and production effectively programmed. As a result the process of production is prone to interruptions due to labour problems, stoppages in the flow of materials, or even bad weather. This tends to increase the already long period between the laying out of money capital by the builder–developer and the realisation of profit.

Second, the price of the final commodity C' raises major problems in actually realising surplus value through sale to the consumer. Housing units are very expensive in relation to the incomes of the vast majority of households, who are unable to purchase them outright and can only pay for the commodity as they consume it over an extended period of time. This realisation problem makes the circulation period of capital C' – M' – M – C particularly long and necessitates the intervention of a specialised form of capital, circulation capital, which enables the household to pay for its housing over a period of many years whilst allowing the builder–developer immediately to recover his investment, realise his profits and begin a new circuit of production.

Circulation capital may be advanced in a variety of ways that are represented in different forms of tenure. For example, a landlord may raise commercial capital by borrowing at the current rate of interest from banks, purchase the house and recover his investment with a profit increment through monthly rental charges. This situation can be represented by the following diagram where the arrows represent exchanges of money or the commodity housing (Boddy, 1980).

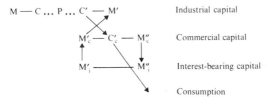

Loan-financed house purchase, on the other hand, can be represented in the following way:

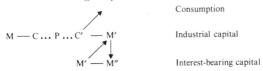

In this case money is directly advanced to the consumer by a financial institution in return for interest and there is no circuit of commercial capital as it does not pass through the intermediary of the landlord.

The above analysis is a relatively straightforward application of Marx's categories of specialised capitals. Lamarche (1976) has gone further and suggested that another specialised form of capital – property capital – should be recognised that is specifically concerned with the spatial organisation of commercial, financial and administrative activities in order to increase their efficiency and contribute towards the reduction of the indirect costs of capitalist production. This form of capital is largely involved in office-complex and shopping-centre developments; private housing development is largely a side-line. The profitability of housing will then largely depend on its integration with office and shopping-centre development. Lamarche's analysis may be more relevant to development processes in North America, although Boddy (1980) has argued that there is no real theoretical justification for distinguishing property capital from commercial capital in general.

These extensions of Marx's discussion of the different forms of capital and their circuits to the field of housing serve to raise some interesting questions and isolate some problems that need deeper analysis. For example, according to Marxist theory surplus value is only created in the process of production within the circuit of industrial capital. Part of this surplus can, however, be appropriated by other capital interests in the secondary circuits of commercial and interest-bearing capital. In this sense part of the surplus value created by building industrial capital does flow to landlords and finance institutions. However, the matter is complicated by the fact that housing transactions are dominated by a thriving second-hand market and a continuing excess of demand over supply in the housing market. As a result the largest mass of interest-bearing capital is provided to finance the re-sale of already completed houses whose prices reflect current replacement costs and market conditions and deviate more and more from their original prices of production. In so far as those rising costs are borne by workers, leading to increasing wage demands, they represent a transfer of surplus value from capital as a whole and not just from building industrial capital (Lamarche, 1976; Boddy, 1980). The relative dominance of the secondary circuits of capital within the housing system leads, therefore, to complex patterns of realisation of surplus value within the economic system as a whole.

The discussion so far has concentrated on the interpretation of industrial capital and secondary circuits of circulation capital. However, housing also requires land and this fact brings the landowner into the picture as a further complicating factor. Land, in the Marxian scheme, is not a commodity but it does command a price (selling price or groundrent) that represents a claim upon surplus value produced within the sphere of commodity production. Landowners possess private property rights and can exact a price for the release of their land. Evidence presented in Part II has shown that land costs form a significant proportion of total housing costs. However, as Castells points out, this certainly does not mean that landowners are the cause of high prices and the housing problem (Castells, 1977a, Chapter 9). Problems rooted in the production process itself, the costs involved in overcoming the realisation problem, and the semi-permanent imbalance between supply and demand create ideal conditions for speculative gain by landowners in urban areas. In this respect landowners exacerbate but do not ultimately cause the housing problem.

HOUSING AND THE REPRODUCTION OF LABOUR POWER

So far we have discussed the interconnection between the housing system and the wider social system by concentrating on housing as a form of commodity production. Housing is also a part of the necessary consumption of workers. In this respect housing is tied into the processes of reproducing labour power and is of vital importance for capital as a whole in so far as higher housing costs raise the value of labour power. If the value of housing can be reduced, then, other things being equal, the value of labour power for capital in general will be reduced, providing the opportunity for an increase in the rate of profit and a higher rate of capital accumulation. Higher housing costs in relation to income may benefit certain capitals such as building industrial capital or landed capital but conflict with the interests of industrial capital as a whole. Conflicts within the housing system thus spill over to affect the system as a whole.

HOUSING AND THE REPRODUCTION OF SOCIAL RELATIONS

A capitalist system is dependent for its functioning and stability on certain forms of property relations, authority relations and attitudes towards consumption. These relations are increasingly maintained by ideological factors. Thus the tenure forms we referred to above partly represent different ways in which surplus value is appropriated by different forms of capital, but they also function to mould and reinforce certain patterns of social relations through their ideological effects. Owner-occupation, for example, tends to reinforce certain attitudes towards private property and private ownership, and an extended period of debt repayment may encourage certain attitudes in the workforce with respect to job stability, career advancement and deference to authority. At a broader level the form in which housing is provided is also tied to the role of the family in capitalist society. The family is the main location for the socialisation of the next generation of workers and is an important source of attitudes and values over the whole field of work and social relations. Adequate housing is a precondition for the stability of the family and changes in family form and family functions may well necessitate changes in the structure of the housing stock.

HOUSING, CLASS CONFLICT AND THE STATE

The housing system is part of a contradictory social system and is an arena for class conflicts rooted in those contradictions. The pattern of conflict will ultimately reflect the fundamental contradictory relationship between capital and labour. However, a series of secondary conflicts within and between classes revolve around this central conflict. Conflicts within the capitalist class over housing issues can be related to the different forms of capital discussed earlier. The laws governing the circuits of specialised capitals also define certain places to be filled by different categories of institutional agents (builders, financial intermediaries, exchange professionals, etc.) and the functions to be performed by those agents in the circuits. In this sense those institutional agents pursue their own specific interests which are structured by the underlying processes of capital accumulation, and these interests, like the underlying processes, may be contradictory. For example, building industrial capital benefits from lower land prices, higher house prices and an even flow of low-interest loans to purchasers. Landowners, on the other hand, benefit from higher land prices, and the returns to loan finance are geared to higher interest rates and the length of repayment. Higher house prices or rents may serve the interests of a number of housing agents but conflict with the longer-term interests of industrial capital as a whole. It is easy to conceive of conditions in the urban housing market where rising land costs eat into builders' profits, builders seek to raise house prices, loan finance capital is not available in adequate amounts because interest rates attract funds to other sectors, and industrial capitalists are under pressure from rising wage demands to cover rising housing costs. We are here a long way from the idea of independent actors interacting in a competitive, but ultimately harmonious and self-regulating, market. The contradictory nature of the system means that individual capitalists, in pursuing their own specific interests, create situations that threaten the reproduction of capital as a whole.

The importance of housing for the system will tend to attract the attention of the state in an attempt to regulate or repress the contradictory forces at work. The state may intervene in the processes of production or realisation/consumption at the economic, political or ideological level and different forms of intervention will favour different classes or fractions of classes. The state may intervene, for example, primarily in the process of production, perhaps to encourage rationalisation or mechanisation and a lowering of the value of housing. This could take the form of placing large public housing contracts and the simultaneous encouragement of prefabricated or industrialised forms of production. The state may intervene primarily in the secondary circuits of housing finance by stabilising the flow of funds through financial institutions or by maintaining a low real rate of interest through tax concessions and subsidies or by controlling the price of housing through rent controls. State intervention will obviously not simply reflect the problems of commodity production and realisation; it will also be geared to the reproduction of social relations through the encouragement of certain forms of housing tenure (typically owner-occupation has emerged as the favourite form of consumption). These different types of intervention will favour different classes, fractions and sub-fractions of capital and explorations of the exact balance of state housing policies must depend on linking these policies to an adequate theory of the state in general.

HOUSING AND SPACE

This survey has sketched out some of the major fields of enquiry of a Marxist approach to housing and their interconnections. Before taking the discussion further, to explore some of these issues in depth, it is worth raising explicitly the role of space and spatial theory. Spatial structures and spatial relations make a number of appearances in these problem areas. An exploration of rent is important for any analysis of urban rent surfaces and the distribution of housing prices and house types within urban areas. Residential differentiation in space is interwoven with class divisions, different modes of consumption and the broad field of the reproduction of social relations. The role of the state is reflected in the spatial patterning of public housing and the effects of various forms of intervention in the land and property markets. The list could be extended indefinitely. The key point to stress, however, is that theories of spatial structures and spatial relations must be linked to wider theories of social and economic structure. Social and spatial relations interpenetrate each other (as later examples will show) and spatial patterns are not just the passive imprint of wider social forces. It is a question of developing theories that simultaneously explain the social and spatial forces and their interaction. As we will see, space is a vital element in most Marxist approaches to housing and the city.

Chapter 10

Integrated theories of housing, urbanisation and capital accumulation: the work of Castells and Harvey

The previous chapter sketched in a number of major themes in a Marxist approach to housing. In this section we explain the inter-connections between these themes through a review of the work of Castells and Harvey. These authors have attempted to relate analysis of housing problems to more general theories of urbanisation in advanced capitalist countries and their differing presentations draw together various perspectives on the themes of capital accumulation, demand for labour power, the restructuring of urban built forms, patterns of urban conflict, and changes in urban politics and planning.

It is one of the major strengths of the Marxist approach that it forces the discussion away from an attempt to understand urban housing systems in isolation and requires a more general theory of the city in capitalist societies. The structure of the modern metropolis cannot be conceived simply as a product of technological changes such as transport improvements, innovations in construction techniques and forms of communication which facilitate decentralisation, specialisation and segregation in urban areas. In the Marxist perspective urban patterns of production, consumption, exchange and administration are linked to evolving processes of capital accumulation and the interrelated problems of the realisation and circulation of surplus value. Of course, urban form and structure is not a simple automatic reflection of the needs of capital accumulation. Certain variations in urban forms may be quite compatible with the basic needs of capital accumulation so that within limits urban forms can vary among advanced capitalist countries. More importantly, urban forms will always be an expression of contradictory processes and will be partly shaped by the outcome of political conflicts as they vary from country to country.

We will see that within this broad framework these two authors adopt different perspectives and place different emphasis on different processes. In Chapter 11 we will take up some of these points of controversy in more detail.

Monopolville **and** *The Urban Question*:
the work of Manuel Castells

The work of Castells (1977a, 1977b, 1976c), and Castells and
Godard (1974) represents a major attempt to construct a new
theoretical perspective on capitalist urban systems, a perspective
which incorporates housing, residential structure and spatial
relations in general as major theoretical elements. We will briefly
summarise the major concepts and theoretical tools developed by
Castells in *The Urban Question* (and related articles) and then
illustrate their application and modification in *Monopolville*, a lengthy
analysis of an actual urban system.

CONCEPTS AND THEORETICAL TOOLS FOR THE ANALYSIS
OF URBAN SYSTEMS

Castells defines the urban system as a unit of collective consumption,
a conclusion which is reached after the following chain of argument.
In order to survive, a capitalist system must reproduce its means of
production, its labour power and its relations of production. To put
it crudely, it must reproduce its factories, offices, a workforce
available to work in those locations, and a workforce prepared to
accept the social relations of capitalism at home and in the
workplace. The means of production are increasingly organised and
reproduced at the regional, national or even international levels.
The urban unit is less and less a unit of production or spatially
defined 'workshop'; but it is a unit of residence for a labour force, a
spatial unit within which labour power and the relations of production are organised and reproduced.

Consumption is necessary for the reproduction of labour power
and consumption can be individual or collective. Individual consumption is the form most familiar to us, although mass production
technology and advertising have generated important changes in
patterns of household consumption, particularly since the war.
Indeed, in a later section we will discuss arguments linking evolving
patterns of mass consumption to residential suburbanisation and
changing urban form. However, it is collective consumption that
Castells considers to be more and more important for specifying the
identity of urban systems today. As capital concentrates and
centralises, the labour process becomes more and more inter-
dependent, and production relies more and more upon a range of
consumption needs that cannot be met efficiently or profitably by
private capital. In this broad sense the process of production is

becoming more and more socialised, dependent on the back-up of public transport, public housing, health and education services. Within the modern city the workforce must be appropriately housed in relation to the workplace, assembled daily at the factory gates or office doors, provided with the right skills and education for the jobs available. Its efficiency needs to be serviced with health care and its ideology (its 'world view') needs to be moulded through education and the media so that capitalist social relations are accepted as 'natural'. As cities grow in size and complexity collective goods become more and more necessary for production to be carried on efficiently, but the difficulty of actually realising profit from their provision throws the responsibility for providing them increasingly on the state.

Thus we arrive at the concept of the urban unit as a unit for the collective reproduction of labour power. This is not to argue that other activities such as production or administration do not go on in cities, only that a focus on urban units conceptualised in these terms provides a means for grasping the real nature of present-day urban problems which are increasingly bound up with those processes of collective consumption.

Having defined an urban system, Castells then develops theoretical tools to analyse it. Such a system can be analysed in terms of structures or practices, although the two are in reality intimately related. Starting with *structures* Castells draws heavily upon the theoretical writings of Althusser (1969), Althusser and Balibar (1970) and Poulantzas (1973) to distinguish an economic, a political/juridical and an ideological level to social systems. These levels are interrelated by a particular form of structural causality. The economic level is considered to be 'determinant in the last instance' in the sense that it conditions the structure of the other levels and their interrelationships without mechanically determining them. They are considered to have a relative autonomy and their structures are not simple reflections of contradictory forces at work within the economic level (see Glucksman, 1974, for a detailed exposition).

For more detailed analysis these levels are broken down into elements. *The economic level* is a combination of the following:

Element P (Production) – refers to processes related to the reproduction of the means of production, represented in spatial terms by activities producing goods and services (factories, offices, etc.)

Element C (Consumption) – refers to processes related to the reproduction of labour power, represented in spatial terms by activities concerning individual and collective consumption (housing, public facilities, etc.)

Element E (Exchange) – refers to processes of exchange between P and C and within P and C, represented in spatial terms by journey-to-work flows, commodity flows, etc.

Element A (Administration) – refers to processes regulating relations between P, C and E (urban planning, etc.)

The political level is represented by the institutional organisation of space which reflects the way the state divides up space by fragmenting certain powers between administrative units of varying levels in the interests of overall regulative control. Finally, *the ideological level* is represented at the urban level by the symbolic marking of different areas within the city. For example, through a multiplicity of signs certain residential areas indicate class membership and status differentiation.

Castells suggests a further detailed breakdown into sub-elements of these levels, but this need not concern us here. It is important to emphasise, however, that levels, elements and sub-elements are articulated in a particular causal structure in which the economic level is only determinant in the last instance, and that within the economic level it is the element P, representing the processes of production, that is the crucial element. The fundamental contradictions of the economic level (the collision between the forces and relations of production, the tendency for the rate of profit to fall, etc.) will find expression throughout the structure at the economic, political and ideological levels. The urban system is a system of contradictions.

The urban system can also be approached in terms of an analysis of the *practices* of the agents occupying different positions in the structure. These practices are ultimately class practices and class conflicts, and class relations are expressions at the level of practices of the structural contradictions of the system. Thus the study of urban structures leads to the study of urban politics. Castells focuses firstly on a study of *planning* (the political processes whereby the state attempts to regulate conflicts and contradictions and reproduce the social system) and secondly on a study of *urban social movements* (the conditions leading to a mobilisation of social forces within urban areas that seek to change the structure of the system).

The above is only a sketch of Castells's massive (and often unwieldy) theoretical structure, but it is sufficiently detailed for the moment to situate housing and housing problems within a contradictory system of structures and practices bound together by a particular form of structural causality. Housing is obviously a sub-element of the element C and appears as a form of private consumption and collective consumption (public housing), although the boundaries between these two forms of consumption are often not clearly demarcated. However, the daily flow of labour between home and workplace simultaneously locates housing within the structure of exchange. The spatial form of housing – residential differentiation – is also intimately related to the symbolic structuring of space and the ideological level in general. Finally, the institutional organisation of space often expresses the political power of groups to preserve exclusive residential areas through zoning and maintain status differentials and property values. Given the contradictory nature of the system, crises will be thrown up at all three levels leading to an inadequate reproduction of labour power and social relations, and the sporadic development of urban social movements focusing on housing issues, such as housing quality and high prices and rents, increasing separation of home and workplace, etc.

These arguments are still at too high a level of generality to sound convincing at this stage. Castells provides some concrete examples of his approach in *The Urban Question*, but a clearer and more revealing analysis can be found in *Monopolville*, Castells and Godard's study of the Dunkirk urban system, where theories, concepts and empirical material are cleverly interwoven to give an integrated picture of contemporary urban problems (Castells and Godard, 1974).

Monopolville: HOUSING IN THE URBAN SYSTEM

Monopolville is the study of the recent development of the Dunkirk urban system. This development is based upon a new industrial-port complex designed as a site for large multinational firms, with the French state financing and organising much of the urban infrastructure and related residential development. *Monopolville* is not, however, just a study of Dunkirk; it is an attempt to understand the basic processes of urbanisation in an advanced capitalist country in the kind of situation (the creation of a new urban complex) where the contradictory processes of capital accumulation and the generation of urban problems can be most clearly seen. The analysis unfolds through an hierarchy of explanations, following the theoretical structure and using the concepts and tools of *The Urban Question*. Thus housing is a major element of consumption within the system, and its characteristics, spatial patterns and problems are intertwined with the broader problems of the reproduction of labour power and social relations. This in turn demands a preliminary analysis of the processes of capital accumulation which shape the system and structure the formation of classes and class relations.

The location of housing within a system of contradictions leads on to an analysis of local politics and planning. We will trace through this hierarchy of explanation in a little more detail to see how it helps us to understand housing patterns, problems and policies.

CAPITAL ACCUMULATION AND THE ORGANISATION OF THE MEANS OF PRODUCTION

The study begins with the fundamental patterns of capital accumulation and capital movement in the current stage of state monopoly capitalism in France. The development of industrial-port complexes such as Dunkirk is linked to the search for strategic sites for production and distribution by multinational companies. Such favoured locations can only be exploited by monopoly capital with the help of massive state intervention to lay down urban infrastructure, assemble an adequate labour force, and take charge of the reproduction of labour power and social relations through the provision of collective goods and services and the creation of new institutions for planning and political control.

With this broad background it is possible to look in detail at the movement and organisation of capital at the local scale, or in other words the organisation of the means of production. Local capital is divided into fractions whose interests by no means coincide, and Castells and Godard trace out the conflicting demands for infrastructure, locations and labour supplies by the major monopolies, small and medium capitals, subcontractors and traditional local producers.

CLASS AND IDEOLOGY

This analysis of the processes of capital accumulation and the organisation of production is an essential basis for the discussion of social class relations in the area. The authors draw heavily upon the writings of Poulantzas at this point to distinguish the main lineaments of class structures. The different fractions of the capitalist class are reflected in divisions within the working class so that it is possible to distinguish different strata and levels within the workforce according to skill differentials (position within the work process) and income levels (position in the process of distribution).

After defining the economic structuring of classes it is possible to look at the interrelationship of class and ideology. Ideologies are here defined broadly as 'modes of life' or specific articulations of values and practices that structure households' everyday life and their pattern of activities. Ideologies are ultimately rooted in class relations and the economic structure that underlies them, but there is no simple one-to-one correspondence between economic structure, class fraction and matching ideology. Castells and Godard distinguish between an ideology of mass consumption (the dominant ideology, shaped by the needs of the dominant fraction of monopoly capital), a pre-capitalist ideology (associated with petty-bourgeois or traditional artisan life-styles), a traditional working-class subculture and an ideology of struggle. Different classes and fractions appropriate and absorb elements from different ideologies and, although certain relations are relatively clear (e.g. managers and top administrators tend to adopt a mass-consumption ideology), there is no mechanical correspondence of class and ideology implied.

THE URBAN SYSTEM AND ITS CONTRADICTIONS

It is only now possible, within this hierarchy of explanation, to make the transition to the urban system as such as a focus for enquiry. This involves a shift in perspective towards the reproduction of labour power and social relations. In order for capital accumulation to proceed at all it is necessary that labour power be continually reproduced, not simply in terms of a total quantity but also in terms of the different components of labour (varying in skills, education and social values) that are required by different branches of industry. The problems that emerge at varying levels within the urban system ultimately reflect the failure to give the same emphasis to the reproduction of labour power and social relations as to the reproduction of the means of production. The basic needs of private capital accumulation and profit always dominate, setting the pace and form of urban growth, as the system of private production draws towards itself capital and resources. The objective socialisation of the process of production and the interdependencies it generates within the urban system is not matched by investment in necessary collective facilities. The emergence of crises and bottlenecks, of a state of permanent disequilibrium, forces the state to intervene to try and regulate or repress the contradictory forces at work. Intervention will be primarily, though not entirely, on behalf of dominant fractions of capital but state crisis management is always partial and ultimately unsatisfactory because of the contradictory pressures on the state's activities, its inability to interfere too closely in the processes of private production (the real source of the problems) and the checks and limitations imposed upon its revenues and expenditures by the demands of the market.

HOUSING IN THE URBAN SYSTEM

The urban system as a system of contradictions is approached through a study of the elements and sub-elements of consumption, exchange, administration and symbolic structure and their interconnections. Housing, as a major element of consumption, now makes its first appearance. It is the weight of the preceding analysis however which gives it its meaning and place within the system and specifies the questions to be posed and the lines of analysis that need to be pursued.

The provision of new housing is not just a quantitative problem of mechanically meeting a demand. The provision of housing is also a qualitative problem in the sense that (a) housing must contribute to the reproduction of the different components of labour power with their different incomes and housing needs, (b) housing must contribute to the reproduction of social relations through a correspondence between signs of residential status and position within a social hierarchy based on class divisions, (c) housing also has a more overtly political role in isolating and disorganising potential working class movements through a dispersal of working-class concentrations and a fragmentation of social areas by status differentials and modes of consumption.

As a result of the contradictory forces at work within the system, housing needs are not met in a rational way, and the result is bottlenecks and crises. Adequate finance is a continuing problem because of the low incomes of the majority in relation to the costs of housing and the attraction of investment away from the housing sector towards more profitable outlets in industrial production. The process of housing production is also threatened by the bidding up of land prices by new industries and the movement of construction labour out of the housebuilding industry into factory construction, where wages are higher. In the short run firms may rely upon a variety of limited strategies to head off crises. Labour may be drawn in from surrounding areas where it is already housed; large corporations may fund housing for key workers and temporary housing may be built for single workers. Ultimately, however, rapid growth of production leads to a growing need for housing for a stable labour force of process and production line workers who cannot be housed in temporary barracks on the one hand or provided with company loans as are managerial or administrative staff on the other. The emergence of a housing crisis in the shape of overcrowding, property deterioration, the spread of slums and the proliferation of temporary accommodation threatens the maintenance of a stable and trained workforce for the major corporations.

In this context some form of state intervention becomes vitally necessary. In the Dunkirk case, where finance, land, labour and managerial expertise are all lacking in the housing field, the typical response has been the building of 'grands ensembles', hastily erected concentrations of flats and blocks, poorly provided with services and amenities. This form of provision is shown to be quantitatively inadequate for the reproduction of the labour force and qualitatively inadequate for the reproduction of social relations.

At the level of the system as a whole capital accumulation and the reproduction of the means of production are thus continually threatened by crises in the reproduction of labour power and social relations, crises that are ultimately rooted in the very dominance of private accumulation and production. Castells and Godard trace through the interconnections by first listing the various kinds of bottlenecks in the system (such as land shortages, labour scarcity, a backward building industry, etc.) and then linking them to a set of underlying contradictions (such as the conflict between big corporations and the local building industry over construction labour). Different bottlenecks, which may appear on the surface to be independent problems, are shown to be manifestations of various combinations of underlying contradictions. A similar kind of analysis is carried out on the bottlenecks and contradictions that underlie related crises in the provision of neighbourhood services and transport.

The residential differentiation of housing is brought into the picture by a consideration of the symbolic structuring of space and its relationship to the reproduction of social relations through the intermediary of ideologies. The analysis proceeds through several stages. First, the authors identify a typology of spatial forms based on the distinctive spatial units which are perceived by the population. Thus it is possible to speak of 'prestige zones', 'ghetto zones', 'traditional working class areas', etc. Second, the authors postulate four underlying dichotomous axes which serve to structure the spatial images already identified. These axes contrast the 'new' against the 'old', 'bourgeois' against 'working class', the 'traditional port town' against the 'outsiders', and 'suburbs and town' against 'country'. The spatial units already identified represent certain combinations of signs. For example, the new suburban prestige zones to the west of the city are defined by the intersection of the signs 'new', 'bourgeois', 'outsiders', and 'town'. Third, the authors seek to establish relationships between different ideologies or 'cultural models' and the axes which differentiate the spatial units. The previously identified ideology of consumption, for example, is expressed at the semantic level by the predominance of 'new' over 'old', 'bourgeois' over 'worker', 'outsiders' over the 'traditional' population and 'town' over 'country'.

The validity of this analysis is partly tested by looking finally for correspondences between different ideologies and the different spatial units. The argument is that spatial units emit certain signs associated with certain ideological practices or modes of life and are the locations for the different social groups who are the supports of these ideologies. Different zones are therefore associated with four major ideologies – the ideology of consumption, the petty-bourgeois/ artisan ideology, the traditional working-class ideology, and the ideology of struggle.

This symbolic structure of the urban system is also riven by contradictions. Ideologies are intertwined with the broader issues of the reproduction of labour power and the reproduction of social relations. However, in Dunkirk the organisation of social space fails to do this adequately, precipitating conflicts and struggles rather than stabilising social relations. For example, the emergency response of building 'grands ensembles' concentrates the new, more militant workers into poorly equipped, one-class neighbourhoods clearly demarcated in space from the middle-class prestige zones with their obviously superior cultural and recreational facilities. This overly sharp spatial segregation represents a symbolic bottle-neck in the sense that spatial patterns reinforce at the neighbour-hood level the class divisions established in the workplace, rather than functioning to mute class antagonism and fragment potential working-class solidarity by offering a status ladder of carefully graded residential areas that gives the illusion of a possible, steady upward progress in the social hierarchy. Bottlenecks such as these can in turn be traced back to contradictions at the level of housing production.

URBAN POLITICS AND PLANNING

The analysis so far has indicated the need for state intervention in one form or another and at the same time the inadequacy of the state's response. The latter aspect is taken up in more detail in the next stage of enquiry, the study of urban politics. Crises do not obviously call forth automatic and rational responses by the state on behalf of capital. Responses are mediated through the changing balance of class forces at the local and national level so that policies shift to accommodate interests of different fractions, although only within the limits set by the need to reproduce the power of capital as a whole and as far as possible serve the interests of the dominant capital fractions. Thus the Dunkirk area has seen the emergence of new types of local institutions, new forms of urban government and new systems of planning – each represented as being in the best interests of the community as a whole, but each reflecting a shifting pattern of class forces at the local, regional and national level.

HOUSING ISSUES AND URBAN SOCIAL MOVEMENTS

The logic of analysis and presentation finally converges on the consideration of urban social movements. State action may be temporarily successful in diffusing crises but only by displacing them to other levels within the system. In so far as the basic contradictory forces remain they will tend to be manifested in new forms of crisis which may be made more difficult to contain by the very fact of state involvement. Castells and Godard focus on certain issues that have broken out of the institutional moulds within which they are usually confined, leading to various forms of direct action. In the sphere of housing, group action has begun to emerge on issues relating to rent, housing costs and inadequate neighbourhood facilities. Although these struggles have been relatively short lived they are indicative of new forces at work. Traditionally, even violent conflicts over wages and working conditions at the workplace have not spilled over into neighbourhood conflicts over housing and collective facilities. The two areas of conflict – one relating to industrial struggle in the sphere of production, the other to 'urban problems' in the sphere of consumption – have generally been kept separate. Workplace struggles have been handled by trade unions, and neighbourhood crises have been channelled through local political institutions where they have been effectively defused. Such a separation of working life from home life, or industrial problems from urban problems, of processes of production from processes of consumption, conceals the increasing domination of the whole system by monopoly capital. However, the increasingly close involvement of the state in urban problems on behalf of monopoly capital also serves to politicise issues and make plain the links between problem areas.

This highly condensed presentation of the work by Castells and Godard has only sketched in the major themes and lines of argument, and the original work should be consulted for its wealth of ideas and details (see also Lebas, 1977, for further comments). Nevertheless, our sketch serves to highlight the kinds of questions that a Marxist approach raises and the way in which a diversity of themes can be integrated in a broad theoretical structure. Before drawing out some of these themes for a more critical examination we will briefly present an alternative framework, with somewhat different emphases, represented in the work of Harvey. This will help to show some of the differences in viewpoint even within the Marxist framework.

Finance capital and urban housing markets: the work of David Harvey

Harvey's work has been presented in a developing series of books and articles rather than a completed text and this accounts for some of the inconsistencies and shifts of position in his work. Nevertheless it is possible to integrate the main themes of his analyses into a broad theoretical framework. Harvey's work has grown out of his research on American urbanisation and his empirical material focuses mainly on the Baltimore housing market.

RENT THEORY

Harvey first attempted to apply Marx's theory of rent to urban areas in *Social Justice and the City* (Harvey, 1973, Chapter 5), and although he has modified his original position a theory of rent runs through much of his work.

We have seen that rent plays a central role in neo-classical theories of urban spatial structure where it appears as the marginal productivity of a scarce factor of production (land) under equilibrium conditions. Harvey attacks this apparently 'innocent' concept as essentially ideological because it conceals an underlying pattern of social class relations. He resurrects Marx's theory of rent laid out in Volume III of *Capital* and attempts to apply it to modern urban conditions.

Marx's discussion of rent applied to the role of the landowner in the agricultural sector of a capitalist mode of production. To Marx the landowner was essentially parasitic; he did not produce value but because of his ownership of a necessary means for production he was able to intercept part of the flow of surplus value that would otherwise have gone to the capitalist or worker. This surplus value was intercepted in the form of rent. Marx went further and distinguished three forms of rent representing the different ways that surplus value could be appropriated.

His concept of *differential rent* was essentially derived from Ricardo. Differential rent arises when capital is applied to lands of varying fertility or distance from the market (Differential Rent 1) or when differing amounts of capital are used on different pieces of land (Differential Rent 2). In the case of DR1, values and prices of production are determined by the labour required for production on the worst-quality soil. Because production on more fertile land, or land closer to the market, requires less labour, more surplus value is produced and hence more profit could accrue to the farmer. If the land is owned by landowners, however, part of this surplus value can be extracted by them in the form of rent, since farmers will compete for the more fertile land and land closer to market, driving up its price. As the result of competitive bidding by farmers the landowner takes this rent and the capitalist farmer obtains an average rate of profit. A similar analysis could be applied to the case of DR2.

Monopoly rent is received by landowners who let out land for the production of goods sold under monopoly conditions at monopoly prices. Marx provides the example of a vineyard producing unique, high-quality wine which due to lack of competition can be sold at a price well above its value. Since the land is an essential component of production, the landowner could obtain some of this surplus profit in the form of a monopoly rent extracted from the capitalist producer.

Marx's third category of rent is *absolute rent*. In his discussion of differential rent Ricardo had argued that no rent accrued to the most distant or marginal lands where only an average rate of profit could be recovered. Marx, on the other hand, argued that landowners could withhold land from production until a rent was obtained even on this marginal land. Absolute rent thus arises from the power of a landowning class to maintain scarcity. More specifically, landowners could restrict the flow of capital into the agricultural sector, preventing a rise in the organic composition of capital and maintaining the conditions for higher-than-average profits. (The rate of profit is inversely related to the organic composition of capital.) A proportion of these surplus profits could be extracted in the form of absolute rent whose upper limit, Marx argued, was set by the values of the agricultural commodities produced. However, Marx did not provide a satisfactory explanation of why landowners could not force prices above values, thus extracting monopoly rent.

Harvey's application and modification of these rent categories in a contemporary urban context is not clear at several points, but the major lines of argument seem to be as follows. The distinction between monopoly rent and absolute rent can be restated as a difference between the monopoly power of an individual to extract rent and the power of a class as a whole to extract rent because of more general conditions of production. The conditions of scarcity for the extraction of monopoly and absolute rents are established in urban areas by the manipulation of the land market by landowners; in other words, scarcity is determined by social rather than natural limits to the use of land. The high rental values of land in central areas of cities is not necessarily a reflection of the higher marginal productivity of land. It is rather the case that central areas provide excellent opportunities for the extraction of monopoly and absolute rents. In nineteenth-century cities, under more competitive land market conditions, higher central city land values may well have primarily reflected differential rents but in contemporary metropolises, with the growth of monopoly power, it is more likely that prices reflect the charging of monopoly and absolute rents. 'In practice, of course, rent arises out of all three circumstances and it is often difficult to determine what portion of the overall rental value arises out of which circumstance' (Harvey, 1973, p. 188).

The peaking of land values is also, of course, explained by the neo-classical rent models but their apparent empirical relevance is largely a function of their assumptions concerning centricity and distance decay. In so far as they abstract from underlying class and property relations, attributing land values to the land's marginal productivity, they are a 'disconcerting mixture of status quo apologetics and counter-revolutionary obfuscation' (ibid., p. 193). Marxist rent theory therefore helps to uncover the deeper processes of exploitation at work within contemporary capitalist cities.

In a later paper Harvey (1974) has introduced a new term, 'class monopoly rent', which represents a restatement of his position. Class monopoly rent arises because there exists a class of owners of resource units (land, houses, etc.) who are willing to release the units under their command only if they receive a positive return above some arbitrarily determined level. Harvey admits that it is not clear whether this form of rent should be included in the category of absolute or monopoly rent but on balance feels that it should be treated as an expression of the former. However, it is clearly a broader concept than Marx's concept of absolute rent which was originally applied to the situation of a class of agricultural landowners at a particular phase of development in the capitalist system. In order to explain how class monopoly rents are realised Harvey integrates his approach to rent into a broader theory of residential differentiation and the role of financial institutions in contemporary capitalism.

FINANCIAL INSTITUTIONS AND RESIDENTIAL
DIFFERENTIATION

The urban housing market is increasingly controlled by a network of public and private financial institutions that channel loans and investments to different segments of the housing market. These institutions form a hierarchy extending from the national and regional levels down to the local levels, transmitting downwards the broad concerns of national policy to ensure (a) orderly relationships between construction, economic growth and household formation, (b) short-run stability and reduction of cyclical swings in the economy by using the construction sector as a Keynsian regulator and (c) social stability and the reproduction of capitalist social relations. The institutions interact at the urban level to create a geographical structure of housing submarkets with boundaries that are relatively stable over time. In the case of Baltimore Harvey identified no less than thirteen such submarkets each characterised by different income and house-price levels, different forms of tenure, different social and ethnic patterns and the involvement of different combinations of financial institutions with their different lending and financing rules (Harvey, 1977).

This institutional and geographical structure of the urban housing market permits the extraction of class monopoly rents. For example, within the inner city submarkets a class of professional landlords controlled the supply of cheaper rented accommodation. Low-income tenants, denied access to owner-occupation and public housing by financial barriers, formed a trapped population. In this kind of context landlords assured themselves a high return on their investments through creating artificial scarcities, by leaving some units vacant, overcrowding others, undermaintaining, and switching investment elsewhere. In certain high-turnover submarkets, in contrast, a different class of agents was able to extract class monopoly rents through the exploitation of Federal Housing Agency programmes introduced in the 1970s to encourage black, low-income home-ownership. Speculators encouraged an outflow of whites from these areas, purchased their houses cheaply, carried out a few cosmetic improvements and sold the houses at inflated prices to incoming blacks who had access to FHA insured mortgages. Class monopoly rents could then be further extracted from middle-income whites fleeing to the suburbs by yet another class of agents, the speculator developers, who provided a variety of suburban housing geared to carefully fostered differences in social prestige and status. In these kinds of ways the extraction of class monopoly rent in one submarket is linked to the extraction of rent in another market, with rent generally filtering upwards through the institutional hierarchy from landlords to developers, and spatially from central areas to suburbs. The residential structure of Baltimore takes the form of a series of man-made islands, or 'absolute spaces', the result of the manipulation of scarcities conducive to the generation and appropriation of class monopoly rents.

This structuring and restructuring of the residential environment by government and financial institutions also functions to mould consumption patterns and fragment class relations, and contributes to the social stability of the system. The dichotomous class division between capital and labour is blurred by a variety of overlapping secondary forces of class structuration. Harvey, following Giddens (1973), has divided these into residual forces (reflecting the survival of social relations from previous stages or modes of production) and derivative forces (Harvey, 1975b). The derivative forces are a function of (a) the developments in the division of labour and the specialisation of the labour force leading to distinctive strata within the working class, (b) the development of different consumption patterns or 'life-styles' based upon the manipulation of consumption needs, (c) the development of authority relations at the workplace, (d) the development of new ideological forms of consciousness that cut across class divisions, and (e) the development of inter-generational barriers to mobility. The segmentation of the housing market and the division of the city into residential communities functions to reinforce many of these divisions in so far as the community as a social milieu is the source of socialisation experiences that equip residents with distinctive values, attitudes towards work, goals and consumption needs. Therefore, the institutional structuring of residential space simultaneously produces distinctive 'consumption classes', 'distributive groupings' and 'housing classes'. This fragmentation into separate communities fosters community-based organisations that cut across objective class lines and encourages separate intercommunity conflicts that are less of a threat to the system than class-wide conflicts based on an emerging awareness of an identity of class interests.

HOUSING AND THE CIRCUITS OF CAPITAL

Harvey's approach places great emphasis on the interlock between financial institutions and the government in the management of urban systems. In fact Harvey suggests in his 1974 paper that the role of financial institutions in urban areas is just one expression of the growing hegemony of finance capital in the latest stage of capitalism (Harvey, 1974). He supports Lefebvre's assertion

(Lefebvre, 1970) that the development of urbanism as the dominant feature of modern capitalist society has gone hand in hand with the increasing dominance of finance capital over industrial capital. An increasing proportion of surplus value is now realised in speculation, real estate and construction, as finance capital reaches out to control the processes of production, realisation and consumption. Put another way, urban processes reflect the growing dominance of secondary circuits of capital over the primary circuit of capital involved in production.

This position seems to have been modified in one of his most recent papers (Harvey, 1978a), which develops further the idea of interrelated circuits of capital but appears to attach less importance to the hegemony of finance capital. Harvey distinguishes a primary circuit of capital involved in production, a secondary circuit of capital flowing into fixed capital investment and consumption funds, and a tertiary circuit of capital flowing into investment in science and technology and the reproduction of labour power. A proportion of fixed capital investment and consumption fund expenditure (the secondary circuit) flows into the urban built environment to provide the necessary physical framework for production and consumption (the provision of urban infrastructure, housing, etc.). The flow of capital into the secondary circuit is now linked much more firmly to the rhythms of capital accumulation in the primary circuit. Crises in the primary circuit are expressed in terms of an overaccumulation of capital, and sudden flows of this surplus into speculative property investment in the built environment may often reflect a last ditch attempt to stave off the crisis. However, investment is also related to the economic lifetime of the different elements of the built environment. Empirical evidence points towards definite cycles of building activity with a length of fifteen to twenty-five years.

Housing investment is obviously a particular component of investment in the built environment and a component of investment in the reproduction of labour power. It is therefore linked to the rhythms of the secondary and tertiary circuits of capital and their interrelations with the primary circuit. Harvey does not develop these interconnections in detail in this paper beyond pointing to the relationship between suburbanisation, the opening up of housing as a profitable outlet for private investment, and the spread of home-ownership as a source of social stability and the reproduction of social relations. The rapid expansion of the suburbs and suburban styles of consumption in the United States since the war may have played a major part in offsetting tendencies towards overaccumulation and crisis in the primary circuit. This is a theme that we will return to later.

Comment

We have reviewed the work of these two authors in some detail
because of the weight of their contributions and because it is a
convenient way of exploring some of the interconnections between
different aspects of a Marxist approach to housing. Castells's work
appears to have a more coherent and integrated theoretical structure which may be partly the result of the close links between his
work and the extensive theorising of Althusser and Poulantzas.
However, their theories represent particular interpretations of
Marxism which have been severely criticised in some quarters. For
example, Althusser's concept of a structural causality binding
together a mode of production has been criticised as simply a form of
functional determination which denies any independent effectivity
to class struggle (Cutler, Hindess, Hirst and Hussain, 1977; see also
Geras, 1972 and Glucksman, 1974). Poulantzas's conception of
class structure and the role of the state has been similarly criticised
for its 'structural superdeterminism' (Milliband, 1973). There is
indeed a strong 'structuralist' tinge to Castells's writings, and parts
of *The Urban Question*, in particular, give the reader the feeling of
being trapped in an unwieldy, deterministic strait-jacket. However,
the imaginative and flexible use of many of the concepts in *Monopolville* goes a long way to counteract such criticisms, and Castells has
also sought to reply at a more theoretical level in a Postscript to the
English edition of *The Urban Question*. Nevertheless, the many points
of contact between Castells's work and the specific and controversial
interpretation of Althusser and Poulantzas should not be forgotten
even though they are much less in evidence in Castells's more recent
writings.

Harvey's work appears less of an integrated theoretical structure
although, as we shall discuss later, some of his ideas derive from
Baran and Sweezy's theory of monopoly capitalism which stresses
an underconsumptionist interpretation of capitalist crisis (Baran
and Sweezy, 1966). His work is more immediately approachable
than Castells's but also marked by certain ambiguities and inconsistencies on important issues. Nevertheless, it is always provocative
and lively and his most recent work appears to be breaking new and
important ground.

In the next section we will take up a number of the themes touched
upon by Harvey and Castells, look at the work of other writers on
these themes, and try and pull out the main sources of controversy
and debate.

Chapter 11

Themes and controversies in Marxist approaches to housing

Urban rent theory and residential land markets

The basic elements of Marx's approach to rent theory have already been introduced in the review of Harvey's work. The Marxist theory of rent also preoccupied a number of French authors in the early 1970s, although their contributions have not until recently received the attention devoted to Harvey's formulations (see Scott, 1976, for a review of their work). The last two or three years has seen a vigorous debate on a number of aspects of rent theory and in this section we expand on some of the main points of controversy.

First, it is worth considering some of the criticisms that have been directed at Marx's original formulations in the context of agricultural commodity production, before looking at the problems of applying the concepts to the urban field. A number of writers (e.g. Edel, 1976; Emmanuel, 1972; S. Clark and Ginsburg, 1975) have questioned Marx's statement that in the agricultural sector, when the organic composition of capital is low and prices of production are potentially below values, landlords are restricted to a maximum absolute rent equal to the difference between prices and values. If landowners have the power to push prices up to values by withholding land from the market, surely they have the power to push prices above values if they choose? Marx's arguments for a clearly defined category of absolute rent do not seem too clear here but Edel (1976) has pulled together four possible arguments in its favour. Three are admittedly weak, but the fourth does provide some justification for an upper limit where prices approximately equal values. It is argued that if rents drove prices above values for a large set of goods, profits would reflect the rate of surplus value in the high organic composition of capital industries alone. The depressing effect on the rate of profit would reduce investment and the demand for land and would also reduce the opportunity for landowners to achieve high returns in rent.

In spite of such attempts to give the concepts more precision Marx's arguments do not seem entirely convincing on a number of points, and some authors (Broadbent, 1975; Scott, 1976) have attempted a more general restatement. Scott, for example, sets up a hypothetical situation with a given demand for commodities and a shortage of land to produce them and shows how a form of absolute rent accrues to marginal and intramarginal producers. However, this rent is interpreted simply as a rent that reflects the global scarcity of land relative to production rather than absolute rent in the strict Marxian sense. In fact Scott suggests that absolute rent in the Marxian sense should be restricted to limited and historically specific circumstances. It is a transitory phenomenon and largely peripheral to the evolution of the capitalist mode of production.

Murray (1977) has argued that to ignore Marx's specific conception of absolute rent is to ignore the labour theory of value. Some authors consider this to be quite justified. Tribe (1977), for example, suggests that conceptual difficulties cannot be rectified by a simple clarification of hypotheses; the source of the difficulty lies in the labour theory of value itself. Howard and King (1975) have suggested that value theory as a whole should be retained, but that its application in the specific context of rent theory is redundant. They argue that the price of land, like any other monopolised commodity, can be explained by the laws of supply and demand not by values. Rent is then just a form of monopoly profit and Marx's value theory of rent is largely redundant (Howard and King, 1975, pp. 139–41).

If there is some confusion about the validity of some of Marx's concepts within a theory of value, and even doubts about the necessity for a value theory approach at all even among Marxists, it is not surprising that there have been considerable disagreements about the application of these concepts to the contemporary urban system. A number of criticisms have taken Harvey's initial formulations as a starting point.

General criticisms have been directed against Harvey's confusion of bourgeois concepts such as prices and Marxist value concepts such as exchange values; his vague and non-Marxian use of the term class in 'class monopoly rent'; and his overemphasis on an almost conspiratorial tie-up between government and finance capital under the hegemony of the latter. In the context of rent theory more specific criticisms have been directed against his interpretation of Marx and his application of Marx's rent concepts. For example, Clark and Ginsburg (1975), Bruegel (1975) and Edel (1976) all question Harvey's use of the term absolute rent in the context of housing submarkets within urban areas. To apply Marx's concept in the strict sense it is necessary to show that the organic composition of capital is low in the construction sector and that there are barriers to the flow of investment into submarkets preventing the equalising of the rate of profit over the system as a whole. This provides the conditions necessary for the appropriation of surplus profits as absolute rent. However several authors do not feel that Harvey makes a strong enough case to justify the use of the term absolute rent in the context of his housing sub-markets. Bruegel does not feel that in most cases submarket barriers are as strong as Harvey suggests. Edel does list six kinds of barriers to investment flows in urban areas, such as the presence of large estates, fragmented holdings, land speculation, planning controls, etc., but is doubtful about the extent to which absolute rent is generated in the urban system as a whole. Edel also argues that Harvey's class monopoly rents are really just monopoly rents and not a form of absolute rent. Both Bruegel and Edel suggest that differential rents are more important than Harvey claims in the context of inner city sites, and monopoly and absolute rents of less importance.

A somewhat different use of a concept of absolute rent has been used by Lamarche (1976). Lamarche links the development of absolute rent in urban areas to the evolution of a specialised form of capital, property capital. Property capital deals in the commodity floor space and concentrates on the construction of office and commercial centres linked to upper-income housing. New office and commercial centres reduce communication and transaction costs between enterprises and ultimately increase the rate of turnover of capital which contributes towards an increase in the rate of profit. This enables property capital to claim a share of the surplus value produced in the productive sector. However, landowners can also lay claim to a share of surplus value by withholding their land from the market, basing their selling price on the anticipated profitability of property capital. The share of profit accruing to landowners is absolute rent and is a function of private property in land. Absolute rent is paid out of what Lamarche terms Differential Rent 1, which is the rent that the developer can obtain from the site after he has created its locational advantages in the city through his investments in shops, offices and houses. As Lamarche puts it, absolute rent 'does not yield actual and immediate profits to the landowner. It is based on time and results in fact from the action of the owner who, by withholding his land from exploitation, encourages the increase in expected differential rents (the only ones to constitute hard cash)' (Lamarche, 1976, p. 108). This ability of the landowner to capture a part of surplus value as absolute rent by withholding land helps to explain why areas close to city centres or strategic nodes are often characterised by housing decay, declining maintenance and vacant lots. Landlords can still extract payment from tenants even for decaying property whilst the landowner awaits the moment when absolute rent can be realised when redevelopment is launched under the direction of property capital. Lamarche's analysis applies largely to the development of new commercial and luxury housing complexes but the effects on differential rents in the immediate vicinity will be rapidly transmitted throughout the urban area.

Although much of the discussion and debate has centred around the concept of absolute rent in particular, a number of authors have touched upon issues that have as yet barely been explored. For example, both Harvey (1973) and Byrne and Beirne (1975) have pointed to the increasing difficulty of distinguishing groundrent from interest as a return on capital improvements in land, since capital improvements tend to become capitalised in land values. With fixed groundrents and long leases, and with the spread of owner-occupation, gains from rising land and building values may accrue to the builder, leaseholder or owner-occupier rather than the landowner. The situation is made more complex in some cases by the fact that builders and the institutions of finance capital are themselves increasingly becoming major landowners in urban areas.

One is forced to conclude that rent theory is at present in an unsatisfactory and transitional state. The attacks mounted against the neo-classical position from the Marxian standpoint have been well directed and in many cases have struck home with considerable effect. But the task of developing an alternative Marxist theory of urban rent has proved difficult and many inconsistencies remain to be cleared up. There are three major questions that yet await a satisfactory answer. First, is a value theory approach to rent theory necessary to Marx's system? Second, if it is necessary, is Marx's formulation of rent theory adequate even for the kinds of agricultural phenomena he was trying to explain? Third, can Marx's concepts be applied with appropriate modifications to the capitalist city (in particular, the contemporary capitalist city) or are they too specific to a nineteenth-century economic and class context that bears little resemblance to the situation prevailing today. Whatever the answers to these questions, the urban rent problem remains and necessitates *some* answer from Marxists, perhaps through the development of quite new concepts within a broad Marxist tradition.

Housing, collective consumption and the reproduction of labour power

The concept of collective consumption and its role in the reproduction of labour power plays a central part in the theories of a number of French writers. We have already encountered this concept in the work of Castells and we will now look at it more critically and in greater depth, asking a number of related questions: What is meant by collective consumption? In what sense is housing a form of collective consumption? In what sense is housing necessary for the reproduction of labour power?

Castells's approach has the following aspects. First, collective means of consumption (public transport, schools, parks, health facilities, public housing, etc.) are increasingly important for the efficient reproduction of labour power and social relations in contemporary capitalist cities. The inability of private capital to provide these goods and services on the scale required means that what we commonly call urban problems are increasingly problems of collective consumption.

Second, collective consumption does not refer to some natural characteristic of certain goods and services that implies they have to be collectively consumed. Capital's voracious search for surplus value can make commodities out of any goods and services unless their production involves a lower-than-average rate of profit or their benefits cannot be monopolised by one capital (schools, the police, etc.).

Third, the inability of private capital to provide certain collective means of consumption necessary for its own survival and expansion in the urban environment, calls for greater and greater state intervention to the extent that the institutions of the state (national and local) become increasingly responsible for the management of everyday urban life. Yet state intervention to meet collective-consumption needs is always partial, inadequate and contradictory. Resources are limited, geared primarily to the rhythms of production, and distributed in response to the conflicting demands of different capital fractions and working-class pressure.

Fourth, there is no clear-cut and permanent boundary between collective and individual forms of consumption. There is a permanent tendency for capital to claim back sectors from the state for private exploitation whenever changes in supply and demand and relative profit rates favour renewed private investment. There is also a tendency for the principles of the private market to invade the public sector, leading to more 'realistic' pricing and a stratification of provision according to ability to pay.

Finally, Castells also argues that state expenditures on collective consumption also have an important effect in counteracting the tendency of the rate of profit to fall. This thesis rests heavily on the work of Boccara (1974) who argues that the overaccumulation of capital which accompanies the tendency of the rate of profit to fall can be partially offset by the advancement of capital by the state at zero or near zero rates of profit (such capital is termed 'devalorised capital'). This devalorisation of part of capital enables remaining private capital to maintain an average rate of profit in the private sector, although there are obvious limits to how far this process can continue. It certainly does not offer a long-term solution to declining profits in a capitalist economy.

Lojkine (1976, 1977) and Preteceille (1973, 1977) also lay great stress on the role of collective consumption, but there are important differences in emphasis in their respective approaches. Lojkine, for example, agrees that collective consumption is an important aspect of modern capitalist urbanisation but criticises Castells for throwing too much weight on this dimension of urban problems. State intervention should not be reduced to the management of the reproduction of labour power; the state is also heavily involved in the reproduction of the means of production through the provision of basic economic infrastructure, grants and subsidies. Indeed, this economic role often pre-empts the resources needed for social expenditure.

Lojkine's definition of collective means of consumption also differs to some degree from Castells's. Collective means of consumption differ from private because collective means of consumption (schools, parks, etc.) are (a) not strictly commodities, or use values sold as objects, (b) they are durable and their consumption does not involve their destruction (as in the case of food), and (c) their mode of consumption is collective as opposed to private, or individualised appropriation. Again, Lojkine argues that such goods and services are not usually provided by private capital because of low profit rates, the slow speed of rotation of capital, discontinuous demand and high risks. State expenditure on collective means of consumption are termed 'expenses capital' by Lojkine to signify the fact that they are unproductive expenditure (they do not generate surplus value) and are deductions from the surplus value produced by productive capital. Lojkine then argues, somewhat contentiously, that the expansion of expenses capital acts in the same way as the increase in constant capital in production; it tends to increase the organic composition of capital and increase the tendency of the rate of profit to fall. Private capital accumulation in modern cities is thus bound up with contradictory processes that on the one hand tend to expand state expenditures to maintain the bases for capital accumulation yet on the other hand tend simultaneously to undermine the rate of profit, the mainspring of that accumulation.

Preteceille (1977) has recently reviewed some of these ideas and concepts and explored yet further layers of complexity. However, we have provided enough detail to indicate the diversity of themes subsumed under this broad heading. This diversity of viewpoints has prompted Pahl (1977b) to suggest that the concept has been used in a confused and ambiguous way and adds little to our understanding of the state's role in consumption. Some of Pahl's criticisms are very fair, but Preteceille's defence of the concept (Preteceille, 1977) also has much to commend it. The concept of collective consumption, he argues, is not to be judged (as Pahl seems to imply) by its ability to *classify* forms of consumption. It is rather a question of developing, deepening and refining a theoretical concept that may or may not enable us to grasp the complex problem of explaining those forms and variations of state intervention in urban systems. Nevertheless, it must be admitted that at the moment the concept remains in a relatively unrefined state, includes many areas of ambiguity and is only partly integrated into a wider theory of the state and urbanisation processes. Given this interim state, can the concept get us very far in an analysis of housing problems and housing policies?

Castells, Lojkine and Preteceille all make references to state subsidised housing at various places in their discussions, although often to make different points. Combining aspects of their work leads us to the following broad themes.

First, to what extent is housing a collective means of consumption and how does this explain state intervention? Castells seems to argue that public housing is a collective means of consumption because it is provided by the state. State intervention is demanded because private capital cannot meet the housing needs of a sizeable sector of the population at a profit because of the slow speed of rotation of capital and the high prices of housing in relation to income. Applying Lojkine's definitions, public housing could be construed as a collective means of consumption because public housing units are not sold as a commodity, are durable and are collectively consumed by tenant households. There are several areas of ambiguity here that can perhaps be clarified in the following way.

At the level of production public housing could be said to be *collectively provided* in the limited sense that the state advances devalorised capital and plans the overall production of housing. However, the actual process of production itself is usually organised by private firms for a profit. Preteceille (1973) has further argued that different forms of devalorised capital advanced by the state have different requirements attached to them with respect to expected rates of return, turnover time, etc. and this affects the kind of housing that is provided. His own study of large public housing developments in France (the 'grands ensembles') shows how different combinations of state devalorised capital, private property capital and loan capital have shaped the type and quality of public housing developments and associated facilities.

After housing units have been produced with devalorised capital, or with private capital and subsequently acquired by the state, in what sense is this housing *collectively consumed*? In practice housing is consumed by individual family units who often remain in occupation of a house or flat for a longer period of time than is common in the private sector. State housing is perhaps a collective means of consumption in the sense that (a) it is collectively and not privately owned, (b) housing consumption is subject to certain social rules and regulations that determine access to and allocation of public housing units, and (c) the costs of housing are shared through subsidies from taxpayers and transfers between tenants (rent-pooling schemes, etc.).

Public housing is perhaps an easy example to take. But state intervention may also take place at arm's length through the intermediary of housing associations or co-operatives, and in many cases the state may content itself by and large with subsidising owner-occupiers to compete in the private market. In practice there is a continuum of state intervention represented by various degrees of socialisation of ownership, management and control, subsidisation and cost-sharing. Although state intervention in housing has certainly increased in all capitalist countries, the forms of socialisation and the degree of socialisation have varied markedly, for example between the United States and the United Kingdom.

Obviously there is no simple, unfolding, logic of capital accumulation which determines particular forms and levels of collective consumption except in the most general terms. Can we extend the analysis by taking up a second and related theme, the relationship between state housing provision and the reproduction of labour power? It could be argued that the way the state intervenes to provide housing is partly related to the need to reproduce certain key components of the labour force. This line of argument has been explored by Pinçon (1976) who has attempted to explain the over-representation of some occupations (skilled manual workers, public employees) in state subsidised housing in Paris and the under-representation of other occupations by arguing that certain types of labour power are more precious for capital than others. This form of explanation has been criticised by Pickvance (1977a) along with the general concept linking housing to the reproduction of labour power. At a detailed level he argues that Pinçon's empirical findings could be just as well explained by the operation of access and allocation rules that reflect other political factors, such as the attempt to keep down state housing subsidies, defuse potential conflicts over housing issues or even encourage suburban areas to take more tenants from congested inner areas. Pickvance concludes that the reproduction of labour argument is not supported by the evidence in this case.

At a more general level Pickvance then goes on to reject the reproduction of labour argument as an explanation of state intervention except in very special cases. First, housing has a small role to play in the reproduction of labour power compared to collective means of consumption such as schooling or technical training. Reproduction of labour power does not simply imply the availability of certain numbers of workers at certain places. It implies the reproduction of a labour force with appropriate skills, attitudes towards authority, ideological perspectives, and so on. Educational and cultural institutions and the workplace itself as a source of social relations, are more important in reproduction than the provision of dwellings. Second, housing as a use value is only weakly linked to the process of reproducing labour power. To argue a strong link between the quality of dwellings and (say) labour productivity would be a form of physical determinism, although there are obviously minimum standards below which a worker's efficiency is likely to be impaired. Third, given the improvement in housing standards over the last half-century in most capitalist countries, the quality of housing is likely to be a minor constraint on that part of the reproduction of labour power that takes place in the home. Finally, the spread of single-family dwellings has defused the kinds of political problems once associated with overcrowding and enforced communal living in the overcrowded towns of the turn of the century. Pickvance concludes that only in the case of new housing provision in association with industrial expansion into greenfield areas is there a clear relationship between state housing policies and the reproduction of labour power.

It could be countered that Pickvance takes his argument too far and overstates his case. It appears frequently to have been the case that public housing in Britain has been provided to meet the labour needs of suburbanising industries. It could also be argued that rising housing standards are incorporated in what labour comes to regard as the minimum subsistence wages. The reproduction of labour in general thus requires the reproduction of increasingly high housing standards. Nevertheless, Pickvance's critique, linked with our earlier comments, does cast doubts on explanations of state intervention in housing in terms of a necessary increase in the provision of collective means of consumption for the reproduction of labour power. This is not to argue for the abandonment of the whole concept of collective consumption. There is clearly a trend towards the socialisation of consumption activities as well as production in advanced capitalist cities, but the form that socialisation takes and the boundaries between collective and individual consumption clearly shift in response to a complex of political factors.

The reproduction of social relations: tenure forms and residential differentiation

The survival of a capitalist system depends upon the reproduction of certain social relations just as much as the reproduction of labour power and means of production. It is necessary to reproduce certain relations of property and authority, so that individuals accept capitalist relations as somehow 'natural' and inevitable. In modern bourgeois democracies ideology plays the crucial role in moulding appropriate attitudes and values, although the underlying tensions of class conflict means that the adoption of the dominant ideology is always precarious, and ideological processes are ultimately backed by the repressive power of the state. In this section we will look at the relationship between forms of housing consumption and the reproduction of social relations.

The interconnection of workplace, home and community has perhaps been clearest in the case of isolated communities, dependent on local, paternalistic firms. Newby (1977) gives the example of certain cotton towns in the late nineteenth century where a coherent, unified elite of paternalistic millowners provided jobs and built houses, churches, recreational and cultural facilities for the associated workforce. Effectively, the relations of dependence and authority were extended outwards beyond the factory gates to embrace the whole pattern of community living, and the encouragement of a strong sense of locality undermined wider class relations with surrounding communities. However, such close interlinking of factory and community has been reduced by many developments in capitalist production in the twentieth century, and the relationship between housing and the reproduction of social relations is now more indirect and more complex. We explore some of these interconnections by looking first at ideology and tenure forms and then at residential differentiation and class divisions.

The point has already been made that there are complex problems of realisation and consumption associated with housing as a commodity. Different forms of tenure intervene between production and consumption, determining the form of housing finance and the rights and obligations attached to occupation of the housing unit. Ball (1978) has suggested that different tenure forms should be looked at in terms of (a) the prospects they offer for the extraction of surplus value by different agents in the realisation process, (b) their effect on the productivity of housebuilding, and (c) their political and ideological effects (i.e. the reproduction of social relations). For example, owner-occupation provides opportunities for the extraction of surplus value by various exchange professionals but does not lead to mass production of standardised housing types and major productivity increases. Public housing provides opportunities for the extraction of surplus value by loan capitalists, and the placing of large contracts for standardised housing units tends to have more impact on the production technology of the building industry. However, political and ideological factors appear to play an increasingly important role in the official encouragement of certain tenure forms.

Owner-occupation is becoming the dominant form of housing tenure in most (but not all) advanced capitalist countries, with the financial and ideological backing of the state. The explicit ideological objectives behind the official encouragement of owner-occupation in the 1930s in Britain and America has been noted by Boddy (1976b), Dickens (1977) and Harvey (1975a). A reading of Ball (1976 and 1978), Boddy (1976b), Castells (1977a), Harvey (1975a), and S. Clark and Ginsburg (1975) suggests that owner-occupation may have the following advantages for the capitalist system:

(a) Owner-occupation chimes with the dominant ideology of private property ownership. It gives the household the feeling of a stake in society and encourages social stability.

(b) Owner-occupation is typically associated with the expansion of single-family housing and the individual consumption of a variety of household consumer goods. Owner-occupation thus has desirable multiplier effects for industries providing mass-consumption goods.

(c) Owner-occupation is basically a form of debt encumbrance for the mass of households in this sector. Repayment of the debt demands work discipline and job stability. When the house is paid for the worker is usually nearing retirement and lower housing costs lowers the cost of maintaining the retired and unproductive population.

(d) Owner-occupation does not lead easily to the politicisation of housing issues. Housing costs are experienced through the intermediary of anonymous market mechanisms and undesirable effects are not obviously seen as the responsibility of particular capital fractions.

(e) Owner-occupation tends to divide and fragment the working class. Access to owner-occupation is usually open only to the more privileged strata of the working class, typically driving a wedge between skilled manual workers and white-collar workers on one side and less skilled manual workers in more unstable employment on the other. Owner-occupation thus cuts across class boundaries though not to the extent that owner-occupiers can be identified as a particular social category in Poulantzas's sense of the term (Ball, 1976).

Some of the writers who claim to see these advantages also point out certain disadvantages. The creation of a mass of debt-encumbered households is not entirely beneficial. The increasing instability of mortgage funds and interest rates in recent years has brought the owner-occupier more and more into contact with the forces of finance capital and encouraged a more critical frame of mind. The sheer volume of debt now locked up in property poses a threat to the stability of the financial system as a whole should real income level off or begin to fall and defaulting on debt repayments increase. The defensive attitudes of owner-occupiers may also lead to more community resistance to the speculative property activities of various financial institutions attempting to manipulate the urban property market to maximise rents and profits.

Public housing, on the other hand, has certain advantages in that mass-production techniques may lower the costs of housing, but it also has ideological drawbacks. Public housing implies a certain socialisation of housing costs and undermines the principles of private-property ownership. It provides a certain challenge to the principles that govern the operation of the system as a whole. The socialisation of costs encourages the development of social solidarity and class unity. The direct involvement of the state in the setting of rents and standards politicises the whole issue of housing provision to a greater extent than owner-occupation.

The two tenure forms described should not, however, be seen in isolation. In America, and to a lesser extent in Britain, public housing is provided in such a way that it often reinforces the advantages of the owner-occupied sector. Public housing is regarded as a safety net for lower-income groups and public emphasis on the state's subsidy to public housing tenants reinforces the virtues and status of owner-occupation for the upwardly mobile.

Nevertheless, it is important not to see owner-occupation on a large scale as somehow necessary for the reproduction of certain social relations. We have already pointed to the wide variations in tenure forms between different advanced capitalist countries. Owner-occupation is not such a dominant feature in many successful European capitalist countries, and public housing has a much greater importance in some countries than in others. Private renting, a declining problem sector for marginal economic groups in some countries, is of considerable importance for a wide range of social classes in others. This is not to deny the ideological advantages outlined above, only to stress that the same kind of ideological effects may be created by other mechanisms that are of greater importance in some systems. It is also important to emphasise that whatever the ideological advantages of owner-occupation this does not mean that owner-occupied housing is provided automatically according to some functionalist perspective. The balance of tenures, and the proportion of public housing in particular, is also the result of conflicts reflecting a changing balance of class forces. Such effects need to be drawn out and explained through historical analysis of housing policy in each country.

RESIDENTIAL DIFFERENTIATION

Differences in tenure are obviously one of the major axes of residential differentiation and a degree of residential segregation is necessary for the kinds of ideological effects outlined above. However, the question of residential differentiation is more complex than that, involving a wider variety of forces.

We have already touched upon residential differentiation in the theories of Castells and Harvey. For Castells residential structure is a reflection of (a) economic factors such as the individual's place in the relations of production which largely determines his income, job security and credit worthiness, (b) politico-institutional factors, such as the institutionalised forms of suburban exclusion found in American cities to preserve property values and social status, (c) ideological factors related to the way in which certain residential units become symbols of modes of consumption and ways of life and function to fragment class consciousness, and (d) class-struggle factors which may lead at one extreme to 'forbidden ghettos' and at the other to the residential mixing of social classes – a form of 'ecological paternalism' reflecting class incorporation.

Harvey, on the other hand, lays greater stress on the role of financial institutions in the structuring of residential space to extract absolute rent. Such structuring and restructuring of residential space could well provoke community resistance, and conflict with the broader requirements that residential differentiation should help to reproduce existing social relations. However, Harvey also develops two lines of argument that place more emphasis on reproduction of social relations. First, he draws upon Giddens's categorisation of secondary factors of class structuration to indicate a variety of factors leading to residential segregation of different groups in space and, second, he explores the links between the segmentation of housing markets and the development of community based consciousness. This tends to undermine class unity and deflect class struggles into the kind of intercommunity conflicts that are less of a threat to the system.

Harvey's views are open to several criticisms. His emphasis on the power of financial institutions to create housing submarkets may well be an exaggeration in the American context and does not appear to be true in the British case, although financial institutions may well have a considerable effect in reinforcing certain trends in the housing market or influencing change in certain marginal situations (in inner city areas, or on the boundaries between different areas). The effect of residential segregation and community-based consciousness in fragmenting class consciousness may also be exaggerated. Other factors operating at the workplace and at a broader political level are probably of far greater importance. Finally, the secondary factors of class structuration that Harvey derives from Giddens refer to a variety of processes operating at the workplace and in the sphere of consumption and it is not clear how these factors are necessarily reflected in forms of residential segregation. Castells's list of factors influencing residential structure is even wider than Harvey's and although the analysis in *Monopolville* traces fairly convincingly the linkages between economic, politico-institutional, ideological and class-struggle factors, the directness of the connections may be a function of the peculiar conditions prevailing in the Dunkirk urban system at the time of analysis.

Several themes need to be clarified. First, the relationship between labour market processes and household consumption needs to be clarified in terms of their relevance to the reproduction of social relations. It could be argued, for example, that the negative effects of de-skilling and the homogenisation of the labour process in modern capitalist production (see Braverman, 1974), are partly offset by the proliferation of status differentials in the sphere of consumption. This could find expression in subtle distinctions between residential areas. On the other hand, it could be argued that there is a tendency towards the segmentation of the labour process in capitalist units of production (Bowles and Gintis, 1977); segmented labour markets do not just reflect differences in skill and productivity, they are intimately related to the problems of reproducing capitalist social relations within the workplace. The labour force is effectively fragmented into separate bargaining groups which can be more effectively controlled by the imposition of different work norms, privileges and sanctions. It is possible that shifts in labour market segmentation, with corresponding changes in income, status, job security and creditworthiness, may be behind shifts in residential status and differentiation.

Second, more work is needed on the actual processes of residential differentiation through which social classes are segregated in space. Godard and Pendariés (1978) have recently attempted a reformulation of the theory of segregation in terms of social relations of consumption. The social relations of consumption of housing encompass two interrelated aspects. First, there are ownership relations which determine the process whereby surplus value is realised in the marketing of the commodity housing. Ownership relations determine the costs of housing consumption, forms of payment and the legal rights associated with occupation of the dwelling unit. Second, there are relations of real appropriation which refer to the way in which a family unit actually consumes the use-value housing. This includes certain labour processes (cleaning, maintenance, etc.) carried out by the family and the use of certain services (electricity, heating, etc.) which may be individually or collectively consumed.

Ownership relations and relations of real appropriation are linked to a theory of segregation. Segregation is defined as a process of exclusion that operates through two processes. The first of these processes of segregation stems from a situation of 'antagonism', which is defined at the level of the ownership relations. For example, this form of segregation may occur as the result of property owners asking rents above the level certain categories of family can afford. Typically, this process of segregation operates through the exclusion of lower income groups by denying them access to certain types of housing. The second process of segregation stems from a situation of 'incongruence' which is defined at the level of real appropriation. In this case the consumption practices of households conflict with the investment strategies of property owners or controllers, for example, in the case where households trying to maintain a certain mode of consumption are faced with disinvestment and undermaintenance strategies by their landlords. Typically, this process of segregation operates to exclude both high- and low-income groups from certain areas, and affects families already resident as well as those seeking to gain access to areas.

Situations of antagonism or incongruence need not automatically result in exclusion (expulsion or voluntary movement). Households may respond to changing housing costs or the investment strategies of owners by adapting their patterns of consumption. For example, this may take the form of reducing expenditure on other forms of consumption to offset rising housing costs or substituting their own labour on maintenance and repairs for that of the landlord. Even when the limits of adaptation are reached households may still resist exclusion through co-ordinated action to oppose rent increases or demand maintenance work.

The approach of Godard and Pendariés does attempt to forge some links between the social relations of consumption and patterns of residential differentiation. However, the social relations of consumption also have to be seen in the context of the social relations of production which shape them. Certain links in the complex chain of relationships remain to be forged.

Third, the impact on the reproduction of social relations of the forms of residential differentiation produced by the above processes of segregation need to be explored. Certain forms of residential segregation may undermine social stability by threatening certain strands of the dominant ideology. For example, too great a degree of social class segregation may lead to stark visual contrasts between rich and poor areas, and rigid exclusion policies may increase a sense of relative deprivation. Elite areas of conspicuous consumption may serve as ever-present symbols for wider class struggles. On the other hand, an increase in social class mixing within residential areas may undermine the carefully nurtured status differentials of middle-income groups and raise a lower-income group's awareness of the real extent of income and consumption differences between classes.

There is not a great deal of empirical data currently available on the relative importance of residential differentiation and tenure forms in the reproduction of social relations compared to the writings on workplace factors and wider political and ideological processes. Some evidence suggests that the importance of tenure and residential differentiation should not be exaggerated. For example, Goldthorpe et al.'s study of affluent workers in Luton attempted to evaluate the effects of changing technology, labour processes and new patterns of industrial relations on traditional working class attitudes (Goldthorpe *et al.*, 1969). This study simultaneously examined the effect of social class mixing on new private estates on attitudes, values and social relations. Many of the new 'affluent' workers were owner-occupiers on estates with considerable occupational diversity. Affluent manual workers lived alongside clerical and sales workers, schoolteachers, department managers, industrial chemists and professional engineers. Although there was some evidence of convergence towards a more privatised family life-style, the authors of the study concluded that economic, technological and ecological changes had had little effect on traditional working-class attitudes and values. Affluent manual workers did not see residence on new private estates as a sign of status advancement and did not adopt middle-class attitudes towards education, individual advancement or the class structure. The authors conclude, 'affluence, and even residence in localities of a "middle class" character do not lead, in any automatic way, to the integration of manual workers and their families into middle class society' (Goldthorpe *et al.*, 1969, pp. 158–9). However, this study refers to only one point in time and the longer-term effects are unknown.

The discussion here has been pitched at a fairly general level. A number of Marxist writers have used arguments relating residential structures to the reproduction of social relations in more detail in an examination of the phenomena of suburbanisation. Suburbanisation is also bound up with other factors, however, and the topic warrants a separate section to review the considerable literature in this field.

Suburbanisation, underconsumption and crises

The sprawling growth of suburban housing estates around major cities has been one of the most striking aspects of post-war urban development, particularly in the United States. Suburbanisation has been more than the physical construction of new housing: it has been associated with rising car-ownership, new roads, new social infrastructure and changes in modes of consumption and patterns of family life. Suburbanisation thus poses interesting questions for Marxist theory and a large number of writers in the Marxist tradition have touched upon this theme at one time or another. A common starting point is the rejection of any explanation of suburbanisation that argues that it reflects changing consumer preferences (the drive for contact with nature, for example) or technological developments (the development of the car as a cheap, mass-produced form of transport). It is true that preferences have changed and technological developments have been important, but Marxists argue that the real questions relate to changes in social relations of production and consumption that underlie and structure the choices that are made available and the technological possibilities that are exploited. This necessitates the integration of any theory of suburbanisation within a wider theory of social and economic change in advanced capitalism.

The earlier discussions on housing and the reproduction of labour power, and housing and the reproduction of social relations, are obviously of relevance here. As industry has sought greenfield sites and employment has decentralised suburban housing developments, public and private, have played a vital role in the supply of necessary labour power. Suburban development has also been associated with the spread of single-family, owner-occupied dwellings, a pattern of living that a number of writers consider to have had important effects on commodity consumption. Castells has claimed that the search by individual households for self-sufficiency in terms of a widening range of domestic goods and consumer durables has made the single-family home in the suburbs 'the perfect design for maximising capitalist consumption' (Castells, 1977a, p. 388). Furthermore, 'the social relationships in the suburban neighbourhood also expressed the values of individualism, conformism and social integration, reducing the world to the nuclear family and social desires to the maximisation of individual (family) consumption' (ibid.). These themes of suburbanisation and changing patterns of commodity consumption have been integrated, particularly in the American context, into a broader theory of economic crises under monopoly capitalism. It is worth tracing these links in more detail.

We have already briefly outlined Marx's theories of crises, distinguishing crises associated with the tendency of the rate of profit to fall from realisation crises (disproportionality crises and crises of underconsumption). Much of the writing on the theme of suburbanisation within the Marxist tradition has related suburbanisation in its many forms to an underconsumptionist perspective. This is particularly true of the American tradition which finds its roots in the work of Baran and Sweezy (Baran and Sweezy, 1966). Their book *Monopoly Capital* is a major attempt to explain the long boom of post-war capitalist prosperity in terms of a theory of monopoly capitalism. Their explanation revolves around the concept of economic surplus and an underconsumptionist theory of crisis. Their general theory of monopoly capitalism, in some respects a drastic revision of Marx's theory of competitive capitalism, has important spatial implications in terms of suburbanisation.

The economic surplus is the difference between what a society produces and the socially necessary costs of producing it. Baran and Sweezy argue that there is a tendency in the monopoly capitalist stage for the economic surplus to rise as the large firms that dominate the market collude to maintain price stability whilst competing through the introduction of cost-saving productivity improvements. They then argue that the rising surplus cannot all be absorbed by capitalists' consumption or new investment outlets or increases in workers' income, so that the productive capacity to produce consumption goods expands faster than the effective demand for such goods. As a result the rising economic surplus manifests itself not only in terms of aggregate profits but also in the form of unemployment and excess capacity. The monopoly capitalist system has a built-in tendency towards stagnation. The real problem is now not so much the production of surplus value (the problem that dominated the stage of competitive capitalism) but its realisation in the form of profit.

Two major mechanisms have evolved in an attempt to absorb the surplus. First, there is what Baran and Sweezy term 'the sales effort'. This embraces a variety of strategies – the creation of new needs through advertising, the encouragement of mass consumption, planned obsolescence, etc. – aimed at increasing effective demand. Second, there is the increasing role accorded to the state. Given the power structure of monopoly capitalism, the major form of government expenditure that is tolerated is military expenditure; many forms of civilian expenditure clash with the interests of one or more of the major monopolies. An exception is state expenditure on highways, for this directly favours the complex of powerful industries involved in the production of cars and related products such as petrol, rubber and steel.

Although there is a long-term tendency towards stagnation, monopoly capitalism has experienced waves of rapid economic expansion as the result of epoch-making innovations which have created vast new investment outlets. The automobile has been one such innovation and this has had important consequences for suburbanisation. The first wave of expansion in car production and sales dated from around 1915 and it propelled a surge of suburbanisation with the attendant growth of housebuilding, home consumption goods and related secondary industries. This wave of expansion was not, however, strong enough to offset the underlying tendency towards stagnation which manifested itself strongly after 1925 with the onset of the Great Depression. The second wave of expansion of car-ownership and suburbanisation followed the ending of the Second World War and was reinforced by federally subsidised mortgages and easier consumer credit. The massive increase in aggregate demand associated with this wave, coupled with a high level of military expenditure, served to launch the American economic system into a prolonged post-war boom which, when Baran and Sweezy were writing, showed no sign of coming to an end. In Baran and Sweezy's model, then, suburbanisation is an integral part of the absorption of the economic surplus and its major phases of growth are closely tied in with state expenditure encouraging car-ownership and owner-occupation.

Suburbanisation is also an integral part of O'Connor's approach to monopoly capitalism, an approach which also incorporates an underconsumptionist theory of crisis (O'Connor, 1973). O'Connor's model revolves around the distinction between the monopoly sector, the competitive sector and the state sector on the one hand, and the division of the state's role into aiding capital accumulation and legitimising social relations on the other. O'Connor in fact develops quite a complex categorisation of state expenditure (Figure 11.1). Social capital expenditures are expenditures required for profitable private accumulation and they are thus indirectly productive for capital, and in particular for monopoly capital. Social expenses, on the other hand, are not even indirectly productive for capital, but are necessary for the preservation of social harmony. Social capital is further subdivided into social investment which increases labour productivity (for example, state-financed industrial development, transport and education) and social consumption which lowers the reproduction costs of labour (social insurance, etc.). Of course, as O'Connor recognises, many forms of state expenditure fall simultaneously into several of these categories.

State expenditure is bound up with the basic contradictions of the monopoly capitalist system. Monopoly sector growth is increasingly dependent upon state expenditure on social capital as the processes of production and consumption become more and more socialised. But expansion of social capital encourages the growth of the monopoly sector and the productive capacity of the monopoly sector expands faster than the demands for its output, leading to surplus capacity and unemployment. This in turn leads to the expansion of state expenditure on social expenses, such as welfare payments and military expenses, to permit the expansion of overseas outlets. But state expenditure tends to rise faster than the taxes needed to pay for this expenditure leading to inflation and what O'Connor terms the 'fiscal crisis of the state'.

The process of suburbanisation is interlinked with several categories of state expenditure in O'Connor's model. State expendi-

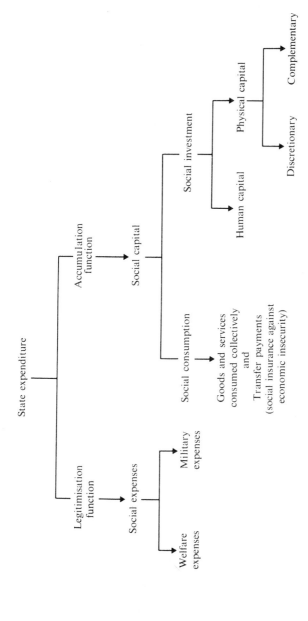

FIGURE 11.1 *Categorisation of state expenditures (After O'Connor, 1973)*

ture on roads is a type of physical capital expenditure, a component of social investment, and indirectly productive for capital. Road expenditure has been actively supported by the powerful 'auto-complex', and related industries which have derived profits from rising car-ownership and suburban expansion. 'It is now widely recognised that economic growth in recent decades has been spear-headed by automobiles and related production, decentralisation of industry and commercial activities, suburban residential construc-tion, and a vast expansion of recreational facilities' (O'Connor, 1975, p. 106). But suburban roads, schools and state-subsidised mortgages are also an aspect of social consumption expenditures by the state, functioning simultaneously to lower the reproduction costs of labour. In fact O'Connor takes the argument further, arguing that the important disparities between social consumption expenditures in central cities and suburbs is one aspect of the division between the monopoly sector and the competitive sector. The key monopoly sector workers have now joined the middle and upper classes in suburbia and share in the advantages of superior state-subsidised social consumption facilities. The economically more peripheral and politically less powerful competitive sector workers are largely confined to poorer paid and insecure jobs in central city areas where social consumption expenditures are limited. Central city suburban disparities are thus an expression of the bifurcation of the workforce into monopoly and competitive sectors. In conclusion, suburban expansion is tied up with various forms of state social investment and social consumption expenditures that are indirectly productive for monopoly capital. Suburban expansion therefore expresses the forces that simultaneously lead to the fiscal crisis of the state.

Harvey's work is in the same tradition and is even more explicit about the role of suburban development in combating under-consumption. Suburbanisation is seen as a deliberate creation of the capitalist state to prevent a repetition of the underconsumption crisis of the 1930s (e.g. Harvey, 1977). State intervention since the New Deal has been largely indirect, working through the inter-mediary of financial institutions to subsidise new homes in the suburbs. Single-family housing, low-density urban sprawl and individualised family consumption – encouraged by the state – have had important multiplier effects on a wide range of industries, particularly those involved in the mass consumption of consumer goods. In effect, the post-war American city has become a con-sumption artifact, designed to stimulate consumption, rather than a workshop designed for industrial production. Castells (1977a) has recently developed the same line of argument, although with rather more emphasis on the relationship between suburbanisation and the development of the highway-auto-transport system and also more emphasis on the role of suburbanisation in the reproduction of social relations and the maintenance of social stability.

Although these various authors see suburban sprawl as a form of urbanisation functional for capitalism, they also agree that such developments are not permanently successful in staving off capitalist crises. Suburbanisation under capitalism has contradictory political, economic and ideological effects that are becoming more apparent as the present economic crisis develops. O'Connor points to the increasing conflict between central cities and suburbs as central cities deteriorate and state expenditure rises. Harvey and Castells point to the threat to the mass of mortgage debt as real incomes stagnate, and the increasing instability of housing finance markets as inflation rates and interest rates rise. Harvey goes further in suggesting that the present form of the American city makes it inefficient as a place of production and circulation of commodities. Yet entrenched suburban interests can resist any attempts at a more rational reorganisation of space that would threaten their suburban tax advantages and property values.

It is significant that most Marxist writers who have sought to link suburbanisation and underconsumption have come from America or have studied in America, and most of the illustratory empirical detail refers to the American urban context. British writers, for example, have placed far less emphasis on this link for a number of reasons. At an empirical level it is evident that the state in Britain has attempted since the war actually to contain the sprawl of suburban growth through planning controls and has subsidised the redevelopment of the central cities with public housing. At a more theoretical level British writers have rejected underconsumptionist theories of crisis and placed much greater emphasis on the tendency of the rate of profit to fall as the key underlying factor. Gamble and Walton (1976) have argued that capital accumulation crises are simultaneously realisation crises, but that realisation is only the appearance of crisis and not its most critical dimension. Fine and Harris (1976) have defended the theory of the tendency of the rate of profit to fall and placed most of their emphasis on the role of industrial restructuring in the recovery from economic crisis rather than an expansion of demand. Gough suggests that the American preoccupation with underconsumptionist theories of crisis reflects American conditions (Gough, 1975a). In America public expenditure patterns seem to have more closely reflected the needs of the dominant class rather than taking the form of concessions wrested by a well-organised labour movement. In Britain state policy has been a response to a different pattern of class conflicts and urban planning and public investment has been less obviously connected to the stimulation of demand for monopoly sector goods.

In conclusion, it is evident that the precise relationship between suburbanisation, economic crisis and state policy is a controversial subject. Theories of suburbanisation are here entwined with wider debates within Marxism over theories of economic crisis and theories of the state.

Housing policy and the role of the state

Public housing policies of one sort or another are obviously of great importance in advanced capitalist systems. We have encountered the different roles of the state at various points in this chapter and we can now try to bring together this material in a more general perspective. Explaining the general role of the state and linking this to its specific role in housing markets is a crucial problem for Marxist theory.

A fully developed theory of the state does not appear in the work of Harvey although a variety of roles are ascribed to the state at different points. In some of his earlier papers (e.g. Harvey, 1974) the state appears as subservient to the hegemonic interests of finance capital. Elsewhere state intervention is linked more broadly to the interests of monopoly capital through a variety of policies designed to maintain aggregate demand and reproduce the social relations of capitalism (e.g. through the various policies designed to stimulate suburbanisation). In a more recent paper Harvey (1978b) has portrayed the state as an agent of private capital intervening in conflicts over the built environment between labour, the appropriators of rent and the construction faction. Capital in general cannot afford the outcome of struggles around the built environment to be determined simply by the relative powers of these three groups. The role of the state in encouraging private home-ownership, 'rationalising' consumption patterns and maintaining suburban environments is here linked to the need for capital to 'dominate labour not simply in the work process, but with respect to the very definition of the quality of life in the consumption sphere' (Harvey, 1978b, p. 14).

The role of the state receives even more emphasis in the work of Castells, where it is related to a theory of the growth of collective consumption. At various points in *Monopolville* Castells and Godard draw explicitly upon the theories of Poulantzas outlined in *Political*

Power and Social Classes (Poulantzas, 1973). The state is assumed to function primarily as a mechanism for organising the interests of the dominant classes (the 'power bloc'), and the interests of the hegemonic fraction of this bloc in particular. However, the state apparatus retains a relative autonomy in order that it can arrange compromises between capital fractions with varying interests and arrange concessions where necessary to the dominated classes to defuse situations of mounting class conflicts. Such concessions are nevertheless designed to preserve the overall, long-term political power of the dominant classes.

In a later paper Castells seems to present a more instrumentalist view of the state. State intervention is 'functional and necessary to the monopolies' (Castells, 1975, p. 178). It assures the reproduction of the labour force, eases demands and, in so far as public investment involves the devaluation of social capital, it counteracts the tendency for the rate of profit to fall. State intervention in the housing field is subordinated to the interests of the monopolies in two ways. First, social investments only come after the needs of industrial enterprises for direct aid have been satisfied, and, second, there is a constant tendency to make publicly subsidised sectors profitable so that they can be transferred to private sector interests.

There is some evidence that both Harvey and Castells shift their emphasis on the different roles of the state in different papers, and it is difficult to categorise their views in a precise fashion. As Jessop (1977) has pointed out, there is a wide range of viewpoints on the state within the Marxist tradition. In the work of Poulantzas the role of the state appears to be mainly political in so far as it acts as a factor of cohesion in the social formation. The theory of state monopoly capitalism developed by a number of writers in the French Communist Party places more stress on the economic role of the state and its close links with the interests of the major monopolies. One could also point to the perspectives offered by neo-Ricardians (e.g. Gough, 1975b), fundamentalists (e.g. Yaffe, 1973), 'state derivation' theorists (Holloway and Picciotto, 1978) and underconsumptionists (Baran and Sweezy, 1966). These perspectives place different emphases on economic factors, political factors, ideological factors and class conflicts in determining the forms of state intervention. A large part of the literature on the state is taken up by debates between the protagonists of these different perspectives. Poulantzas (1975) has attacked the state monopoly capitalist position for its instrumentalist view of the state as simply an agent of monopoly capital. Lojkine (1975) has criticised Poulantzas's views as a 'functionalist' view of state regulation. Neo-Ricardians such as Gough have attacked the economic determinism that they see implicit in the views of the fundamentalists. It should also be added that the arguments between different writers are sometimes founded upon misunderstandings and polemical oversimplifications. Pickvance (1977b), for example, has pointed out the considerable areas of overlap between the views of Poulantzas and Lojkine that are concealed by their polemical exchanges on one or two major points of controversy.

The positions espoused at various times by Harvey and Castells do not fit neatly into one or another of these broad categories. At times Harvey seems to take an instrumentalist view of the state serving the interests of finance capital or the major monopolies, but at other times state policy seems more a response to changing patterns of class conflict. Castells makes many explicit references to Poulantzas in some of his work but at other times his position seems closer to the theory of state monopoly capitalism.

This diversity of viewpoint is also evident in the contributions of a number of other writers within the Marxist tradition who have explored various other aspects of state housing policies. We can best summarise these contributions in three broad areas of enquiry.

CATEGORISING STATE INTERVENTION

Marcuse's paper provides a good example of an attempt to categorise the wide range of state housing activities and link them to the wider functions of the state (Marcuse, 1977). In Figure 11.2 the state's activities are broadly defined in terms of 'accumulation' and 'legitimisation', the former relating to the state's economic role and the latter to its political role. The accumulation-oriented actions of the state are in turn divided into four subcategories. Efficiency-related activities refer to state actions designed to rationalise land assembly and housing production, usually in the interests of promoting the conditions for private profit. Consumption-related activities are closely connected to the maintenance of aggregate demand (subsidising mortgages, encouraging suburbanisation, etc.). Exploitation-related activities often operate through the legal system to support the activities of housing agents such as landlords (e.g. enforcement of eviction laws). Redistribution-related activities include policies such as public housing programmes brought about by pressure from the dominated classes.

Legitimisation activities are divided into three components. Integration activities are essentially reforms originating within the dominant class designed to co-opt the dominated classes (tenant participation schemes, etc.). Repression is represented by policies that sustain ghettoisation and restrictive zoning. Delegitimation covers concessions forced from the state by class-wide or community-based organisations.

Even though many state policies fall simultaneously into several of these categories such a categorisation does provide useful links between housing policies and the broader roles of the state apparatus. It is one thing, however, to categorise state activities in this way and quite another to explain why certain combinations of state activity should dominate in certain countries and in certain

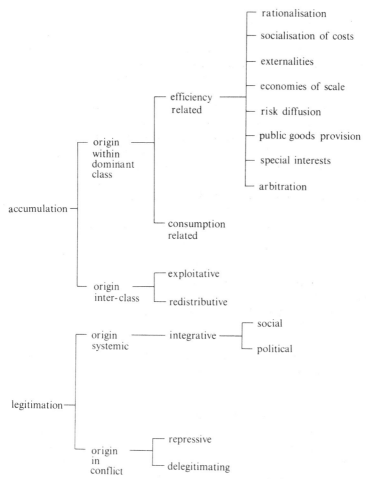

FIGURE 11.2 *Categorisation of state housing policies (After Marcuse, 1977)*

time periods. A second broad area of enquiry has concentrated on an historical analysis of the evolution of state housing policies in different countries, drawing upon a number of Marxian theories and concepts.

ACCOUNTING FOR THE EVOLUTION OF STATE HOUSING POLICIES

Various aspects of the evolution of British housing policy since 1918 have been explored in varying detail by (among others) S. Clark and Ginsburg (1975), Byrne and Beirne (1975), Boddy (1976a and b), and Dickens (1977). Although there are differences in perspective there is broad agreement that state intervention can be related to three major sources of pressure. First, state policies reflect the attempt to reconcile the differing interests of different fractions of capital (industrial capital, landed capital, finance capital, and various subfractions of building capital). Second, state policies reflect working-class pressures. This pressure may be exerted directly in the housing field, or it may be exerted at the workplace, in which case housing reforms may reflect an attempt to grant concessions in the sphere of consumption in order to divert a more serious threat to the system of production. Third, state policies reflect the global role that the state assumes in preserving the overall stability of the social system. Ideology provides an important cement to the social structure and certain forms of tenure facilitate the reproduction of the dominant ideology.

The problems arise when this broad perspective is applied to the evolution of actual policies. It is often difficult to disentangle the exact combination of factors that underlies a particular policy change. Major pieces of legislation, for example the 1919 Addison Act, may be explained in terms of economic necessity (the collapse of the housebuilding industry), working-class pressures, reform by the state in anticipation of rising demands or as the necessary consequences of previous pieces of state legislation (the 1915 Rent Act which froze rents and cut off the flow of investment into rented property). Different authors place different emphasis on these factors.

There are two important dangers that it is difficult for such historical reconstructions to avoid. The first is the danger of over-rating the importance of housing to different fractions of capital or capital as a whole. This brings us back to the issue of the importance of housing for the reproduction of labour power and social relations, an issue that has not been satisfactorily resolved. The second is the danger of *post-hoc* rationalisation whereby different fractions or subfractions of capital are invented in order to explain a piece of legislation in terms of specific capitalist interests. The loose way in which Marxists tend to talk about fractions and subfractions without a firm theoretical justification has been pointed out by S. Clarke (1978). In spite of these problems this re-working of historical data is likely to become a major field of research.

THE LOCAL STATE

We have explored some of the local-national relationships and the determinants of local policies from an institutionalist perspective in Chapter 7. From a Marxist perspective local government is part of the state apparatus, but variations in local policies will reflect the relative autonomy of the local state and the local configuration of class forces. This perspective is apparent in the work of Castells and Godard (1974) and in a number of other French studies of local urban policy reviewed by Pickvance (1977b). Broadly speaking, local policy is seen as the outcome of the local state's function in enforcing the domination of the local bourgeoisie and maintaining the cohesion of the urban social system. This involves the regulation of contradictions between the dominant and dominated classes and contradictions between different fractions of local capital. Although there are few good case studies using this framework to analyse local housing policies (as opposed to other policy areas), Cockburn's approach is of general relevance, extends the Marxist analysis of the local state, and touches upon a number of housing issues (Cockburn, 1977).

Cockburn distinguishes state interventions designed to aid capitalist production, and intervention designed to aid reproduction (either the reproduction of productive forces or the reproduction of social relations). Housing is necessary for the reproduction of the productive forces (e.g. labour power) and the reproduction of social relations (certain forms of housing are necessary for the efficient functioning of the bourgeois family, a crucial source of capitalist values and motivations). Whereas the national state is primarily involved in economic aid and regulation to facilitate capitalist production, the local state has an increasingly important role in legitimating capitalist relations and diffusing conflict. Traditions of local autonomy and local democracy help to obscure class relations and the class role of the state. Cockburn's analysis of the twin programmes of corporate management reform and community participation in Lambeth in the early 1970s is located within this broader perspective.

Cockburn argues that corporate management reform was designed to bring local government more under central control both locally and nationally, increase efficiency and permit expenditure cuts at a time of increasing economic difficulties and mounting urban problems. However, unemployment and local housing shortages precipitated family instability, family breakdown, squatting and communal living. These developments in turn led to the breakdown of social control over children, rising juvenile crime and the growing involvement of women in militant protest organisations. The housing crisis was thus part of an interconnected series of events that partly undermined the ability of the bourgeois family to fulfil its traditional role in the reproduction of social relations and threatened the management functions of local government and the legitimacy of local political democracy. This threat to the local state was a major factor in the launching of community participation programmes to increase the flow of local information to decision-makers and find new ways of establishing the legitimacy of local government policies. A proliferation of tenants' groups and neighbourhood organisations was one result of this new policy. According to this perspective the kinds of community housing actions we discussed in Chapter 7 are linked to a broader theory of class incorporation and control through this fragmentation of class activity and the defusing of local political conflicts.

CONCLUSION

The role of the state and the determinants of state policy constitute a fascinating and critical area of Marxist controversy. The theories touched upon in this section are certain to receive even more attention from writers in various 'schools' in the future. There are signs that some of this attention will be focused more on the local state and the determinants of local policies. First, there is the question of the nature of the relationship between the local and the central state and the precise role of the local state within the state apparatus. Second, there is the problem of identifying the objective interests of local classes and class fractions. Third, there is the problem of tracing the relationship between objective class interests and the way in which these interests are represented (or not represented) in political terms through party and pressure-group activity. Finally, there is the problem of relating the actual pattern of policy outputs to the economic and political interests of the different classes and fractions. Our brief survey suggests that this perspective has only just begun to be applied to the specific field of housing policy.

Housing conflict

It is evident that a variety of conflicts are centred around various housing issues in advanced capitalist countries, many of them located at the neighbourhood or local community level. We have already noted in Chapter 7 that the level of conflict has increased since the mid-1960s, at least in Britain and America. Marxists have shown an increasing interest in such conflicts, their determinants, their effects, and their relationship to wider social and political forces.

One effect of this increased interest has been a number of explorations into the long neglected and poorly researched history of housing struggles. Corrigan and Ginsburg (1975) and Schifferes (1976) have pulled together some of the most accessible information on housing struggles in Britain since 1918 that permit some preliminary empirical generalisations. It would appear that housing struggles have been comparatively low key and disorganised compared to militant activities centering around the workplace. They have tended to be based on particular localities and communities, their leadership has often not involved the more class-conscious workers, and they have involved more women in active work than most industrial struggles. They have often been directed at local authorities (particularly over rent issues) and have not often posed any direct threat to any major capitalist interest. It is not as yet clear whether this pattern has changed or is likely to change in the 1970s.

At a more theoretical level Marxists have been concerned over the precise relationship between housing and neighbourhood conflicts, industrial conflicts, and the wider processes of class structuration and class conflict. We have already noted how these themes are treated by Harvey and Castells. Both authors comment on the apparent separation of workplace-based struggles on the one hand and housing and neighbourhood-based struggles on the other. Such a separation is to the advantage of capital in contributing towards a fragmentation of working-class interests through the development of community-consciousness and inter-community conflict. Nevertheless, both authors maintain that at a deeper level work-based and community-based conflicts are interrelated and are rooted in the basic contradictions of the capitalist system, although the work of tracing out the interconnections is not easy.

Castells presents perhaps the most developed theoretical framework for studying housing struggles. The concept of urban social movements encompasses the broad ranges of protest activities that have become an increasingly important feature of contemporary urban systems. In Castells's framework urban social movements are traced back to the structural contradictions inherent in the urban system (Castells, 1976c). It is hypothesised that the potential for mobilisation is related to the number of accumulated contradictions that underlie the movement and the extent to which these contradictions are rooted in the economic system. An appropriate organisation is necessary to fuse the protest into an effective force; if it remains at the level of urban protest it is capable only of achieving reforms. Olives's study of protest activities centering around urban renewal in Paris provides an example of this approach in practice (Olives, 1976). Olives' procedure involves the identification of the stakes involved (e.g. evictions), the social base of the action (the groups involved), its organisational characteristics, the social force that can be mustered, the opponents of the protest (e.g. landlords or the council), the specific demands, the global demands, the actions taken, the forms of repression encountered, the urban effects of the protest (e.g. stopping evictions or redevelopment) and the political effects (e.g. the politicisation of the local population). Olives's empirical analysis of sixteen protest activities suggests that the primary factors in successful mobilisation are the size of the stake and the degree to which the social base can be mobilised into a social force through the intermediary of organisations linking local struggles to wider political struggles.

A considerable literature has begun to emerge on the themes of urban social movements, either extending Castells's framework or criticising it (see, for example, the regular 'Urban Praxis' reports in the *International Journal of Urban and Regional Research*). Pickvance has raised some doubts about the general applicability of Castells's framework to the British urban situation. Castells, he argues, seems to imply that urban social movements are the only source of major change (Pickvance, 1976). Pickvance refers to the studies by Dennis, Gower Davies, Ferris and Muchnick that we discussed in Chapter 7 to suggest that significant policy change can also come about through the actions of local governments responding to local pressure groups, or through inter-departmental conflicts within the local government structure. Dunleavy (1977) further points out that many urban protests may be unsuccessful not because the stake is small or through a failure to organise and link contradictions but because of the considerable power that resides with the local authority particularly in the field of housing. The failure of the Beckton protest (see Chapter 7) provides a classic example of the unequal distribution of power between local government and prospective public housing tenants in British urban systems.

Dunleavy's argument is, however, partly undermined by the

evidence presented by Cockburn in her work on Lambeth (Cockburn, 1977). The local authority was here forced into the official encouragement of various forms of public participation partly to improve local government efficiency, partly to find new means of legitimating local policies at a time of worsening housing crisis. In most cases the various forms of community action were safely incorporated in the government system but Cockburn provides several examples of neighbourhood-based organisations of tenants that built themselves up as an effective social force and threatened to break out of the officially prescribed organisational mould, with some effect on local housing policy.

A second line of criticism has been directed against Castells's assumption that housing issues may be the basis for a broad anti-capitalist alliance. Saunders (1978) has revised the Weberian concept of 'housing classes' and suggested that tenurial divisions between owner-occupiers and non owner-occupiers provides the basis for real divisions of economic interest within the housing field. Saunders argues that owner-occupation brings real material advantages that provide a basis for housing class formation and political divisions between tenure groups. Owner-occupiers may ally themselves with non owner-occupiers in resisting commercial developments by private capital that threaten property values; they may also come together to resist an increase in council house provision in suburban areas if this too threatens property values. These real political differences are based on real economic differences established within the housing field. They cannot be dismissed as ideological divisions stemming from a 'false consciousness' that hides an underlying class unity established at the level of the relations of production. Saunders's argument amounts to an attack on the assumed underlying unity of community based conflicts and housing conflicts.

Bibliography

ABRAMS, C. (1965), *The City is the Frontier*, Harper & Row, New York.
ABU-LUGHOD, J. L. and FOLEY, M. M. (1960), 'Consumer strategies', in Foote, N. N. *et al.* (eds), *Housing Choices and Housing Constraints*, McGraw-Hill, New York.
ADAMS, J. S. (1969), 'Directional bias in intra-urban migration', *Economic Geography*, 45, 303–23.
AGNEW, J. (1978), 'Market relations and locational conflict in crossnational perspective', in Cox, K. R. (ed.), *Urbanisation and Conflict in Market Societies*, Methuen, London.
ALIHAN, M. A. (1938), *Social Ecology*, Columbia University Press, New York.
ALONSO, W. (1964), *Location and Land Use*, Harvard University Press, Cambridge, Mass.
ALT, J. (1977), 'Politics and expenditure models', *Policy and Politics*, 5 (3), 83–92.
ALTHUSSER, L. (1969), *For Marx*, Allen Lane, London.
ALTHUSSER, L. and BALIBAR, E. (1970), *Reading Capital*, New Left Books, London.
AMBROSE, P. (1976), 'The land market and the housing system', *Working Paper 3, Dept. of Urban and Regional Studies*, University of Sussex.
AMBROSE, P. and COLENUTT, B. (1975), *The Property Machine*, Penguin, Harmondsworth.
ANDERSON, J. (1977), 'Engels' Manchester: Industrialisation, worker's housing and urban ideology', *Political Economy of Cities and Regions* No. 1, Architectural Association, London.
ANDERSON, P. (1976), *Considerations on Western Marxism*, New Left Books, London.
BACHRACH, P. and BARATZ, M. (1962), 'Two faces of power', *American Political Science Review*, LVI, 947–52.
BACHRACH, P. and BARATZ, M. (1963), 'Decisions and non-decisions; an analytical framework', *American Political Science Review*, 57, 632–42.
BALL, M. J. (1976), 'Owner occupation', in Political Economy of Housing Workshop, *Housing and Class in Britain*, London.
BALL, M. J. (1978), 'British housing policy and the house-building industry', *Capital and Class*, 4, 78–99.
BALL, M. J. and KIRWAN, R. M. (1975), *The Economics of an Urban Housing Market*, Research Paper 15, Centre for Environmental Studies, London.

BALL, M. J. and KIRWAN, R. M. (1977), 'Accessibility and supply constraints in the urban housing market', *Urban Studies*, 14, 11–32.

BARAN, P. and SWEEZY, P. (1966), *Monopoly Capital*, Penguin, Harmondsworth.

BARBOLET, R. H. (1969), *Housing Classes and the Socio-ecological System*, Univ. Working Paper 4, Centre for Environmental Studies, London.

BARRAS, R. and CATALANO, A. (1975), 'Investment in land and the financial structure of property companies', *Conference Paper 17*, Centre for Environmental Studies, London.

BASSETT, K. and HAUSER, D. (1976), 'Public policy and spatial structure: housing improvement in Bristol', in Peel, R. F., Chisholm, M. and Haggett, P. (eds), *Processes in Physical and Human Geography: Bristol Essays*, Heinemann, London.

BASSETT, K. and SHORT, J. R. (1978), 'Housing improvement in the inner city: a case study of changes before and after the 1974 Housing Act', *Urban Studies*, 15, 333–42.

BATLEY, R. (1972), 'An explanation of non-participation in planning', *Policy and Politics*, 1, 96–110.

BATTY, M. (1976), *Urban modelling: algorithms, calibrations and predictions*, Cambridge University Press.

BELL, W. and MOSKOS, C. C. (1964), 'A comment on Udry's "Increasing scale and spatial differentiation" ', *Social Forces*, 42, 414–17.

BENTON, T. (1978), *Philosophical Foundations of the Three Sociologies*, Routledge & Kegan Paul, London.

BERRY, B. J. L. and REES, P. H. (1969), 'The factorial ecology of Calcutta', *American Journal of Sociology*, 74, 445–91.

BIRD, H. (1976), 'Residential mobility and preference patterns in the public sector of the housing market', *Transactions of the Institute of British Geographers*, New Series, 1, 20–33.

BOADEN, N. (1971), *Urban Policy-Making*, Cambridge University Press.

BOCCARA, P. (1974), *Le Capitalisme monopoliste d'etat, sa crise, et son issu*, Editions Sociales, Paris.

BODDY, M. (1976a), 'The structure of mortgage finance: building societies and the British social formation', *Transactions of the Institute of British Geographers*, New Series, 1, 58–71.

BODDY, M. (1976b), 'Building societies and owner occupation', in Political Economy of Housing Workshop, *Housing and Class in Britain*, London.

BODDY, M. (1980), 'Finance capital commodity production and the production of urban built form', in Dear, M. J. and Scott, A. J. (eds), *Urbanization and Urban Planning in Capitalist Societies*, Maaroufa Press, Chicago.

BOURNE, L. (1976), 'Housing supply and housing market behaviour in residential development', in Herbert, D. and Johnston, R. (eds), *Social Areas in Cities* Volume 1, *Spatial Processes and Form*, John Wiley, London.

BOWLES, S. and GINTIS, H. (1977), 'The Marxian theory of value and heterogeneous labour: a critique and reformulation', *Cambridge Journal of Economics*, 1 (2), 173–92.

BOWLEY, M. (1945), *Housing and the State*, Allen & Unwin, London.

BOYER, B. D. (1976), 'Bad dreams in the night: the American housing con game', in Mendelson, R. E. and Quinn, M. A. (eds), *The Politics of Housing in Older Urban Areas*, Praeger, New York.

BRAVERMAN, H. (1974), *Labour and Monopoly Capital*, Monthly Review Press, New York.

BROADBENT, T. (1975), *An Attempt to Apply Marx's Theory of Ground Rent to a Modern Urban Economy*, Research Paper 17, Centre for Environmental Studies, London.

BROWN, L. A. and MOORE, E. G. (1970), 'The intra-urban migration process: a perspective', *Geografiska Annaler*, 52B, 1–13.

BROWN, T., VILE, M. and WHITMORE, M. (1972), 'Community studies and decision taking', *British Journal of Political Science*, 2, 133–54.

BRUEGEL, I. (1975), 'The Marxist theory of rent and the contemporary city: a critique of Harvey', in Political Economy of Housing Workshop', *Political Economy and the Housing Question*, London.

BURGESS, E. W. (1925), 'The growth of the city', in Park, R. E., Burgess, E. W. and McKenzie, R. D. (eds), *The City*, University of Chicago Press; reprinted in Stewart, M. (1972).

BURNETT, J. (1978), *A Social History of Housing, 1815–1870*, David & Charles, Newton Abbot.

BURNEY, E. (1967), *Housing on Trial*, Oxford University Press.

BURNS, L. and GREBLER, L. (1977), *The Housing of Nations: Analysis and Policy in a Comparative Framework*, Macmillan, London.

BYRNE, D. and BEIRNE, P. (1975), 'Towards a political economy of housing rent', in Political Economy of Housing Workshop, *Political Economy and the Housing Question*, London.

CASTELLS, M. (1975), 'Advanced capitalism, collective consumption, and urban contradictions: new sources of inequality and new models for change', in Lindberg, L., Alford, R., Crouch, C., and Offe, C. (eds), *Stress and Contradiction in Modern Capitalism*, Lexington Books, Massachusetts.

CASTELLS, M. (1976a), 'Is there an urban sociology?' in Pickvance, C. G. (ed.), *Urban Sociology: Critical Essays*, Tavistock, London.

CASTELLS, M. (1976b), 'Theory and ideology in urban sociology', in Pickvance, C. G. (ed.), *Urban Sociology: Critical Essays*, Tavistock, London.

CASTELLS, M. (1976c), 'Theoretical propositions for an experimental study of urban social movements', in Pickvance, C. G. (ed.), *Urban Sociology: Critical Essays*, Tavistock, London.

CASTELLS, M. (1977a), *The Urban Question: A Marxist Approach*, Edward Arnold, London.

CASTELLS, M. (1977b), 'Towards a political urban sociology', in Harloe, M. (ed.), *Captive Cities*, John Wiley, London.

CASTELLS, M. and GODARD, F. (1974), *Monopolville*, Mouton, Paris.

CDP (1976a), *Profits against Homes*, Community Development Project Information and Intelligence Unit, London.

CDP (1976b), *Whatever Happened to Council Housing?*, CDP Information and Intelligence Unit, London.

CHAC (Central Housing Advisory Committee) (1969), *Council Housing:*

236 *Bibliography*

Purposes, Procedures and Priorities, 9th Report of the Housing Management Sub-Committee, HMSO, London.

CIS (undated), *The Recurrent Crisis of London*, Counter Information Service, London.

CLARK, C. (1940), *The Conditions of Economic Progress*, Macmillan, London.

CLARK, S. and GINSBURG, N. (1975), 'The political economy of housing', in Political Economy of Housing Workshop, *Political Economy and the Housing Question*, London.

CLARK, T. N. (1972), 'The structure of community influence', in Hahn, H. (ed.), *People and Politics in Urban Society*, Sage Publications, London

CLARK, T. N. (1974), 'Community autonomy in the national system: federalism, localism and decentralisation', in Clark, T. N. (ed.), *Comparative Community Politics*, John Wiley, New York.

CLARKE, S. (1978), 'Capital, fraction of capital and the state: neo-Marxist analyses of the South African State', *Capital and Class*, 5, 32–77.

CLAWSON, M. and HALL, P. (1973), *Planning and Urban Growth: an Anglo-Saxon Comparison*, Johns Hopkins University Press, Baltimore.

CLEMENTS, R. (1969), *Local Notables and the City Council*, Macmillan, London.

COCKBURN, C. (1977), *The Local State*, Pluto Press, London.

COMMITTEE ON THE MANAGEMENT OF LOCAL GOVERNMENT (1967), Volume 5 *Local Government Administration in England and Wales*. HMSO, London.

CONZEN, M. R. G. (1960), 'Alnwick, Northumberland: a study in town plan analysis', *Transactions of the Institute of British Geographers*, 27.

COONEY, E. (1974), 'High flats in local authority housing in England and Wales since 1945', in Sutcliffe, A. (ed.), *Multi-Storey Living*, Croom Helm, London.

CORINA, L. (1976), *Housing Allocation Policy and its Effects: A Case Study of Oldham*, CDP, Papers in Community Studies no. 7, Department of Social Administration and Social Work, University of York.

CORRIGAN, P. and GINSBURG, N. (1975), 'Tenants' struggle and class struggle', in Political Economy of Housing Workshop, *Political Economy and the Housing Question*, Cambridge.

COURSEY, R. (1977), *The Debate on Urban Policy: Decentralisation v. Improvement*, Retailing and Planning Associates, Corbridge.

COX, K. R. (1978), 'Local interests and urban political processes in market societies', in Cox, K. R. (ed.), *Urbanisation and Conflict in Market Societies*, Methuen, London.

COX, K. R. and AGNEW, J. (1974), *The Location of Public Housing: Towards a Comparative Analysis*, Discussion Paper No 25, Department of Geography, Ohio State University.

COX, K. R. and REYNOLDS, D. R. (1974), 'Locational approaches to power and conflict', in Cox, K. R., Reynolds, D. R. and Rokkan, S. (eds), *Locational Approaches to Power and Conflict*, John Wiley, New York.

CULLINGWORTH, J. B. (1963), *Housing in Transition*, Heinemann, London.

CULLINGWORTH, J. B. (1965), *English Housing Trends*, Bell, London.

CULLINGWORTH, J. B. (1966), *Housing and Local Government*, Allen & Unwin, London.

CUTLER, A., HINDESS, B., HIRST, P. and HUSSAIN, A. (1977, 1978), *Marx's Capital and Capitalism Today*, Vols I and II, Routledge & Kegan Paul, London.

DAHL, R. (1961), *Who Governs?*, Yale University Press, New Haven.

DAMER, S. (1974), 'Wine Alley: the sociology of a dreadful enclosure', *Sociological Review*, 22, 221–48.

DARKE, R. and WALKER, R. (eds) (1977), *Local Government and the Public*, Leonard Hill, London.

DAVIES, J. G. (1972), *The Evangelistic Bureaucrat*, Tavistock, London.

DEARLOVE, J. (1973), *The Politics of Policy in Local Government*, Cambridge University Press.

DENNIS, N. (1970), *People and Planning*, Faber & Faber, London.

DENNIS, N. (1972), *Public Participation and Planner's Blight*, Faber & Faber, London.

DENNIS, N. (1978), 'Housing policy areas: criteria and indicators in principle and practice', *Transactions of the Institute of British Geographers*, New Series, 3, 2–22.

DESAI, M. (1974), *Marxian Economic Theory*, Cray-Mills, London.

DICKENS, P. (1977), 'Social change, housing and the state: some aspects of class fragmentation and incorporation', in Harloe, M. (ed.), Centre for Environmental Studies *Second Conference on Urban Change and Conflict*, London.

DINGEMANS, D., BROTHERS, T., HICKOK, F. and STANIEE, N. (1978), 'Residential mortgage lending patterns: a case study of Sacramento in 1976', Institute of Government Affairs, *Monograph Series 11*, University of California, Davis, California.

DOBB, M. (1973), *Theories of Value and Distribution since Adam Smith: Ideology and Economic Theory*, Cambridge University Press.

DOE (1977a), *Housing Policy Technical Volume*, HMSO, London.

DOE (1977b), *Unequal City: Final Report of the Birmingham Inner Area Study*. HMSO, London.

DOE (1977c), *Change or Decay: Final Report of the Liverpool Inner Area Study*. HMSO, London.

DRAKE, S. T. and CAYTON, H. (1962), *Black Metropolis*, Harper & Row, New York.

DUCLAUD-WILLIAMS, R. (1978), *The Politics of Housing in Britain and France*, Heinemann, London.

DUNCAN, S. S. (1974), 'Cosmetic planning or social engineering?' *Area*, 6, (4), 259–70.

DUNCAN, S. S. (1976), 'Self help: the allocation of mortgages and the formation of housing submarkets', *Area*, 8, 307–16.

DUNCAN, T. (1973), *Housing Improvement Policies in England and Wales*, Research Memorandum 28, Centre for Urban and Regional Studies, University of Birmingham.

DUNHAM, H. W. (1937), 'The ecology of functional psychoses in Chicago', *American Sociological Review* 2, 467–79.

DUNLEAVY, J. (1977), 'Protest and quiescence in urban politics', *International Journal of Urban and Regional Research*, 1 (2), 193–218.

DYE, T. (1975), *Understanding Public Policy*, Prentice Hall, London.

DYOS, H. J. (1961), *Victorian Suburbs*, Leicester University Press, Leicester.

DZUS, R. and ROMSA, G. (1977), 'Housing construction, vacancy chains and residential mobility in Windsor', *Canadian Geographer*, 21, 223–36.

EDEL, M. (1976), 'Marx's theory of rent: urban applications', in Political Economy of Housing Workshop, *Housing and Class in Britain*, London.

EICHLER, E. P. and KAPLAN, M. (1967), *The Community Builders*, University of California Press, Berkeley and Los Angeles.

ELKINS, S. (1974), *Politics and Land Use Planning*, Cambridge University Press.

ELKINS, S. (1975), 'Comparative urban politics and interorganisational behaviour', in Young, K. (ed.), *Essays on the Study of Urban Politics*, Macmillan, London.

ELLIOT, B., and MCCRONE, D. (1975), 'Landlords as urban managers: a dissenting opinion', *Conference Paper 14*, Centre for Environmental Studies, London.

ELLIOT, J. (1975), 'Political leadership in local government: T. Dan Smith in Newcastle upon Tyne', *Local Government Studies*, 1, 33–44.

EMMANUEL, A. (1972), *Unequal Exchange*, Monthly Review Press, New York.

ENGELS, F. (1958 edition), *The Condition of the Working Class in England*, Blackwell, London.

ENGELS, F. (1970 edition), *On the Housing Question*, Progress Publishers, Moscow.

ENGLISH, J. MADIGAN, R. and NORMAN, P. (1976), *Slum Clearance: the Social and Administrative Context in England and Wales*, Croom Helm, London.

ERICKSON, E. G. (1949), 'Review of "The social areas of Los Angeles"', *American Sociological Review*, 14, 699.

EVANS, A. W. (1973), *The Economics of Residential Location*, Macmillan, London.

EVANS, M. (1975), *Karl Marx*, Allen & Unwin, London.

EVERSLEY, D. (1975), 'The landlords' slow farewell', *New Society*, 31, 119–21.

EXPENDITURE COMMITTEE (1973), *Tenth Report from the Expenditure Committee, House Improvement Grants*, 3 vols, HC 345, HMSO, London.

FERRIS, J. (1972), *Participation in Urban Planning: the Barnsbury Case*, Bell, London.

FINE, B. (1975), *Marx's Capital*, Macmillan, London.

FINE, B. and HARRIS, L. (1976), 'Controversial issues in Marxist economic theory', in Milliband, R. and Saville, J. (eds), *The Socialist Register*, Merlin Press, London.

FIREY, W. (1945), 'Sentiment and symbolism as ecological variables', *American Sociological Review*, 10, 140–8.

FORD, J. (1975), 'The role of the building society manager in the urban stratification system: autonomy versus constraint', *Urban Studies*, 12, 295–302.

FORM, W. H. (1954), 'The place of social structure in the determination of land use', *Social Forces*, 32, 317–23; reprinted in Stewart (1972).

GAMBLE, A. and WALTON, P. (1976), *Capitalism and Crisis*, Macmillan, London.

GANS, H. (1972), *People and Plans*, Penguin, Harmondsworth.

GARNER, B. (1967), 'Models of urban geography and settlement location', in R. J. Chorley and P. Haggett (eds), *Models in Geography*, Methuen, London.

GERAS, N. M. (1972), 'Althusser's Marxism: an account and assessment', *New Left Review*, 71, 57–86.

GIDDENS, A. (1973), *The Class Structure of the Advanced Societies*, Hutchinson, London.

GITTUS, E. (1976), *Flats, Families and the Under Fives*, Routledge & Kegan Paul, London.

GLUCKSMAN, M. (1974), *Structuralist Analysis in Contemporary Social Theory*, Routledge & Kegan Paul, London.

GODARD, F. and PENDARIÉS, J. (1978), 'Rapports de propriété, ségrégation et pratique de l'éspace résidentiel', *International Journal of Urban and Regional Research*, 2 (1), 78–100.

GOLDTHORPE, J., LOCKWOOD, D., BECHHOFER, F., PLATT, J. (1969), *The Affluent Worker in the Class Structure*, Cambridge University Press.

GOTTDIENER, M. (1977), *Planned Sprawl: Private and Public Interests in Suburbia*, Sage, Beverly Hills, California.

GOUGH, I. (1975a), 'Review of "The Fiscal Crisis of the State" ', *Bulletin of the Conference of Socialist Economists*, IV (2).

GOUGH, I. (1975b), 'State expenditure in advanced capitalism', *New Left Review*, 92, 53–92.

GOULD, P. (1972), Pedagogic review: *Entropy in Urban and Regional Modelling*, Annals Association of American Geographers, 62, 689–700.

GRANFIELD, M. L. (1975), *An Econometric Model of Residential Location*, Ballinger, Cambridge, Mass.

GRAY, F. (1975), 'Non-explanation in urban geography', *Area*, 7, 228–35.

GRAY, F. (1976a), 'Selection and allocation in council housing', *Transactions of the Institute of British Geographers*, New Series, 1, 34–46.

GRAY, F. (1976b), 'The management of local authority housing', in Political Economy of Housing Workshop, *Housing and Class in Britain*, London.

GREEN, G. (1976), 'Property exchange in Saltley', in Political Economy of Housing Workshop, *Housing and Class in Britain*, London.

GREVE, J. (1965), *Private Landlords in England*, Bell, London.

GUELKE, L. (1974), 'An idealist alternative in human geography', *Annals Association of American Geographers*, 64, 193–202.

GYFORD, J. (1976), *Local Politics in Britain*, Croom Helm, London.

HADDON, R. F. (1970), 'A minority in a welfare state society: location of West Indians in the London housing market', *New Atlantis*, 2, 80–133.

HALL, P., GRACEY, H., DREWETT, R., and THOMAS, R. (1973), *The Containment of Urban England*, PEP and Allen & Unwin, London.

HAMNETT, C. (1973), 'Improvement grants as an indicator of gentrification in inner London', *Area*, 5, 252–61.

HAMPTON, W. (1970), *Democracy and Community: A Study of Politics in Sheffield*, Oxford University Press.

HARLOE, M. (1977), 'Introduction', in Harloe, M. (ed.), *Captive Cities*, Wiley, London.

HARLOE, M., ISSACHAROFF, R., and MINNS, R. (1974), *The Organisation of Housing*, Heinemann, London.

HARRISON, A. and WEBBER, R. (1977), 'Capital spending on housing: control and distribution', *CES Review* (1), 31–6.

HARVEY, D. (1969), *Explanation in Geography*, Edward Arnold, London.

HARVEY, D. (1973), *Social Justice and the City*, Edward Arnold, London.

HARVEY, D. (1974), 'Class monopoly rent, finance capitals and the urban revolution', *Regional Studies*, 8, 239–55.

HARVEY, D. (1975a), 'The political economy of urbanization in advanced capitalist societies: the case of the US', in Gappert, G. and Rose, H. M. (eds), *The Social Economy of Cities*, Urban Affairs Annual Review, Vol. 9, Sage Publications, Beverly Hills, California.

HARVEY, D. (1975b), 'Class structure in a capitalist society and the theory of residential differentiation', in Peel, R. Haggett, P. and Chisholm, M. (eds), *Processes in Physical and Human Geography: Bristol Essays*, Heinemann, London.

HARVEY, D. (1977), 'Government policies, financial institutions and neighbourhood change in United States cities', in Harloe, M. (ed.), *Captive Cities*, Wiley, London.

HARVEY, D. (1978a), 'The urban process under capitalism', *International Journal of Urban and Regional Research*, 2 (1), 101–31.

HARVEY, D. (1978b), 'Labour, capital and class struggle around the built environment in advanced capitalist societies', in Cox, K. R. (ed.), *Urbanisation and Conflict in Market Societies*, Methuen, London.

HARVEY, D. and CHATTERJEE, L. (1974), 'Absolute rent and the structuring of space by Government and Financial institutions', *Antipode*, 6, 22–36.

HATCH, J. C. S. (1973), 'Estate agents as urban gatekeepers', Paper read at British Sociological Association Urban Sociology Meeting, Stirling.

HAWLEY, A. H. (1950), *Human Ecology*, Ronald Press, New York.

HAWLEY, A. H. (1971), *Urban Society: an Ecological Approach*, Ronald Press, New York.

HAWTHORN, G. (1976), *Enlightenment and Despair: a History of Sociology*, Cambridge University Press.

HAYES, E. (1972), *Power Structure and Urban Policy: Who Rules in Oakland?*, McGraw-Hill, New York.

HEIDENHEIMER, A., HECLO, H. and ADAMS, C. (1975), *Comparative Public Policy: The Politics of Social Choice in Europe and America*, Macmillan, London.

HILL, A. G. (1973), 'Segregation in Kuwait', in Clark, B. D. and Gleave, M. B. (eds), *Social Patterns in Cities*, 123–42, Institute of British Geographers Special Publication No. 5.

HILL, M. (1972), *The Sociology of Public Administration*, Weidenfeld & Nicolson, London.

HOLLIS, M. and NELL, E. (1975), *Rational Economic Man: a Philosophical Critique of Neo-classical Economics*, Cambridge University Press.

HOLLOWAY, J. and PICCIOTTO, S. (1978), 'Introduction: towards a materialist theory of the state', in Holloway, J. and Picciotto, S. (eds), *State and Capital: A Marxist Debate*, Edward Arnold, London.

HOLMES, C. (1977), 'Islington's tough approach works', *Roof*, 2 (2), 81–83.

HOWARD, M. C. and KING, J. E. (1975), *The Political Economy of Marx*, Longman, London.

HOYT, H. (1939), *The Structure and Growth of Residential Neighbourhoods in American Cities*, Federal Housing Administration, Washington D.C.

HUNTER, F. (1953), *Community Power Structure*, University of North Carolina Press.

HURD, R. M. (1903), *Principles of City Land Values*, The Record and Guide, New York.

JENNINGS, H. (1962), *Societies in the Making*, Routledge & Kegan Paul, London.

JENNINGS, J. (1971), 'Geographical implications of the municipal housing programme in England and Wales', *Urban Studies*, 8 (2), 121–38.

JESSOP, B. (1977), 'Recent theories of the capitalist state', *Cambridge Journal of Economics*, 1 (4), 353–74.

JEVONS, R. and MADGE, J. (1946), *Housing Estates*, J. W. Arrowsmith, Bristol.

JOHNSTON, H. G. (1971), 'The Keynesian revolution and the monetarist counter revolution', *American Economic Review*, 16, 1–14.

JOHNSTON, R. J. (1966), 'The location of high status and residential areas', *Geografiska Annales*, 48B, 23–35.

JOHNSTON, R. J. (1969a), 'Population movements and metropolitan expansion: London 1960–61', *Transactions of the Institute of British Geographers*, 46, 69–91.

JOHNSTON, R. J. (1969b), 'Processes of change in the high status residential districts of Christchurch, 1951–64', *New Zealand Geographer*, 25, 1–15.

JOHNSTON, R. J. (1971), *Urban residential patterns*, Bell, London.

JOHNSTON, R. J. (1972), 'Towards a general model of intra-urban residential patterns: some cross-cultural observations', *Progress in Geography*, 4, 83–124.

JOHNSTON, R. J. (1976), 'Residential area characteristics: research methods for identifying urban sub-areas – social area analysis and factorial ecology', in Herbert, D. T. and Johnston, R. J. (eds), *Social Areas in Cities*, Vol. 1, Wiley, London.

JONES, G. (1975), 'Varieties of local politics', *Local Government Studies*, 1 (2), 1–16.

JOYCE, F. (ed.) (1977), *Metropolitan Development and Change*, Teakfield, Westmead.

KAIN, J. F. (1962), 'The journey to work as a determinant of residential location', *Papers and Proceedings, Regional Science Association*, 9, 137–60.

KANTOR, P. (1976), 'Elites, pluralists and policy areas in London: towards a comparative theory of city policy formation', *British Journal of Political Science*, 6, 3, 311–34.

KARN, V. (1976), *Priorities for Local Authority Mortgage Lending: A Case Study of Birmingham*, Research Memorandum No. 52, Centre for Urban and Regional Studies, University of Birmingham.

KEAT, R. and URRY, J. (1975), *Social Theory as Science*, Routledge & Kegan Paul, London.

KELLETT, J. R. (1969), *The Impact of Railways on Victorian Cities*, Routledge & Kegan Paul, London.

KESSELMAN, M. (1974), 'Research perspectives in comparative local politics: pitfalls, prospects, and notes on the French case', in Clark, T. N. (ed.), *Comparative Community Politics*, Wiley, New York.

KIRK, W. (1951), 'Historical geography and the concept of the behavioural environment', *Indian Geographical Journal, Silver Jubilee volume*, 152–60.

KIRK, W. (1963), 'Problems of geography', *Geography*, 48, 357–71.

KIRWAN, R. M. and BALL, M. J. (1973), 'The micro-economic analysis of a local housing market', *Papers from the Urban Economics Conference*, Centre for Environmental Studies, Conference Paper 9, London.

KIRWAN, R. M. and MARTIN, D. B. (1972), *The Economics of Urban Residential Renewal and Improvement*, Centre for Environmental Studies, London.

KUHN, T. S. (1962), *The Structure of Scientific Revolutions*, University of Chicago Press.

LAMARCHE, F. (1976), 'Property development and the economic foundations of the urban question', in Pickvance, C. G. (ed.), *Urban Sociology: Critical Essays*, Tavistock, London.

LAMBERT, C. (1976), *Building Societies, Surveyors and the Older Areas of Birmingham*, Working Paper 38, Centre for Urban and Regional Studies, University of Birmingham.

LAMBERT, J. (1970), 'The management of minorities', *New Atlantis*, 2, 49–79.

LAMBERT, J. (1975), 'Housing class and community action in a redevelopment area', in Lambert, C. and Weir, D. (eds), *Cities in Modern Britain*, Collins, London.

LEBAS, E. (1977), 'Regional policy research: some theoretical and methodological problems', in Harloe, M. (ed.), *Captive Cities*, Wiley, London.

LEFEBVRE, H. (1970), *La Revolution urbaine*, Gallimard, Paris.

LEY, D. (1977), 'Social geography and the taken-for-granted world', *Transactions of the Institute of British Geographers*, New Series, 2, 498–512.

LOJKINE, J. (1975), 'Stratégies des grands entreprises, politiques urbaines, et mouvements sociaux urbains', *Sociologie du Travail*, 18–40.

LOJKINE, J. (1976), 'Contribution to a Marxist theory of capitalist urbanisation', in Pickvance, C. G. (ed.), *Urban Sociology: critical Essays*, Tavistock, London.

LOJKINE, J. (1977), 'Big firms' strategies, urban policy and urban social movements', in Harloe, M. (ed.), *Captive Cities*, Wiley, London.

LOWENTHAL, D. (1961), 'Geography, experience and imagination: towards a geographical epistemology', *Annals Association of American Geographers*, 51, 241–60.

LOWRY, I. S. (1964), *A Model of Metropolis* RM – 4035 – Re. RAND Corporation, Santa Monica, California.

LUKES, S. (1974), *Power: a Radical View*, Macmillan, London.

MARCUSE, P. (1977), 'The myth of the benevolent state: notes towards a theory of housing conflict', in Harloe, M. (ed.), Centre for Environmental Studies *Second Conference on Urban Change and Conflict*. Centre for Environmental Studies, Conference Papers.

MASON, T. (1977), Community action and the local authority: a study in the incorporation of protest. In Harloe, M. (ed.), Centre for Environmental Studies: *Second Conference on Urban Change and Conflict*. Centre for Environmental Studies, Conference Papers.

MCCUTCHEON, R. (1975), 'High flats in Britain 1945 to 1971', in Political Economy of Housing Workshop, *Political Economy and the Housing Question*, London.

MCLELLAN, D. (1971), *The Thought of Karl Marx*, Macmillan, London.

MICHELSON, W. (1977), *Environmental Choice, Human Behaviour and Residential Satisfaction*, Oxford University Press.

MILLER, D. C. (1958a), 'Industry and community power structure: a comparative study of an American and English city', *American Sociological Review*, 23, 9–15.

MILLER, D. C. (1958b), 'Decision making cliques in community power structure: a comparative study of an American and English city', *American Journal of Sociology*, 64, 299–310.

MILLIBAND, R. (1973), 'Poulantzas and the capitalist state', *New Left Review*, 82, 83–92.

MILLS, E. S. (1972), *Studies in the Structure of the Urban Economy*, Johns Hopkins Press, Baltimore.

MINISTRY OF HOUSING AND LOCAL GOVERNMENT (1970), *Moving Out of a Slum: A Study of People Moving from St. Mary's, Oldham*, HMSO, London.

MINNS, R. (1974), 'Who builds more?', *New Society*, 603, 184–6.

MORTIMORE, M. J. (1969), 'Landownership and urban growth in Bradford and its environs in the West Riding conurbation', *Transactions of the Institute of British Geographers*, 46, 99–113.

MUCHNICK, D. (1970), *Urban Renewal in Liverpool*, LSE Occasional Papers in Social Administration, No. 33, Bell, London.

MUNTON, R. (1977), 'Financial institutions: their ownership of agricultural land in Great Britain', *Area*, 9, 29–37.

MURDIE, R. A. (1969), 'Factorial ecology of metropolitan Toronto, 1951–1961', *Research Paper 116*, Dept. of Geography, University of Chicago.

MURIE, A. (1975), *The Sale of Council Houses*, Centre for Urban and Regional Studies, Occasional Paper No. 35, University of Birmingham.

MURIE, A. (1977), 'Council house sales mean poor law housing', *Roof*, 2 (2), 46–50.

MURIE, A., NINER, P. and WATSON, C. (1976), *Housing Policy and the Housing System*, Allen & Unwin, London.

MURRAY, R. (1977), 'Value and theory of rent: Part 1', *Capital and Class*, 3, 100–22.

MUTH, R. F. (1969), *Cities and Housing*, Chicago University Press.

NELL, E. (1972), 'Economics: the revival of political economy', in Blackburn, R. (ed.), *Ideology in Social Science*, Fontana, London.

NEWBY, H. (1977), 'Paternalism and Capitalism', in Scase, R. (ed.), *Industrial Society: Class, Cleavage and Control*, Allen & Unwin, London.

NEWTON, K. (1974), 'Community decision makers and community decision-making in England and the United States', in Clark, T. N. (ed.), *Comparative Community Politics*, Wiley, New York.

NEWTON, K. (1975), 'Community politics and decision-making: the American experience and its lessons', in Young, K. (ed.), *Essays on the Study of Urban Politics*, Macmillan, London.

NEWTON, K. (1976), 'Feeble governments and private power: urban politics and policies in the United States', in Masotti, L. H. and Lineberry, R. (eds), *The New Urban Politics*, Ballinger, Cambridge, Mass.

NEWTON, K. (1977), *Second City Politics*, Clarendon Press, Oxford.

NEWTON, K. and SHARP, L. J. (1977), 'Local outputs research: some reflections and proposals', *Policy and Politics*, 5 (3), 61–82.

NICHOLSON, R. and TOPHAM, N. (1971), 'The determinants of investment in housing by local authorities: an econometric approach', *Journal of the Royal Statistical Society*, Series A, 134 (3), 273–303.

NINER, P. (1975), *Local Authority Housing Policy and Practice*, Centre for Urban and Regional Studies, Occasional Paper No. 31, University of Birmingham.

NORMAN, P. (1975), 'Managerialism: review of recent work', *Conference Paper 14*, Centre for Environmental Studies, London.

O'CONNOR, J. (1973), *The Fiscal Crisis of the State*, St James Press, New York.

OLIVES, J. (1976), 'The struggle against urban renewal in the Cite d'Aliarte (Paris)', in Pickvance, C. G. (ed.), *Urban Sociology: Critical Essays*, Tavistock, London.

OLLMAN, B. (1971), *Alienation: Marx's Conception of Man in Capitalist Society*, Cambridge University Press.

OPENSHAW, S. (1976), 'An empirical study of some spatial interaction models', *Environment and Planning*, 8, 23–41.

OPENSHAW, S. (1977), 'Optimal zoning systems for spatial interaction models', *Environment and Planning*, 9, 169–84.

PAHL, R. E. (1975), *Whose City?* 2nd edition, Penguin, Harmondsworth.

PAHL, R. E. (1977a), 'Managers, technical experts and the state: forms of mediation, manipulation and dominance in urban and regional development', in Harloe, M. (ed.), *Captive Cities*, Wiley, London.

PAHL, R. E. (1977b), 'Collective consumption and the state in capitalist and state capitalist societies', in Scase, R. (ed.), *Industrial Society: Class, Cleavage and Control*, Allen & Unwin, London.

PALMER, R. (1955), 'Realtors as social gatekeepers: a study in social control', unpublished Ph.D. thesis, Yale University.

PAPAGEORGIOU, G. J. (1976), 'On spatial consumer equilibrium', in Papageorgiou, G. J. (ed.), *Essays in Mathematical Land Use Theory*, 145–76, Lexington Books, Lexington, Mass.

PARIS, C. (1974), 'Urban renewal in Birmingham, England: an institutional approach', *Antipode*, 6, 7–15.

PARIS, C. (1977a), 'Housing Action Areas', *Roof*, 2 (1), 9–13.

PARIS, C. (1977b), 'Birmingham: a study in urban renewal', *Centre for Environmental Studies Review*, 1, 54–61.

PARIS, C. (1977c), 'Policy change: ideological conflict and consensus – the development of housing improvement policy in Birmingham', in Harloe, M. (ed.), Centre for Environmental Studies: *Second Conference on Urban Change and Conflict*, Centre for Environmental Studies, Conference Papers.

PARK, R. E. (1936), 'Human ecology', *American Journal of Sociology*, XLII, 1–15; reprinted in Theodorson (1961).

PARRY, G. (1969), *Political Elites*, Allen & Unwin, London.

PEADEN, J. (1977), 'A Sheffield action group', in Darke, R. and Walker, R. (eds), *Local Government and the Public*, Leonard Hill, London.

PEPPER, S. (1971), *Housing Improvement: Goals and Strategy*, Architectural Association Papers, No. 8, Lund Humphries, London.

PICKVANCE, C. G. (1976), 'On the study of urban social movements', in Pickvance, C. G. (ed.), *Urban Sociology: Critical Essays*, Tavistock, London.

PICKVANCE, C. G. (1977a), 'Some aspects of the political economy of French housing or why the reproduction of labour power theory of housing is invalid', paper presented at Political Economy of Housing Workshop, Birmingham.

PICKVANCE, C. G. (1977b), 'Marxist approaches to the study of urban politics: divergences among some recent French studies', *International Journal of Urban and Regional Research*, 1 (2), 219–55.

PINCH, S. (1978), 'Patterns of local authority housing allocation in Greater London between 1966 and 1973: an inter-borough analysis', *Transactions of the Institute of British Geographers*, New Series, 3, 35–54.

PINÇON, M. (1976), *Les HLM: Structure Sociale de la Population Logee: Agglomeration de Paris 1968*, Centre du Sociologie Urbaine, Paris.

PINES, D. (1975), 'On the spatial distribution of households according to income', *Economic Geography*, 51, 142–9.

POULANTZAS, N. (1973), *Political Power and Social Classes*, New Left Books, London.

POULANTZAS, N. (1975), *Classes in Contemporary Capitalism*, New Left Books, London.

PRED, A. (1967), 'Behaviour and location', part 1, *Lund Studies in Geography*, series B, no. 27.

PRETECEILLE, E. (1973), *La Production de Grands Ensembles*, Mouton, Paris.

PRETECEILLE, E. (1977), Equipment collectif et consommation sociale. *International Journal of Urban and Regional Research*, 1 (1), 101–23.

RAVETZ, S. (1974), *Model Estate: Planned Housing at Quarry Hill, Leeds*, Croom Helm, London.

RECKLESS, W. C. (1926), 'Indices of commercialized vice', *Journal of Applied Sociology*, Jan.-Feb.

REVELL, J. (1974), 'UK building societies', in *Housing Finance: Present Problems*, OECD, Paris.

REX, J. (1968), 'The sociology of a zone in transition', in Pahl, R. E. (ed.), *Readings in Urban Sociology*, Pergamon, Oxford.

REX, J. and MOORE, R. (1967), *Race, Community and Conflict*. Oxford University Press.

RHODES, R. (1975), 'The lost world of British local politics?', *Local Government Studies*, 1 (3), 39–60.

RICHARDSON, H. W. (1971), *Urban Economics*, Penguin, Harmondsworth.

RICHARDSON, H. W. (1977), *The New Urban Economics*, Pion, London.

ROBERTS, J. T. (1976), *General Improvement Areas*, Saxon House, Farnborough.

ROBSON, B. T. (1969), *Urban Analysis*, Cambridge University Press.

ROBSON, B. T. (1973), 'Foreword', in Clark, B. D. and Gleave, M. B. (eds), *Social Patterns in Cities*, Institute of British Geographers Special Publication No. 5.

ROWEIS, S. and SCOTT, A. (1978). 'The urban land question', in Cox, K. R. (ed.), *Urbanisation and Conflict in Market Societies*, Methuen, London.

ROWTHORN, R. E. (1974), 'Neo-classicism, neo-Ricardianism and Marxism', *New Left Review*, 86, 63–87.

SAUNDERS, P. (1975), 'They make the rules: political routines and the generation of political bias', *Policy and Politics*, 4 (1).

SAUNDERS, P. (1978), 'Domestic property and social class', *International Journal of Urban and Regional Research*, 2 (2), 233–51.

SCHIFFERES, S. (1976), 'Council tenants and housing policy in the 1930s: the contradiction of state intervention', in Political Economy of Housing Workshop, *Housing and Class in Britain*, London.

SCHNORE, L. F. (1963), 'The socio-economic status of cities and suburbs', *American Sociological Review*, 28, 76–88.

SCHNORE, L. F. (1964), 'Urban structure and suburban selectivity', *Demography*, 1, 164–76.

SCHNORE, L. F. (1965), *The Urban Scene*, Free Press, New York.

SCHNORE, L. F. (1966), Measuring city-suburban status differences, *Urban Affairs Quarterly*, 1, 95–108.

SCHUTZ, A. (1967), *The Phenomenology of the Social World*, Northwestern University Press, Evanston.

SCOTT, A. (1976), 'Land and land rent: an interpretative review of the French literature', *Progress in Geography*, 9, 101–46.

SENIOR, M. L. (1974), 'Approaches to residential location modelling 2: urban economic models and some recent developments (A review)', *Environment and Planning*, 6, 369–409.

SHENTON, N. (1976), *Deneside – A Council Estate*, Papers in Community Studies 8, Dept of Social Administration and Social Work, University of York.

SHEVKY, E. and BELL, W. (1955), *Social Areas Analysis*, Stanford University Press, Stanford, California.

SHEVKY, E. and WILLIAMS, M. (1949), *The Social Areas of Los Angeles*, University of California Press, Los Angeles.

SHORT, J. R. (1977), 'The intra-urban migration process: comments and empirical findings', *Tijdschrift voor economische en sociale geografie*. 68, 362–71.

SHORT, J. R. (1978), 'Residential mobility', *Progress in Human Geography*, 2, 419–47.

SHORT, J. R. (1979), 'Landlords and the private rented sector: a case study', in Boddy, M. (ed.), *Property, Investment and Land*, School for Advanced Urban Studies Working Paper 2, Bristol.

SIMPSON, M. A. and LLOYD, T. H. (eds) (1977), *Middle-Class Housing in Britain*, David & Charles, Newton Abbot.

STARR, R. (1975), *Housing and the Money Market*, Basic Books, New York.

STEDMAN, M. and WOOD, P. (1965), 'Urban renewal in Birmingham', *Geography*, L, 1–17.

STEGMAN, M. A. (1972), *Housing Investment in the Inner City*, MIT Press, Cambridge, Mass.

STERNLIEB, G. and BURCHELL, R. W. (1973), *Residential Abandonment*, Rutgers University Press, New Jersey.

STEWART, M. (ed.) (1972), *The City. Problems of Planning*, Penguin, Harmondsworth.

STONES, A. (1972), 'Stop slum clearance – now', *Official Architecture and Planning*, 107–10.

SUTCLIFFE, A. and SMITH, R. (1974), *History of Birmingham III, 1939–1970*, Oxford University Press.

SWEEZY, P. (1968), *The Theory of Capitalist Development*, Modern Reader Paperbacks, New York.

THEODORSON, G. A. (ed.) (1961), *Studies in Human Ecology*, Harper & Row, New York.

THOMAS, C. (1966), 'Some geographical aspects of council housing in Nottingham', *East Midland Geographer*, 4, pt 2 (26), 88–98.

THOMPSON, A. (1977), *The Role of Housing Associations in Major Urban Areas*, Research Memo 60. Centre of Urban and Regional Studies, University of Birmingham.

THOMPSON, G. (1977), 'The relationship between the financial sector and the industrial sector in the United Kingdom economy', *Economy and Society*, 6, 235–83.

TIMMS, D. W. G. (1971), *The Urban Mosaic*, Cambridge University Press.

TOPALOV, C. (1973), 'Capital et propriété foncièré, *Centre de Sociologie Urbaine*, Paris.

TRIBE, K. (1973), 'On the production and structuring of scientific knowledges', *Economy and Society*, 2, 465–77.

TRIBE, K. (1977), 'Economic property and the theorisation of ground rent', *Economy and Society*, 6, 69–88.

TUCKER, J. (1966), *Honourable Estates*. Gollancz, London.

WARD, D. (1962), 'The pre-urban cadaster and the urban patterns of Leeds', *Annals Association of American Geographers*, 52, 150–66.

WEIR, S. (1976), 'Red line districts', *Roof*, July issue, 109–14.

WILLIAMS, O. P. (1971), *Metropolitan Political Analysis*, Free Press, New York.

WILLIAMS, O. P. (1975), 'Urban politics as political ecology', in Young, K. (ed.), *Essays on the Study of Urban Politics*, Macmillan, London.

WILLIAMS, P. (1976), 'The role of institutions in the inner London housing market: the case of Islington', *Transactions of the Institute of British Geographers*, New Series, 1, 72–82.

WILLIAMS, P. (1978a), 'Urban managerialism: a concept of relevance', *Area*, 10, 236–40.

WILLIAMS, P. (1978b), 'Building societies and the inner city', *Transactions of the Institute of British Geographers*, New Series, 3, 23–34.

WILSON, A. G. (1970), *Entropy in Urban and Regional Modelling*, Pion, London.

WILSON, A. G. (1974), *Urban and Regional Models in Geography and Planning*, Wiley, London.

WILSON, G. and WILSON, M. (1945), *The Analysis of Social Change*, Cambridge University Press.

WINGO, L. (1961), *Transportation and Urban Land*, Johns Hopkins Press, Baltimore.

WIRTH, L. (1938), 'Urbanism as a way of life', *American Journal of Sociology*, 44, 1–24.

WOLMAN, H. (1975), *Housing and Housing Policy in the U.S. and the U.K.*, Lexington Books, Massachusetts.

WOLPERT, J. (1964), 'The decision process in spatial context', *Annals Association of American Geographers*, 54, 537–58.

WOLPERT, J. (1965), 'Behavioural aspects of the decision to migrate', *Papers and Proceedings of Regional Science Association*, 15, 159–69.

WOLPERT, J. (1966), 'Migration as an adjustment to environmental stress', *Journal of Social Issues*, 22, 92–102.

YAFFE, D. (1973). 'The Marxian theory of crisis, capital and the state', *Economy and Society*, 2, 186–232.

YAMADA, H. (1972), 'On the theory of residential location: accessibility, space, leisure and environmental quality', *Papers of Regional Science Association*, 29, 125–35.

YOUNG, K. (1975), 'Urban politics: an overview', in Young, K. (ed.), *Essays on The Study of Urban Politics*, Macmillan, London.

ZIPF, G. K. (1949), *Human Behaviour and the Principle of Least Effort*, Cambridge University Press.

ZORBAUGH, H. W. (1929), *The Gold Coast and the Slum*, University of Chicago Press.

Index

Evans, A. W., 27
Evans, M., 159
Eversley, D., 82
evolution, 9, 10
Expenditure Committee (House of
 Commons), 122

factor analysis, 19
factorial ecology, 19, 21–3, 35
Federal Housing Administration, 89,
 90, 93, 94, 96, 195
Ferris, J., 147, 230
filtering, 13, 15, 22, 23
Fine, B., 159, 168, 221
Firey, W., 15
Foley, M. M., 28
Ford, J., 51
Form, W. H., 2, 45, 46
Fort Smith, 16
France, 3, 6, 151, 152, 206
French Communist Party, 223

Gamble, A., 221
Gans, H., 91
Garner, B., 19
General Improvement Areas, 78,
 121–3, 148
gentrification, 79, 84, 87, 122, 147
Geras, N., 198
Giddens, A., 196, 212
Ginsburg, N., 199, 200, 209, 226, 229
Gintis, H., 213
Gittus, E., 111
Glasgow, 121
GLC (Greater London Council),
 124, 139
Glucksman, M., 183, 198
Goddard, F., 182, 185–7, 189, 191,
 213, 214, 222, 227
Goldthorpe, J., 214, 215
Gottdiener, M., 90
Gough, I., 221, 223
Gould, P., 43
Granfield, M. L., 29
gravity models, 35, 40, 42
Gray, F., 44, 51, 119, 149, 150
Great Depression, 217
Grebler, L., 151
Green, G., 67
Greve, J., 81, 82
Guelke, L., 39
Gyford, J., 132

Habitations à Loyer Modéré, 151,
 152
Haddon, R. F., 49, 50
Hall, P., 60, 65, 71, 90, 91, 104
Hamnett, C., 122, 123
Hampton, W., 132
Harloe, M., 51, 70, 82, 124, 139, 173
Harris, L., 168, 221
Harrison, A., 105
Harvey, D., 1, 2, 6, 32, 40, 46, 93, 96,
 157, 166, 192–202, 209, 211, 212,
 220–2, 224, 229
Hatch, J. C. S., 51, 87
Hawley, A. M., 15, 16
Hawthorn, G., 9
Hayes, E., 153
Heclo, H., 103, 151
Heidenheimer, A., 103, 151
Hill, A. G., 22
Hill, M., 133, 142
Hindess, B., 198
Hirst, P., 198
historical materialism, 1, 2, 4, 160,
 168
Hollis, M., 27
Holloway, J., 223
Holmes, C., 148
Housing Act (1949), 91
Housing Act (1969), 121, 137, 147
Housing Act (1974), 123, 147
Housing Action Areas, 78, 104, 123,
 148
housing associations, 51, 58, 102, 206
housing classes, 48, 49, 100, 106, 145,
 172, 196, 231
Housing Finance Act (1972), 138
housing visitors, 49
Howard, M. C., 159, 200
Hoyt, H., 13–15, 19, 21, 22
Huddersfield, 122–4
Hull, 51, 119, 150
human ecology, 1, 6, 11, 15, 55
human geography, 4, 5, 19, 32, 40
Hurd, R. M., 10, 13
Hussain, A., 198

ideology, 128, 135, 143, 149, 161, 183,
 186, 187, 226
Islington, 79, 84
Issacharoff, R., 51, 124, 139

Jennings, H., 115
Jennings, J., 109